Selected Critical Writings of George Santayana

VOLUME I

NORMAN HENFREY
Assistant Professor of English, Laval University

George Santayana (1863–1952) was one of the leading philosophers of his era. His range of interests was wide; in addition to books and essays on philosophical subjects, he wrote literary criticism of the first rank, cultural criticism that remains fresh and valid today and autobiographical works which reveal a man of great charm with a deep interest and affection for his acquaintances.

Santayana was born in Spain and always considered his Spanish and Catholic origin as the foundation to his intellectual temperament However, he was educated mainly in the United States and spent a large part of his life teaching at Harvard; he later lived in England before retiring to Italy. He wrote entirely in English. The contrast between his latin background and the protestant Anglo-Saxon world he lived in was a fruitful one and contributed to the critical tension of his writing. Santayana's approach is always one of detached interest, appealing to the facts of the case, never forcing the reader to share his views, and always believing that intelligence above all else is 'the highest form of vitality'.

This two-volume selection of Santayana's writing is exceptionally comprehensive; the editor has been careful to provide passages which adequately illustrate Santayana's views on a wide variety of subjects and his selection includes essays and excerpts from books that have long been unavailable. Volume one contains essays on literature and the theory of art, and character studies of Santayana's family and some of his most famous acquaintances. Volume two contains selections of cultural and social criticism and philosophical writing.

In his substantial Introduction, which appears in volume one, Norman Henfrey gives an attractive biographical description of Santayana and a persuasive and enlightening appreciation of his critical approach.

SELECTED CRITICAL WRITINGS OF GEORGE SANTAYANA

VOLUME I

George Santayana

From a Harvard University class photograph, 1886

Reproduced by kind permission of the Library of Harvard University

SELECTED CRITICAL WRITINGS OF GEORGE SANTAYANA

Volume I

EDITED BY

NORMAN HENFREY

Assistant Professor of English
Laval University

CAMBRIDGE
AT THE UNIVERSITY PRESS
1968

Published by the Syndics of the Cambridge University Press
Bentley House, 200 Euston Road, London, N.W.1
American Branch: 32 East 57th Street, New York, N.Y. 10022

Library of Congress Catalogue Card Number: 68–21394

Standard Book Numbers:
521 07103 8 clothbound
521 09463 1 paperback

Printed in Great Britain
at the University Printing House, Cambridge
(Brooke Crutchley, University Printer)

CONTENTS

Contents

ACKNOWLEDGMENTS

The editor and publishers are grateful to Mr Daniel Cory, the literary executor of the Santayana estate, and the following publishers for permission to reprint copyright material by George Santayana:

Constable and Company Limited for selections from *Interpretations of Poetry and Religion, Obiter Scripta, Soliloquies in England and Later Soliloquies, The Life of Reason* (volume IV), *Persons and Places* and *Character and Opinion in the United States.*

J. M. Dent and Sons Limited for selections from *Winds of Doctrine* and *Egotism in German Philosophy.*

Harvard University Press for excerpts from *Three Philosophical Poets* (copyright 1910, 1938).

Charles Scribner's Sons for excerpts from *The Sense of Beauty* and selections from the omnibus edition of *Persons and Places* (copyright 1944, 1945, 1953).

Historic remains and restorations might well be used as one uses historic knowledge, to serve some living interest and equip the mind for the undertakings of the hour. An artist may visit a museum but only a pedant can live there. Ideas that have long been used may be used still, if they remain ideas and have not been congealed into memories. Incorporated into a design that calls for them, traditional designs cease to be incongruous, as words that still have a felt meaning may be old without being obsolete. All depends on men subserving an actual ideal and having so firm and genuine an appreciation of the past as to distinguish at once what is still serviceable in it from what is already ghostly and dead.

GEORGE SANTAYANA, *Reason in Art*, 1905

PREFACE

I have sought to bring together as much as possible of Santayana's best work in literary criticism, moral philosophy, and social and cultural history; to this end, most of the writings drawn upon fall between his thirty-second and fifty-seventh years, when he was at the height of his powers. A notable omission is *Three Philosophical Poets*; it is his best-known work and is in paperback; other criticism has accordingly been preferred, though his general position in that book is set out in the excerpts that have been taken from his Introduction and Conclusion to it.

Essays, and selections from books, are given whole wherever possible, but some curtailment was necessary if the choice was not to be unduly restricted; Santayana was a discursive writer. Where elisions have been made it is on the grounds that the material omitted is not vital, or that it has to do with a subject adequately treated elsewhere in the Selection. In some cases, to avoid breaking up the flow of an argument, I have conflated into one paragraph parts of two which were originally removed from each other by some pages. In three places passages from different chapters of a book have been incorporated into the one excerpt so as to represent Santayana's position satisfactorily: in volume I, the initial excerpt from *The Sense of Beauty* is an amalgam of a section from the first part of that book and three sections from the third, and I supply the title; in volume II, 'The Protestant Heritage' is rounded out with extracts from two later chapters in *Egotism in German Philosophy*, and 'The Belief in a Future Life' with an extract from the ensuing chapter in *Reason in Religion*. Four essays have been cut: 'The Elements and Function of Poetry' and 'Penitent Art' (volume I); 'The Intellectual Temper of the Age' and 'The Philosophy of Mr Bertrand Russell' (volume II).

Santayana made three collections of his essays: *Interpreta-*

tions of Poetry and Religion, 1900; *Winds of Doctrine, Studies in Contemporary Opinion*, 1913; *Soliloquies in England and Later Soliloquies*, 1922.

Justus Buchler and Benjamin Schwartz brought out a further collection, with Santayana's approval: *Obiter Scripta*; Lectures, Essays and Reviews, 1936.

The essays in this Selection are drawn from the following sources:

VOLUME I

Platonic Love in Some Italian Poets: written for the Contemporary Club and read at the meeting of 5 February 1896, under the title 'Platonism in the Italian Poets'. Printed by Paul's Press, Buffalo, 1896, 31 pp. Reprinted with modifications in *Interpretations of Poetry and Religion*, 1900.

The Absence of Religion in Shakespeare: *New World*, December 1896, v, pp. 681–91. Reprinted in *Interpretations of Poetry and Religion*, 1900.

The Elements and Function of Poetry: *Interpretations of Poetry and Religion*, 1900.

The Poetry of Barbarism: *Interpretations of Poetry and Religion*, 1900.

Emerson: *Interpretations of Poetry and Religion*, 1900.

Hamlet: in *The University Press Edition of Shakespeare's Works*, Cambridge, U.S.A., 1908, xxx, pp. ix–xxxiii, under the title 'Introduction to *Hamlet*'. Reprinted with slight modifications in *Life and Letters*, June 1928, I, pp. 17–38, and in *Obiter Scripta*, 1936.

Shelley: or the Poetic Value of Revolutionary Principles: *Winds of Doctrine*, 1913.

Hints of Egotism in Goethe: *New Republic*, 2 January 1915, I, pp. 15–16, under the title 'Goethe and German Egotism'. Reprinted in *Egotism in German Philosophy*, 1916.

Dickens: *Dial*, November 1921, LXXI, pp. 537–49. Reprinted in *Soliloquies in England*, 1922.

A Contrast with Spanish Drama: *Athenaeum*, 11 February

1921, pp. 146–7. Reprinted in *Soliloquies in England*, 1922.

Tragic Philosophy: *Scrutiny*, March 1936, IV, pp. 365–76.

What is Aesthetics?: *Philosophical Review*, May 1904, VIII, pp. 320–7. Reprinted in *Obiter Scripta*, 1936.

Penitent Art: *Dial*, July 1922, LXXIII, pp. 25–31. Reprinted in *Obiter Scripta*, 1936.

VOLUME II

The Intellectual Temper of the Age: *Winds of Doctrine*, 1913.

Classic Liberty: *New Republic*, 21 August 1915, IV, pp. 65–6. Reprinted in *Soliloquies in England*, 1922.

Liberalism and Culture: *New Republic*, 4 September 1915, IV, pp. 123–5. Reprinted in *Soliloquies in England*, 1922.

The Human Scale: *New Republic*, 29 January 1916, V, pp. 326–8. Reprinted in *Soliloquies in England*, 1922.

The Genteel Tradition in American Philosophy: *University of California Chronicle*, October 1911, XIII, pp. 357–80. Reprinted in *Winds of Doctrine*, 1913.

Plotinus and the Nature of Evil: *Journal of Philosophy*, 23 October 1913, X, pp. 589–99, under the title 'Dr Fuller, Plotinus, and the Nature of Evil'. (Review of B. A. G. Fuller, *The Problem of Evil in Plotinus.*) Reprinted with modifications in *Obiter Scripta*, 1936.

The Philosophy of M. Henri Bergson: *Winds of Doctrine*, 1913.

The Philosophy of Mr Bertrand Russell: *Journal of Philosophy*, 3 February 1911, VIII, pp. 57–63; 2 March 1911, VIII, pp. 113–24; 3 August 1911, VIII, pp. 421–32; under the title 'Russell's *Philosophical Essays*'. Reprinted with modifications in *Winds of Doctrine*, 1913: 'Hypostatic Ethics', reprinted in the present Selection, is the fourth and concluding section of the essay.

Where Santayana made or approved modifications in an essay before republication, this later version has been used. Modifications in a title have been similarly retained.

Preface

The Selected Portraits in the first volume come from the following books: the portrait of William James is from *Character and Opinion in the United States*, 1920, and the others are from Santayana's autobiography, *Persons and Places*: the first two from *Background of my Life*, 1944; the next four from *The Middle Span*, 1945; and the two last from *My Host the World*, 1953. The three volumes of the autobiography were written between 1940 and 1944, though Santayana's account of his father and mother may have been drafted as early as 1924: see Santayana's letter to George Sturgis of 29 July 1924 (*The Letters of George Santayana*, ed. Daniel Cory (1955), p. 216).

The selections from *Reason in Common Sense*, *Reason in Society*, *Reason in Religion* and *Reason in Art* are drawn from the first, second, third and fourth volumes of Santayana's five-volume work, *The Life of Reason* (1905–6).

Santayana's footnotes are indicated by asterisks; mine by numerals. In the table of contents and in the Introduction, book-titles are in italics to distinguish them from the essays.

Unless otherwise stated, references to essays by Santayana are to the present Selection.

I should like to express my indebtedness to Dr F. R. Leavis, whose incisive discussions of Santayana's essay on Dickens introduced me to his work. I should also like to thank Dr John Newton for his generous aid in setting this edition on foot, and Mr Daniel Cory, Mr Richard Gooder, Mr Pierre Lefranc and Mr Geoffrey Strickland for help they have given me.

Quebec, Canada N. H.

INTRODUCTION

George Santayana, moral philosopher, critic, poet, essayist and novelist, wrote an English where precision, eloquence and repose weave a harmony that seems native to the language; yet he was pure Spanish. Born in Madrid of Spanish parents on 16 December 1863, he was taken to Avila when he was two; and Avila, where his father, by then in his fifties, was to live out his days, remained into old age the centre of Santayana's 'deepest legal and affectionate ties'. He never relinquished his Spanish nationality, and did not begin to learn English until taken to live in New England when he was a little under nine years old. '...you can't imagine', he writes late in life to an American correspondent, 'what a completely false picture comes to mind if you suggest that my mother was an American. Then, too, she and my [half-] sisters would have been Protestants, and my whole imaginative and moral background would have been different.'[1]

Santayana's mother was in fact Catalan. Her first husband, George Sturgis, had died in 1857 when she was thirty. He was from Boston and she had promised to bring up their children in America. Despite her second marriage, in Madrid in 1862, to Don Augustín Ruiz de Santayana, she felt she must fulfil this promise; in due course she returned to Boston with her three Sturgis children and settled there for good. Later Santayana's father took him to Boston too and left him with his mother. Santayana was to remain in New England for most of the ensuing forty years, though from the age of nineteen he regularly spent his summers in Avila with his father. Thus was set up that conflict which was so to shape his moral outlook, to fix unmistakably its distinctive tone and colour: a Latin mind articulate and sure, strong in the sense

[1] *The Letters of George Santayana*, ed. Daniel Cory (London, 1955), pp. 343–4. All letters from Santayana quoted in the Introduction are from this collection, or from his correspondence with Daniel Cory: *Santayana: The Later Years. A Portrait with Letters*, ed. Daniel Cory (New York, 1963).

of a Mediterranean culture with its age-old habits of living; a Protestant tradition strenuous and absorbing, but deficient in vital form and purpose. '...I was perfectly at home in that [Boston] life', he tells us in the preface to his novel, 'and immensely interested in it...but it always seemed to me a strained, kindly, humorous, somehow fleshless world. Spain ...was after all my real country: when I went back there...I was not happier or better pleased, but decidedly less comfortable physically and morally: yet that old passive passionate way of living, that religion, those very faults and disillusions seemed to me somehow more human, more classical, than all this slavish diligence in modern duties.'

Santayana arrived in Boston in July of 1872. He went through grammar school, high school and Harvard College with distinction, graduating from Harvard *summa cum laude* in 1886. Then, on a Harvard College Fellowship grant, he spent two years studying philosophy at the University of Berlin, with a short interlude at Oxford, before returning to Harvard late in 1888 to embark upon his thesis. He suggested Schopenhauer, the German author who interested him most at the time, and came to wish he had picked Hegel; Josiah Royce successfully advised Lotze for an aspiring doctor of philosophy. Santayana's thesis on him was accepted, he was awarded his doctorate, and in the autumn of 1889, strongly backed by Royce and William James, under whom he had worked, he was appointed to the staff of the Harvard department of philosophy. He was twenty-five. There were doubts about his academic zeal, but he was beginning to express himself eloquently in prose and in verse, and his mind was acknowledged brilliant. A notable career seemed assured.

Santayana was to remain on the Harvard Faculty for twenty-three years, though three of them were spent abroad: 1896–7 at King's College, Cambridge—as an advanced graduate student, dining at high table; 1904–5 on sabbatical in Italy and the East; 1905–6 in Paris as an exchange professor at the Sorbonne. He was appointed full Harvard professor in 1907, and in 1911 A. L. Lowell, the new

College president, agreed to release him from his duties for eight months in every year. But in February of 1912 Santayana's mother died; he was in England at the time and a few months later he sent in his resignation:

The death of my mother...has made a great change in my personal situation, leaving me without a home in Boston and with most of my close friends and relations living in Europe. It seems clearly to mark the moment when I should carry out the plan I have always had of giving up teaching, returning to live in Europe, and devoting myself to literary work. Each of these things is an object in itself sufficient to determine me, and the three conspire together.

The tone is modest, yet firm. He is grateful for the present kindness, but 'although fond of books and young men, [he] was never fit to be a professor'; he hopes the president will not ask him to reconsider his decision. He never returned to America, though some fifteen years later Livingston Lowes, acting for President Lowell and the Harvard committee, essayed to tempt him back with the offer of the Norton Chair of Poetry. The terms were generous and Santayana was conscious of the honour. He remained untempted. In 1931 Harvard tried again: three months as the William James professor. But Santayana was sixty-eight; they should, he regretfully felt, 'look to some younger and fresher quarter'. In 1936, when his novel *The Last Puritan* appeared, age still more prevented him from accepting the Harvard president's cabled invitation to come over and accept a degree of Doctor of Letters. There were handsome offers from other American universities; all were steadily declined.

Most of Santayana's friends and colleagues were astonished by his resignation, for it came at the height of his career. Santayana suggested that his writing and teaching were incompatible; the quality of each hardly bears this out. Indeed, from the turn of the century he had been able to define himself increasingly through his writings: *Interpretations of Poetry and Religion* had appeared in 1900, the five volumes of *The Life of Reason* in 1905–6, *Three Philosophical Poets* in 1910; and *Winds of Doctrine* was to follow in 1913. At the same time, despite his own modest disclaimers, there is evidence that he was a most gifted teacher: interested in his students, and with a rare capacity for analysing philosophies and related poetry with a lucid sympathy while yet judging them by standards that remained rational and humane. Even aesthetic theory in his hands ceased to be an arid metaphysics: it was humanized and related congenially to the life of every day. *The Sense of Beauty* (1896) and *Three Philosophical Poets* were based on two such Harvard courses and are admirable exemplifications of them. We have, as well, the testimony of students.

In his introduction to *The Letters of George Santayana* Daniel Cory quotes a Harvard professor, C. I. Lewis:

> I have never understood how one who taught so well and easily and seemed so perfectly oriented to those occasions when I sat before him, and who chatted so engagingly and graciously with a young and novice assistant, could have failed to enjoy teaching and the contacts that go with it. . . I still feel sure that there was something of satisfaction for him in it—else he would have been a more consummate actor than seems credible.

The Harvard Monthly, of which Santayana had been a founder editor in his undergraduate days, wrote in 1912 that he had 'attained at Harvard a following which in enthusiasm and intensity, if not in numbers, [was] almost impossible to parallel'; students were aware of 'greatness in his presence', of 'completeness and grandeur'. T. S. Eliot himself had been one of his students, taking his course in the *History of Modern Philosophy* in 1908, and then as a graduate student in 1909, electing his *Ideals of Society, Religion, Art and Science in their Historical Development*.[1] In the Preface to his own account of Dante (1929) Eliot acknowledges a debt to *Three Philosophical Poets*, and a yet larger one is manifest in his *Selected Essays*. Locally, there are formulations that remind us of certain of Santayana's own.[2] More pervasively, there is that revolutionary stress Eliot places on tradition at the

[1] See Herbert Howarth, *Notes on Some Figures behind T. S. Eliot* (Boston, 1964), p. 84.

[2] 'Conventions do not arise without some reason, and genius will know how to rise above them by a fresh appreciation of their rightness, and will feel no

expense of romantic egotism and mere personal intensity, the terms and spirit of which compare so interestingly with Santayana's own decisive phrasing of the theme years earlier in such work as 'The Poetry of Barbarism'.

Yet Santayana was ill at ease at Harvard as in America, and his return to Europe was a step he had meditated on with pleasure almost from the moment he began teaching. Part of the reason was that he felt no vocation for imparting philosophy in the lecture-room, his relative success at it notwithstanding. Philosophy could be 'communicated only by being evoked'; the student's mind needed to be 'engaged dialectically in the discussion' (something the lecturing process hardly encouraged), otherwise all that could be taught was 'the literary history of philosophy..., the *phrases* that various philosophers [had] rendered famous'. But besides instructing students, university teachers were supposed to evolve into vigorous academics, and Santayana's strong and independent mind prevented him from doing so: 'Scholarship and learning of any sort seemed to me a means, not an end. I always hated to be a professor.' He was doubly unfortunate in that his period at Harvard coincided with the long presidency of Charles William Eliot, whose administrative innovations had included the 'elective system' (the undergraduate being invited to choose for himself from a generous range of competing subjects), and whose democratic vulnerability to numbers, size and quantitative criteria generally, Santayana dryly memorializes in *Character and Opinion in the United States*:

temptation to overturn them in favour of personal whimsies' (The Elements and Function of Poetry (1900), in vol. I of this Selection); 'A convention is not ridiculous: a subterfuge makes us extremely uncomfortable. The weakness of Elizabethan drama is not its defect of realism, but its attempt at realism; not its conventions but its lack of conventions' ('Four Elizabethan Dramatists' (1924), in T.S. Eliot, *Selected Essays* (London, 1932), p. 112). Of other formulations that seem to have yielded Eliot an interest, let me cite just two: 'The poet's art is to a great extent the art of intensifying emotions by assembling the scattered objects that naturally arouse them' (The Elements and Function of Poetry); 'Even native classics have to be reapprehended by every reader. It is this continual digestion of the substance supplied by the past that alone renders the insights of the past still potent in the present and for the future' (Introduction to *Three Philosophical Poets*, 1910).

The president of Harvard College, seeing me once by chance soon after the beginning of a term, inquired how my classes were getting on; and when I said I thought they were getting on well, that my men seemed to be keen and intelligent, he stopped me as if I were about to waste his time. 'I meant,' said he, '*what is the number* of students in your classes?'

In his autobiography Santayana summarizes the academic environment thus:

Harvard, in those the waning days of Eliot's administration, was getting out of hand. Instruction was every day more multifarious and more chaotic...Eliot, autocrat as he was, depended on the Fellows, half a dozen business men in Boston who were the legal proprietors of Harvard, and especially on one of them, the treasurer, who managed the vast investments of the Foundation...Most numerous and stately, but tamest, in this working menagerie was the Faculty of Arts and Sciences. Although a member of it, I hardly knew what were its attributions or its privileges. The most interesting and clearest business of the meetings was to hear what the President might tell us of the action or prospects of the moment... Sometimes, very rarely, there was clear opposition or even a hostile vote. That might produce a postponement, but could hardly arrest the movement of reform that he had undertaken in the interest of democratic arrangements and quick returns...The end [of education] was service in the world of business.[1]

Such a process, robustly pervasive on the North American continent, is of course not exclusive to it. But at that earlier stage the process might be portentous as well as just disagreeable, especially to a Spaniard like Santayana for whom in any case configurations of material well-being wore a questionable shape and who asked always the Socratic questions: 'why?', 'where to?', 'with what end in view?'; who was concerned that a life should have its own discipline and form; who was convinced, in short, that true progress lay in 'reading or writing fewer and better things, and being fewer and better men'. Such a man must find the vocational drive of American university life uncongenial, not least in New England: conformity of spirit and an irrational

[1] See the informative final chapter, 'Official Career at Harvard', in *The Middle Span* (New York, 1945).

materialism were abetted there where they might most have been confronted.

In saying this I am aware that Santayana's considered accounts of American life are sympathetic as well as tautly perceptive, but the detachment was not easily won. The hostility he felt at the time had sometimes been fierce; he worked to compose it, so that only occasionally, as here in letters to William James around the turn of the century, is the intensity allowed to show through:

You tax me several times with impertinence and superior airs. I wonder if you realize the years of suppressed irritation which I have passed in the midst of an unintelligible, sanctimonious and often disingenuous Protestantism, which is thoroughly alien and repulsive to me...

...I object to and absolutely abhor...the assertion that all the eggs indiscriminately are good because the hen has laid them...

...it seems to me intolerable that we should still be condemned to ...give the parsons and the 'idealists' a monopoly of indignation and of contemptuous dogmatism. It is they, not we, that are the pest; and while I wish to be just and to understand people's feelings, wherever they are at all significant, I am deliberately minded to be contemptuous towards what seems to me contemptible, and not to have any share in the conspiracy of mock respect by which intellectual ignominy and moral stagnation are kept up in our society...

Nor was the hostility all on one side. Santayana was no recluse, he led in fact an active social life; but to President Eliot, an implied humorous modesty about oneself and others, the capacity to discern one's small place on the actual map instead of zestfully losing oneself in the aspiring life around one—this might seem almost disreputable. Why did Santayana not shoulder administrative burdens like his colleagues, marry and loyally put down roots? When in 1897 his promotion to assistant professor came up, the president was dubious:

The withdrawn, contemplative man who takes no part in the everyday work of the institution, or of the world, seems to me a person of very uncertain value. He does not dig ditches, or lay bricks, or write school-books, his product is not of the ordinary useful, though humble kind. What will it be? It may be something of the highest utility; but, on the other hand, it may be something futile, or even harmful because unnatural and untimely.

It took James's insistence that Santayana was 'a very honest and unworldly character—of thoroughly wholesome mental atmosphere', together with the testimony of other senior colleagues that he was a 'strong and healthy man', a 'good, gay, fresh companion', an excellent teacher and author too, for the president to be won over.[1] Eliot retired in 1909 and the new president wished to encourage a more genial climate, but Santayana's mind had long since been made up. '... when I am here', he wrote to his half-sister, Susana Sturgis, a few weeks before his final departure, '...a sort of instinct of courtesy makes me...almost unconscious of how much I hate it all: otherwise I couldn't have stood it for *forty years*!' There is a marked contrast between Santayana's intensity here and that tempered view of America embodied in his writings. The tone of 'The Genteel Tradition in American Philosophy' (1911) is instructively ample, humorous and warm, and in *Character and Opinion in the United States*, written in England some seven years later, it becomes touched with velvet; the edge, though, can cut the more effectively:

Even what is best in American life is compulsory—the idealism, the zeal, the beautiful happy unison of its great moments. You must wave, you must cheer, you must push with the irresistible crowd; otherwise you will feel like a traitor, a soulless outcast, a deserted ship high and dry on the shore. In America there is but one way of being saved, though it is not peculiar to any of the official religions, which themselves must silently conform to the national orthodoxy, or else become impotent and merely ornamental. This national faith and morality are vague in idea, but inexorable in spirit; they are the gospel of work and the belief in progress. By them, in a country where all men are free, every man finds that what most matters has been settled for him beforehand.

When war broke out Santayana was in England and he remained there for the duration, most of the time in Oxford. He of course made a point of comprehending the German senti-

[1] See Margaret Münsterberg, 'Santayana at Cambridge', *American Mercury* (1924), I, p. 70.

ments, but the system they would impose seemed to him strained and artificial, 'a sort of orderly nightmare', and he feared for the Latin tradition 'cut off or disfigured into a Teutonic classicism'. *Egotism in German Philosophy* appeared in 1916 and was translated into French the following year; it was interpreted as a philosopher's contribution to the war effort, whereas Santayana had meant his English-speaking readers to realize that the egotism under attack, so far from being 'exclusively German', was something *they* shared in, too, whenever they turned 'their national ideal into something cosmic..., and felt themselves to be the chosen people'. Still he did not hide, here or elsewhere, that his natural sympathies were warmly engaged on the Allied and English side. 'Of course,' he wrote to an American friend in December 1914, 'the newspapers and political speeches are full of cant, even here; but the living people, especially the young officers, are pure of all malice and intentional passion—really wonderful in their disillusioned courage and humble gallantry. No manufactured hatred here, no politics and philosophy *per order*. Germany was never more studied or better understood'. But the Charles Sorleys were cut down in swathes, and as the war ground on through mud and carnage, its rationale lost in a spawn of lies and cant and artificial hatreds—engendered all at home—Santayana's warm allegiance began to fine away into philosophy. Before the end, the war had been dissolved, desperately, into a historical perspective; he was never to allow himself to be so stirred again.

He led a secluded life in Oxford, though his friendship with Robert Bridges dates from this time, and a little earlier he had renewed an acquaintance with Bertrand Russell, whom he had first met at Cambridge in 1893 through his brother the second Earl Russell, whom he knew well. Lady Ottoline Morrell, too, had wished to draw him into her circle at Garsington, and he liked her; but 'her social and political world', he wrote in his autobiography, '...was the antithesis and scornful enemy of the Oxford I could love', and he 'resisted her invitations'. His 'chief sign of life' during these early war years, he felt, was a series of essays he contributed to *The New Republic*; thirteen appeared between November 1914 and January 1916. He wrote no more of them until, in March 1919, Middleton Murry, newly appointed editor of the revived *Athenaeum*, invited him to contribute. A dozen essays of his appeared that year; nine more in the two following. They were gracefully worked, generally in a meditative-melancholic strain, and increasingly took as their point of departure the English character, climate or countryside. The view of England that emerged was ripely green and airy, very much that of a cultivated appreciative outsider, only more so, and with just enough of aristocratic edge to make the tributes all the more worth having. The essays were popular; before the end of 1919 Robert Bridges, convinced that Santayana 'had things to say that the English needed to hear', was trying hard to secure him for England by attaching him officially to Oxford. Bridges was a member of Corpus Christi College and Santayana was sounded out: Would he care to accept college lodgings in town and become a member for life of the Corpus high table and common-room, where he already had friends? Or would he like actually to teach? Perhaps he would prefer New College, to which Bridges also belonged? Santayana admits in his autobiography that he was tempted, but he declined: 'I loved England only too much. Living there I was in danger of losing my philosophical cruelty and independence.' At bottom was the settled disinclination to be chained as Prose-writer Laureate to any public; in any case the England he loved was of the past, an ideal object, a personal construction even. The current England and the current America were 'variable material complexes'; it would be foolish to wed them even if he had desired: they must elude a secure contemplation.

Bridges told him his abandonment of England was 'deplorable'; by the end of 1919 Santayana was back in Europe anyway. He was to return to England only twice: in 1923 to give the Herbert Spencer memorial lecture at Oxford, and in 1932 to Bloomsbury Square to address the Royal Society of

Literature on John Locke, whose tercentenary it was. His return to England on the first occasion gave him pleasure; but nine years later he was sixty-eight and his English friends were dead. In addition, his reception at Bloomsbury Square was such as perhaps only the well-bred can bring off: a blend of boorishness and civilized ineptitude that he never forgot. It confirmed his sense that his allegiance to England had become exclusively ideal.

After his departure in 1919 he lived for a year or so in Paris with C. A. Strong, a friend and fellow philosopher from Harvard student days. But Italy was coming to seem the most congenial place of retirement, and by 1924 he had taken permanent rooms at the Hotel Bristol on the Piazza Barberini in Rome: he would winter there and move to cooler spots during summer. He had consolidated a reputation in England and America as critic and man of letters: 1920 had seen the publication of *Character and Opinion in the United States* and of Logan Pearsall Smith's selection, *Little Essays drawn from the Writings of George Santayana*, and this was followed in 1922 by *Soliloquies in England and Later Soliloquies*, which brought together his contributions to *The Athenaeum* as well as four of his earlier ones to *The New Republic*. But increasingly now he turned away from specific social or cultural issues into the elaboration and sustenance of a personal philosophical system. *Scepticism and Animal Faith* (1923), and the four long volumes of the *Realms of Being*—the first published in 1927, the last in 1940—attest to the pertinacity of this interest. Yet there is no doubt that he hoped still to appeal to the lay rather than the academic reader. In 1930 he wrote to an American friend:

> ...without pretending that my views are of much importance measured by the standards of absolute truth, which after all is in nobody's hands, I think you might be interested in them as confessions and moral insights of an old friend...I take the greatest pains to be clear, not only in language but in thought...Everybody ought to say: 'Of course: that's what I've always thought, only I didn't expect a philosopher to see it.'

But though Santayana did not waver, ordinary readers could not find purchase in the increasingly remote and generalized flow of his ideas and they turned away. 'The Genteel Tradition at Bay', serialized early in 1931 in Middleton Murry's *Adelphi* and in the American *Saturday Review of Literature*, and then published separately, gained a larger hearing; but it took the publication of *The Last Puritan* in 1935–6, a novel at which he had worked intermittently over the preceding fourteen years, to win back for him a wide attention. The fruit of a long contemplation of certain aspects and inherent tendencies of American and of English life, the novel had, in Santayana's words, 'a vast success'. In England an appreciative Desmond MacCarthy review in the *Sunday Times* helped alert opinion; in America it was a Book-of-the-Month club selection; by August of 1936 148,000 copies had been sold, and Santayana learned he was to get $30,000. Before the end of the year the book had been translated into German and Swedish, in the former version the 'nasty things' about Goethe and the Germans being omitted by agreement. 'The interest taken in the novel by the Nordics', Santayana reported to a friend, 'is entirely scientific. Style, humour, etc., are beneath their notice: but they say the book is an important document on American life; and...they wish it to be studied in their country.' Mere document, of course, it is not, for its themes acquire often an independent life, are embodied in the actual and the particular and there enforce themselves spontaneously, where more and more in his polemical writings now the bones and sinews of things find themselves dissolved away. The life the novelist draws upon, deriving from forty and more years before, has remained substantial and steadily present to him.

In 1939 Santayana's friends urged him to seek asylum in Switzerland, but his Spanish passport was a hindrance and the war found him still in Italy. He was seventy-five and the journey to Spain was dauntingly long; he decided to weather things out in Rome, and in October of 1941 took rooms as paying guest in a nursing home run by Sisters of the Little

Company of Mary. The atmosphere was congenial to a native-born Catholic, who, retracting long since any formal belief in a religious faith, had yet always admired and sympathized with the Catholic tradition. There, on one of the seven hills of Rome and next door to the old Santo Stefano Rotondo, surroundings that made him feel he had been 'miraculously...transported to Avila', he quietly saw out the war. America's entry isolated him from the world outside, but his life of contemplative study was not disrupted and he started on his autobiography. The three volumes were completed before the end of the war, the last remaining unpublished until after his death. In 1942, through the good offices of the Vatican, the manuscript of the first volume was lodged with Scribner's in New York. Published in America in 1944 as *Persons and Places: The Background of My Life*, it too became a Book-of-the-Month club selection; by the autumn of that year the author was being visited by an 'avalanche' of American servicemen and according interviews and photographs. In *Europe without Baedeker* Edmund Wilson has described visiting Santayana the following spring. He had received a signed copy of *Persons and Places* through the post and, now that he was in Rome, imagined Santayana would wish to meet him. He was given a most friendly welcome and the conversation ranged with an easy naturalness, but Santayana had not the least idea who he was; it was enough that his visitor had read his books, common interests could be presumed and congenial ground traversed. The one recent American writer to arouse his interest was Robert Lowell; his *Lord Weary's Castle* he found 'remarkable', a word he allowed its full admixture of tribute.

Gradually—though later there would be friends—the visitors and distinguished callers dropped away. *The Middle Span*, the second volume of his autobiography, appeared in 1945; its insight no less focused than in the first, but a cool view of America appealing less than early reminiscences of Spain and student days in Boston. *The Idea of Christ in the Gospels* followed in 1946, and the absorption in the 'idea' rather than the 'fact' once more deterred home readers; but the work was admired in Europe, where it was translated and reprinted. These had been written in the war, and by now he had started on what was to be his last book, *Dominations and Powers; Reflections on Liberty, Society and Government.* Finished at last in 1950 and published the following year, it reveals a habit of mind that has become pervasively abstract. Here, embalmed in prescriptive generality, are themes he had once known how to quicken into life, to imbue with distinctive form and feeling. He commanded indeed into old age more lucidity and wit than the generality of men can rise to in their prime, as his letters bring home; but he outgrew all wish to renew his thought. And he was, though he did not know it, suffering from intestinal cancer. A few months before his eighty-ninth birthday he endured a last painful illness, dying during the night of 26 September 1952. He was buried, as he had wished, in the Catholic cemetery of Rome in a plot reserved for Spanish nationals.

Santayana's best work is at once ordered and spacious. He combined the training and speculative interest of a philosopher with the live particular response of a literary artist and critic; and he was a Latin, committed by circumstance to the Anglo-Saxon tradition in life and in letters but with his natural affinities elsewhere, so that he seems often to be nourishing in English felicitously un-English things. We do not feel, when he is writing well, that the philosopher is imposing on the critic; rather that the two complete each other: the particular is responded to because felt, and felt with care, yet the whole moral organization is precisely engaged. To respond is to value, and that involves a *scheme* of values which, brought to full consciousness and refined into strength through the discipline of art, expresses our true being.

We can have no pleasure or pain, nor any preference whatsoever, without implicitly setting up a standard of excellence, an ideal of what would satisfy us there. To make these implicit ideals explicit, to catch their hint, to work out their theme, and express clearly to ourselves and to the world what they are demanding in the place of the actual—that is the labour of reason and the task of genius...A failure of reason is a failure of art and taste.[1]

It is

the barbarian...who regards his passions as their own excuse for being; and who does not domesticate them either by understanding their cause or by conceiving their ideal goal...who does not know his derivations nor perceive his tendencies, but who merely feels and acts, valuing in his life its force and its filling...careless of its purpose and its form.[2]

There are two clear poles in Santayana's thought: the 'rebels and individualists are the men of direct insight and vital hope'; but measure is 'a condition of perfection'. No critic saw so clearly that feeling, where it is profound, is an expression of intelligence, not an escape from it; that individualists are what a civilization looks to while it is in health, but that the tense imagination, the consecrated spirit, must subserve a sane art and a rational ideal. Santayana's repeated measuring of romantic against classical, his sifting of both in the interests of a viable tradition, are no exercise in scholastic terminology but a search for true judgment in resolved contraries. He was sufficiently of his time to have 'fed' in his youth, 'by day and by night, on Shelley and Leopardi and Alfred de Musset', and to acknowledge at sixty that he remained a romantic, if only 'north-north-west'. He was also the man who admired the fixed lines of Spinoza's thought and cherished the fact of classical Greek civilization, who regarded Lucretius and Dante as types of consummate poets, and who could observe of the victims of romantic afflatus: 'They measure the profundity of feeling by its intensity, not by its justifying relations; and in the radical disintegration of their spirit, the more they are devoured the more they fancy themselves fed.'[3]

It is thus important to remember not only Santayana's

[1] The Poetry of Barbarism, vol. I.

[2] *Ibid.*

[3] The Elements and Function of Poetry, vol. I.

temperament and racial heritage but the intellectual climate of his day, in which rationalism was a decisive fact—that regretful but deliberate abandonment of religious faith which his own early sonnets seek to describe. The 1890s were the years of his formative manhood, the period he admitted to be his 'spiritual and chronological home': 'You must remember', he wrote to a friend in 1928, 'that we were not very much later than Ruskin, Pater, Swinburne, and Matthew Arnold: our atmosphere was that of poets and persons touched with religious enthusiasm or religious sadness... and not even psychology or the analysis of works of art could take away from art its human implications.' In his own critical writings there is the measured force and confidence we find in Mill, or Arnold, or Taine, that steady enquiry into the ultimate significance and value of life which the dissolution of religious faith made necessary. Arnold's belief that religion is 'morality touched with emotion' has an obvious affinity with Santayana's view of the relation of religion to poetry; and Arnold's eloquent insistence, in *Culture and Anarchy*, on 'right reason', on a 'full and harmonious development of our humanity', and his consequent advocacy of the Hellenic rather than the Hebraic ideal for the society of his time, is taken up by Santayana in a less sanguine temper though with greater singleness of purpose. Greek enlightenment is the standard by which the Protestant tradition is measured and found wanting: sometimes by overt comparison, as in 'The Poetry of Barbarism' or *Egotism in German Philosophy*; sometimes by implication, as in 'The Genteel Tradition in American Philosophy', where the old Puritan ethic with its brooding consciousness of sin is viewed under a cool clear light, and its residue in modern life detected.

A man with so strong an allegiance to the nineteenth-century moralistic tradition, and with so live a sense of the Hellenic achievement, was unlikely to be satisfied with a Pre-Raphaelite code of Beauty and Art as ends in themselves. His rejection of aestheticism was emphatic, as the extracts from *Reason in Art*, the essay 'What is Aesthetics?', and the portrait of Lionel Johnson sufficiently show; on ethical and on logical grounds such a cult was absurd:

The question whether aesthetics is a part of psychology or a philosophic discipline apart is... an insoluble question, because aesthetics is neither. The terms of the problem do violence to the structure of things. The lines of cleavage in human history and art do not isolate any such block of experience as aesthetics is supposed to describe... Aesthetic sensibility and artistic impulse are two gifts distinguishable from each other and from other human gifts; the pleasures that accompany them may of course be separated artificially from the massive pleasures and fluid energies of life. But to pride oneself on holding a single interest free from all others, and on being lost in that specific sensation to the exclusion of all its affinities and effects, would be to pride oneself on being a voluntary fool...There has never been any art worthy of notice without a practical bias and occasion, or without some intellectual or religious function.[1]

The *criticism* of art was accordingly 'a serious and public function': the deliberate investigation of what a work was good for. A moral judgment was a social one as well.

Now a social judgment must always be relative, since values were themselves relative to particular natures: Santayana held, with Spinoza, that we desire nothing because it is good, but that it is good only because we desire it. Ideally a man should spontaneously recognize the ideals natural to him, and nothing was less to the purpose in a critic than a vehement self-insistence. Yet if individual freedom lay in an innate specificity of character, our natures of course expressed themselves within a given society and felt its influence; there was a good relative to each species as well as each individual, and the critic had to perceive what it was. His sympathy, where intelligent, would issue in firm judgment of the actual in the interests of a clearly conceived and relevant ideal. Moreover, there were elements of mind that all men shared, and which were more or less permanent as well as universal, so that 'any deep interpretation of oneself' would have 'a largely representative truth'. Self-knowledge remained the ground of self-fulfilment, and of profitable criticism.

[1] What is Aesthetics?, vol. I.

Santayana would have understood but not accepted the import of D. H. Lawrence's essay on Benjamin Franklin: 'The perfectibility of man, dear God! When every man as long as he remains alive is in himself a multitude of conflicting men. Which of these do you choose to perfect at the expense of every other?' Living well meant living a harmonious because integrated life; rational adjustment was essential if such a life were to be attained; representation not accumulation was the principle of growth:

> The living organism, caught in the act, informs us how to reason and what to enjoy. The soul adopts the body's aims; from the body and from its instincts she draws a first hint of the right means to those accepted purposes...; that sympathetic bias enables her to distinguish events pertinent to the chosen interests, to compare impulse with satisfaction, and, by representing a new and circular current in the system, to preside over the formation of better habits, habits expressing more instincts at once and responding to more opportunities.[1]

Self-knowledge was not *suffisance:*

> In practice, values cannot be compared save as represented or enacted in the private imagination of somebody: for we could not conceive that an alien good *was* a good...unless we could sympathize with it in some way in our own persons; and on the warmth which we felt in so representing the alien good would hang our conviction that it was truly valuable and had worth in comparison with our own good.[2]

Now if these other values are really enacted within us—if our imagination, in other words, is strong—we shall feel a tension, an incipient challenge, and our sense for the scope of the good and the bad will be enlarged accordingly. Browning and Whitman, or aspects of the modern world, are not rejected because Santayana has failed to intuit them; they are rejected, after being characterized truly, in the interests of vital and harmonious life. During his American years, life was too real, his own sympathies too vigorous, for experience to be pictured and calmly transcended. Things were confronted because they were felt; they were judged because re-

[1] *Reason in Common Sense*, vol. II.

[2] The Philosophy of Mr Bertrand Russell, vol. II.

sponded to. A controlled tension, persisting while his mind retained its sap, is what makes Santayana's insight into the contemporary scene so distilled, penetrating and self-possessed. The contemplation goes deep because it has behind it a discipline, an energy that has been banked; for all his independence of mind, the valuer has a great deal of his own at stake in the valuation.

Santayana's retirement to Italy, at fifty-seven, as 'an elderly gentleman of leisure', his permanent removal of the world to a comfortable distance, marks the slackening of the observer into the imperturbable spectator, without stakes in the world that he viewed. Philosophy became a 'consolation', an 'edifice to go and live in for good', and though he continued to address society, the life he wrote out of (for all its declared naturalism) had become thin; in an essay like 'Platonism and the Spiritual Life', written in 1927, it is practically disembodied. 'I was never more entertained and less troubled than I am now', he informed a friend in 1939; '... what is happening interests me like ancient history, and illustrates the same truths', he was assuring another the following year. A philosopher who leans out of his edifice in so self-ministering a mood need not expect to command much of an audience. And even where Santayana's detachment fines to real intensity, as in this passage written in the Second War, 'human life' and 'human interests' have become too much algebraic symbols for the theme to acquire full weight:

> The natural world is indefinitely fertile; but its fertility is not directed by the human will; it is not governed, except in man, by human interests. The sentiment that it would justly inspire about human life and human hopes would be extremely sober. Beings that arise are likely to find means of subsistence and a chance to propagate their kind, because otherwise they would never have arisen; but in no particular case, and at no particular time, can a race or individual be sure of continued good fortune, and no specific hope about distant issues is ever likely to be realized. The ground shifts, the will of mankind deviates, and what the father dreamt of, the children neither fulfil nor desire.[1]

[1] *The Idler and His Works*, ed. Daniel Cory (New York, 1957), pp. 13–14.

The earlier Santayana had not wished to be Olympian; a moralist, he saw, might be too philosophic: he 'might see what sort of life is spontaneous in a given being and how far it may be harmonized with circumstances, yet his heart might remain cold, he might not suffer nor rejoice with the suffering or joy he foresaw'. And Santayana could admire Dickens because Dickens so loved 'the good of others'. Despite the lucid expertise of his philosophy, and the steadfastness with which he lived and expounded it, only in his novel, now, in parts of his autobiography that refer likewise to a distant past, and to friends, does he reveal a large humanity.

Apart from the portraits taken from the autobiography, and the essay on *Macbeth*, this Selection concentrates on Santayana's earlier work: the first volume on his criticism of literature and the arts, the second on his social criticism and moral philosophy—though these fields often shade into one another. Santayana was a man with a broad, unified range of knowledge at command, and the ideal he set himself can be inferred from his criticism of Bertrand Russell for the 'microscopic intensity' he showed, which 'narrowed each of his insights, no matter how varied these insights might be, lost the substance in the visible image, the sense in the logic of the words, and made him, though he might be many-sided, a many-sided fanatic'.

'The Genteel Tradition in American Philosophy' and *Character and Opinion in the United States* are fine examples of Santayana's method: he is a master of narrative that describes the social context with sympathy while embodying a judgment of it:

In the eighteen-eighties a good deal of old-fashioned shabbiness and jollity lingered about Harvard. Boston and Cambridge in those days resembled in some ways the London of Dickens: the same dismal wealth, the same speechifying, the same anxious respectability, the same sordid back streets, with their air of shiftlessness and decay, the same odd figures and loud humour, and, to add a touch of horror, the monstrous suspicion that some of the inhabitants might be secretly wicked. Life, for the undergraduates, was full of droll incidents and broad farce; it drifted good-naturedly from one commonplace thing to another. Standing packed in the tinkling horse-car, their coat collars above their ears and their feet deep in the winter straw, they jogged in a long half-hour to Boston, there to enjoy the delights of female company, the theatre, or a good dinner. And in the summer days, for Class Day and Commencement, feminine and elderly Boston would return the visit, led by the governor of Massachusetts in his hired carriage-and-four, and by the local orators and poets, brimming with jokes and conventional sentiments, and eager not so much to speed the youngsters on their career, as to air their own wit, and warm their hearts with punch and collective memories of youth.[1]

The ethos here is evoked, and the appraisal lodged, with a genial control. We soon feel, of course, a European mind behind that appraisal. Santayana's aim is similar to Arnold's in *Culture and Anarchy*: to reveal a society to itself from an outside viewpoint, to bring other standards to bear than the self-confirming ones it is used to. But though the skill with which he evokes the intellectual and moral background, and the clean focus he offers on the America of his day and place, make *Character and Opinion in the United States* and 'The Genteel Tradition in American Philosophy' valuable as cultural history—they deserve, surely, to be recognized as classics in the genre—much of his analysis has a continuing relevance. This is especially true of *Character and Opinion in the United States*, both in the discussion of Anglo-Saxon pragmatism and in the related appraisal of the *climate* of American life. The account of the former is sympathetic and discerning, but characteristically free of claptrap:

No one considering the English language, the English church, or English philosophy, or considering the common law and parliamentary government, would take them for perfect realizations of art or truth or an ideal polity. Institutions so jumbled and limping could never have been planned; they can never be transferred to another setting, or adopted bodily; but special circumstances and contrary currents have given them birth, and they are accepted and prized, where they are native, for keeping the door open to a great volume and variety of goods, at a moderate cost of danger and absurdity.[2]

[1] *Character and Opinion in the United States*, vol. II.
[2] *Ibid.*

The appraisal of American life is of course the crux of the book, and that life is really revealed; the general reflections derive from insights which are disinterested, ordered and keen. Santayana perceives, and really admires, the directness and warmth of Americans, their pragmatism, energy and self-reliance, but he notes a thinness in the mental climate, a mindless pressure of conformity that results from the absence of a central and living tradition. Education ought to mean the inculcation of distinct and luminous values: the mind was to be grounded in a clear-cut tradition and trained into excellence. The process at Harvard that he describes is the precise antithesis:

No single abstract opinion was particularly tabooed at Harvard; granted industry, sobriety, and some semblance of theism, no professor was expected to agree with any other. I believe the authorities would have been very well pleased, for the sake of completeness, to have added a Buddhist, a Moslem, and a Catholic scholastic to the philosophical faculty, if only suitable sages could have been found, house-trained, as it were, and able to keep pace with the academic machine and to attract a sufficient number of pupils...The teaching required was for the most part college teaching, in college subjects, such as might well have been entrusted to tutors; but it was given by professors in the form of lectures, excessive in number and too often repeated; and they were listened to by absent-minded youths, ill grounded in the humanities, and not keenly alive to intellectual interests...Accordingly, the professor of philosophy had to swim against rather a powerful current. Sometimes he succumbed to the reality; and if, for instance, he happened to mention Darwin, and felt a blank before him, he would add in a parenthesis, 'Darwin, Charles, author of the *Origin of Species*, 1859; epoch-making work.'[1]

Three general essays in volume II are relevant here: 'Classic Liberty', 'Liberalism and Culture', and 'The Intellectual Temper of the Age'. They make clear that Santayana's criticism of American *laisser-aller* in education is part of a larger case against the assumptions of liberal enlightenment.

The extracts from *The Life of Reason* are concerned with the life of the mind, the constitution of thought in particular:

[1] *Character and Opinion in the United States*, vol. II.

The fact that observation involves the senses, and the senses their organs, is one which a naturalist can hardly overlook; and when we add that logical habits, sanctioned by utility, are needed to interpret the data of sense, the humanity of science and all its constructions becomes clearer than day.[1]

The humanity of religion and metaphysics too: all categories of thought, all states of mind, however rapt, were functions of the human system. There were no final causes, or purposes at work in nature; God was an ideal, not a power. This is an ancient and impregnable position, though Santayana found himself in difficulties when he wished to argue for the vital role of religion in rational life. An efficacious dogma that should be avowedly fabulous, a divine spirit that should transparently symbolize the genius of men, such is easier to conceive than to imagine established. Most people, as Santayana recognized, need to believe in the existence of what they worship, in a divinity that is more than a necessary projection of the human mind, in ideals that express an ulterior reality. 'Santayana', said a friend, 'believes God does not exist, and that Mary is His mother'; a difficult act of faith. Spinoza was a man of far narrower sympathies, but he had this advantage as a moralist: he was a thoroughgoing pantheist, and could believe in an existent God.

Yet Santayana's naturalism, just because he faced its implications without compromise, enabled him to deflate metaphysical pretension in a devastating manner. The essay on Bergson is a memorable example: its thought detailed yet beautifully coherent, the expression of a live and organized intelligence in perfect possession of its ground. Bergson's vitalist theories are set out in clean, clear strokes, and their afflatus is dissolved in a cool confrontation:

[M. Bergson conceives that] when Shakespeare was composing his *Antony and Cleopatra*, for instance, he planted himself in the very heart of Rome and of Egypt, and in the very heart of the Queen of Egypt herself; what he had gathered from Plutarch and from elsewhere was, according to M. Bergson's view, a sort of glimpse of the remote reality itself, as if by telepathy he had been made to witness

[1] *Reason in Common Sense*, vol. II.

some part of it; or rather as if the scope of his consciousness had been suddenly extended in one direction, so as to embrace and contain bodily a bit of that outlying experience...In reality, of course,...this transporting oneself into the heart of a subject is a loose metaphor: the best one can do is to transplant the subject into one's own heart and draw *from oneself* impulses as profound as possible with which to vivify tradition and make it over in one's own image...What he conceives instead is that consciousness is a stuff out of which things are made, and has all the attributes, even the most material, of its several objects; and that there is no possibility of knowing, save by becoming what one is trying to know. So perception, for him, lies where its object does, and is some part of it; memory is the past experience itself, somehow shining through into the present; and Shakespeare's Cleopatra, I should infer, would have to be some part of Cleopatra herself—in those moments when she spoke English.[1]

This is an inhospitable clarification, and a return to Bergson enforces that it is a just one. Thought, for him, meant escaping from it, into a realm of portentous suggestion from where the workings of mind looked stale and unprofitable. The more recent success of Teilhard de Chardin—his mysticism less veiled and more crude—shows how we love to respond:

In spite of all evidence to the contrary, mankind may very well be advancing all around us at the moment—there are in fact many signs whereby we can reasonably suppose that it is advancing. But, if it is doing so, it must be—as is the way with very big things—doing so almost imperceptibly.[2]

Santayana is an antidote to such quackery, as to the habits of mind that engender it. And his essay shows another characteristic excellence, which gives it a decisive advantage over the fierce refutations of Bergson by Julien Benda or Jean-François Revel.[3] Both these critics, for all the intensity of their attack, give the impression of assailing the work in order to vent their exasperation at the man, as though their keenest satisfaction would be to kick Bergson—hard, every

[1] The Philosophy of M. Henri Bergson, vol. II.

[2] Teilhard de Chardin, *The Phenomenon of Man* (London, 1959).

[3] Julien Benda, *Le Bergsonisme ou une philosophie de la mobilité* (Paris, 1913); Jean-François Revel, *Pourquoi des Philosophes?* (Paris, 1957).

day of the year. The sharpness of Santayana's own rebuttal shows how he dislikes Bergson's attempt to confuse and invalidate intelligence in the interests of 'old human prejudices' and a vague comfortable faith, 'which he dreads to have stolen from him'; but Santayana's attention is still for the field of enquiry itself, the pursuit of the truth is what absorbs him. And even error, he sees, may fail to recognize itself: 'Derision...is not interpretation, and the better method of overcoming erratic ideas is to trace them out dialectically and see if they will not recognize their fatuity.'

The essays on the philosophy of Bertrand Russell and of Plotinus, and the two extracts from *Egotism in German Philosophy*, are of help in the way that the critique of Bergson is of help: subjects that the common reader is used to thinking unprofitable or inaccessible are shown to have a plain human interest, and a broader application than he had suspected. Russell's belief, for instance, that good and bad are independent of our responses to them, is not in the least esoteric; he was expressing, in deliberate form, sentiments that many adhere to in a conveniently vague way. Santayana surveys the ground from the standpoint of ethical relativity, which he shared—like much else in his morality—with Spinoza,[1] though expressing it in a manner quite his own. The refutation of Russell is admirable in its wit and temper, in its logic too; never was the *principle* of moral absolutism more quietly undermined:

Mr Russell and Mr Moore infer...that the presence of the good must be independent of all interests, attitudes, and opinions. They imagine that the truth of a proposition attributing a certain relative quality to an object contradicts the truth of another proposition attributing to the same object an opposite relative quality. Thus if a man here and another man at the antipodes call opposite directions up, 'only one of them can be right, though it may be very hard to know which is right'...For the human system whisky is truly more intoxicating than coffee, and the contrary opinion would be an

[1] Compare, for instance, the third and fourth paragraphs of Beauty and the Perception of Form, vol. I, with Spinoza's thirty-first Proposition, Demonstration and Corollary in Book III of the *Ethics*.

error; but what a strange way of vindicating this real, though relative, distinction, to insist that whisky is more intoxicating in itself, without reference to any animal; that it is pervaded, as it were, by an inherent intoxication, and stands dead drunk in its bottle! Yet just in this way Mr Russell and Mr Moore conceive things to be dead good and dead bad.[1]

Russell is reported to have said that it was Santayana who caused him to change his ethical doctrine, and we can appreciate that after he had read 'Hypostatic Ethics' the need for real change would have seemed urgent; but it is not a question of just endorsing Santayana as of being driven by him into sharp consideration of a fundamental issue, Russell providing the occasion. The quality of the thinking is borne out by the felicity of the language and the illustration, the entire absence of jargon or 'inner circle' terminology. It is a habitual excellence, in Santayana.

This unwelcome insistence that ideas express themselves, that thoughts be brought and held to their precise issue, is as evident in the work included in the first volume: the portraits, and the criticism of literature and the arts. Santayana is really appreciative of Emerson, for instance, responsive to that rapt and spontaneous sincerity, but the cackle is dryly faced down:

Individuals no doubt exist, he [Emerson] says to himself. But, ah! Napoleon is in every schoolboy. In every squatter in the western prairies we shall find an owner—

> Of Caesar's hand and Plato's brain,
> Of Lord Christ's heart, and Shakespeare's strain.

But how? we may ask. Potentially? Is it because any mind, were it given the right body and the right experience, were it made over, in a word, into another mind, would resemble that other mind to the point of identity? Or is it that our souls are already so largely similar that we are subject to many kindred promptings and share many ideals unrealizable in our particular circumstances? But then we should simply be saying that if what makes men different were removed, men would be indistinguishable, or that, in so far as they are now alike, they can understand one another by summoning up their respective experiences in the fancy. There would be no

[1] The Philosophy of Mr Bertrand Russell: Hypostatic Ethics, vol. II.

mysticism in that, but at the same time, alas, no eloquence, no paradox, and, if we must say the word, no nonsense.[1]

This brings out the interdependence in Emerson of the romantic and the confusedly mystical, and does so in a way that invites extension to that yearning for self-transcendence which characterizes Romanticism in general; the analysis of Bergson is relevant to the study of literature. It is, moreover, instructive to compare this account of Emerson with Henry James's a decade or so earlier. Santayana's portrait here, and those included from his autobiography, embody a real because unflinching viewpoint, as does his appraisal of the New England background in *Character and Opinion in the United States* or in 'The Genteel Tradition', whereas James's finely shaded sense for New Englanders, and for the relations between England and cultured America, protects as much as it reveals them. James, as Santayana once put it, is 'too gentle, too affectionate, too fulsome'. He wraps his New England figures, Hawthorne excepted, in a soft haze that he is far from extending to such as Whitman, or Dickens, or Hardy. In being generous one needs to be just; that Santayana could be both, his portrait of William James brings home.

Santayana was a distinctive literary critic: he only discussed writers who interested him; he concentrated primarily on the *ideas* a work expressed; and he did not illustrate his perceptions by close textual analysis, presuming that his readers would be sufficiently acquainted with the work at hand to test an insight for themselves. In fact, to judge from a letter he wrote in 1922, he did not think very highly of literary criticism at all:

You know Plato's contempt for the image of an image; but as a man's view of things is an image in the first place, and his work is an image of that, and the critic's feelings are an image of that work, and his writings an image of his feelings, and your idea of what the critic means only an image of his writings—please consider that you are steeping your poor original tea-leaves in their fifth wash of hot water, and are drinking slops... What you need is not more

[1] Emerson, vol. I.

criticism of current authors, but more *philosophy*: more courage and sincerity in facing nature directly, and in criticizing books or institutions only with a view to choosing among them whatever is most harmonious with the life you want to lead.[1]

But this was written when Santayana's own philosophy was becoming less expansive, increasingly concerned with self-salvation. Earlier he had been more hopeful that philosophy in the critic might be persuasive philosophy for the world at large, that what D. H. Lawrence termed 'a reasoned account of the feeling produced upon the critic' by a writer's work might have its representative value and so fulfil 'a serious and public function'. The tributes to Shelley, Dickens and *Hamlet*, or the onslaught on Whitman and Browning, are written with an audience very much in view. Yet even in his prime, Santayana's response to literature was restricted by his theory of art; he oversimplified the nature of creative genius because he had an insufficient sense of its scope. Poetry for him was 'discourse', and he is able to talk of the 'music, nobility and tenderness' of the 'medium', and of the poet 'clothing' his characters in 'tragic' or other 'robes'. I need not labour the point, since it has been made persuasively by F. R. Leavis in his essay, 'Tragedy and the *Medium*'. Commenting on Santayana's account of *Macbeth*, Leavis observes:

The critic who falls so complete a victim to the word 'medium'... doesn't, it is plain, understand the poetic—and the essentially dramatic—use of language that Shakespeare's verse supremely exemplifies. He cannot, then, understand the nature of the organization that goes with that use of language: he cannot appreciate the ways in which the themes and significances of the play are dramatically presented... [For] the 'philosophy', moral significance, or total upshot, of the play isn't stated but enacted.[2]

The essay to which this discussion refers, 'Tragic Philosophy', was written in 1936, and is decidedly inferior to the earlier literary criticism included in this Selection, but the weakness it exhibits is perceptible in Santayana's whole approach to literature. It explains why he inclines to view a writer's work

[1] *The Letters of George Santayana*, p. 196.

[2] F. R. Leavis, *The Common Pursuit* (London, 1952), p. 123.

rather than expose himself to it, and why he is so seldom at a loss to find the level of his response: we rarely detect in that response the smallest sign of felt inadequacy.

Yet the training he has undergone makes possible, too, the distinctive excellence of his literary criticism, in which a writer's work, brought to an unfamiliar but spacious focus, renews itself freshly and intelligibly in our minds. The brilliant pith and pungency of the intelligence show particularly well in the short essays: the account of Goethe, say, or of Spanish drama, where the generalizations flow from observation that is witty, forceful and particular:

> Such a people [the Spanish] will not go to the play to be vaguely entertained, as if they were previously bored. They are not habitually bored; they are full to the brim of their characteristic passions and ideas. They require that the theatre should set forth these passions and ideas as brilliantly and convincingly as possible, in order to be confirmed in them, and to understand and develop them more clearly... All eloquence, all issues, all sentiments, if they are not to seem vapid and trivial, must be such as each man can make his own, with a sense of enhanced vitality and moral glory. The lady, if he is to warm to her praises, must not be less divine than the one he loves, or might have loved; the hero must not fall short of what, under such circumstances, he himself would have wished to be. The language, too, must always be worthy of the theme: it cannot be too rapturous and eloquent... those lyrical ladies and entranced gentlemen of the Spanish drama are like filigree flowers upon golden stems; they belong to a fantastic ballet, to an exquisite dream, rather than to sane human society... How vast, how kindly, how enveloping does the world of Shakespeare seem in comparison![1]

The egotism of the romanticist is one of Santayana's most constant themes. And such romanticism is not seen academically, as a peculiar historical phenomenon, but as a life principle: its quickness to direct *our* responses, to control *our* lives, is what Santayana wishes us to feel:

> The attention he [the romantic egotist] bestows on things seems to him to bathe in light their truly interesting side. What he chiefly considers is his own experience—what he cared for first, what second, what he thinks today, what he will probably think tomorrow,

[1] A Contrast with Spanish Drama, vol. I.

what friends he has had, and how they have lost their charm, what religions he has believed in, and in general what contributions the universe has made to him and he to the universe.[1]

Literature, for Santayana, never loses its basis in life: he studies meaning to establish value. And if the more complex forms of art make the elucidation of that meaning a more testing affair than he perceives, his method has the sharpest relevance to the poetry of a Whitman or a Browning: their voluminous raptures are disentangled, contemplated and judged. Even at the level of Dickens or of *Hamlet* we are brought to a keener—and an ampler—understanding. Always, though, the romantic and the classical responses to life are the large points on which his criticism turns.

It is characteristic of Santayana that his critique of Browning should have been formulated when the latter's reputation was at its height, when he was applauded as poet-prophet of the age: the master of passion and the scourge of mediocrity and convention. 'The Poetry of Barbarism', in fact, was first delivered as a talk to the Boston Browning Society, and was not appreciated. It remains, still, the most devastating criticism Browning has been subjected to. Santayana was incapable of Henry James's sort of response to Browning: the effulgent ambiguity of 'splendid hocus-pocus' and so forth that James takes refuge in;[2] the poetry was to be confronted and reported on with honesty. It is just because Santayana has the courage to take Browning and Whitman seriously that his rebuttal has such force. He sees their gifts, but he sees, too, their 'ignorance' of the past, their 'contempt' for the lessons it can teach. No renewal of sensibility was possible on such terms. To canonize a Browning was dangerous folly. And the judgments rest on a real response to the poetry; Santayana does not give us a detailed local analysis, but that does not mean no analysis has been done:

[1] Hints of Egotism in Goethe, vol. I.

[2] See 'Browning in Westminster Abbey' (1890), and 'The Novel in *The Ring and the Book*' (1912). The first essay is to be found in *Robert Browning: A collection of critical essays*, ed. Philip Drew (London, 1966), pp. 11–16; the second in the *Quarterly Review* (1912), CCXVII, pp. 68–87.

Even without reference to ultimate ideals, one may notice in Browning many superficial signs of that deepest of all failures, the failure in rationality and the indifference to perfection. Such a sign is the turgid style, weighty without nobility, pointed without naturalness or precision. Another sign is the 'realism' of the personages, who, quite like men and women in actual life, are always displaying traits of character and never attaining character as a whole. Other hints might be found in the structure of the poems, where the dramatic substance does not achieve a dramatic form; in the metaphysical discussion, with its confused prolixity and absence of result; in the moral ideal, where all energies figure without their ultimate purposes; in the religion, which breaks off the expression of this life in the middle, and finds in that suspense an argument for immortality...; but more careful reflection is necessary to understand the nature of this incapacity, its cause, and the peculiar accent which its presence gives to those ideas and impulses which Browning stimulates in us.[1]

The essay exerted a decisive influence, and Browning's admirers were unable to gainsay it; though Chesterton declared that the description of barbarism was 'an excellent and perfect definition' of the poet's genius, that Santayana had uncovered the 'root virtue of Browning's poetry' and then labelled that virtue 'a vice'.

No other of Santayana's literary essays has quite the same authority and scope, but each challenges our stock outlook: the work is *discussed*, and with a real attentiveness to the ideals it embodies. By the end a distinct viewpoint has been lodged. Even where we find that viewpoint inadequate, Santayana impresses by the severity of his standards and the honesty with which he applies them. We are never allowed to forget that the dignity of poetry lies in 'its fit rendering of the meanings and values of life'. 'Platonic Love in Some Italian Poets' is probably the least accessible of the essays, at least to the Anglo-Saxon reader, and is marred by preciosity. But the description of the Platonic idea of love—'the transformation of the appreciation of beautiful things into the worship of an ideal beauty and ...of the love of particular persons into the love of God'—with its illustration in the work of particular

[1] The Poetry of Barbarism, vol. I.

Italian poets, establishes that such an ideal is not the bloodless and refutable thing contemporary idiom makes it; that Dante and Michelangelo, for instance, felt it as a living power, and that it is possible to talk too glibly of self-fulfilment. The theme is given a convincing extension in 'The Absence of Religion in Shakespeare'. We are accustomed to think that in *Macbeth* and *King Lear*, supremely, Shakespeare shows himself a religious dramatist. Santayana reminds us that 'religious' is not a rhetorical, vague term, but that it involves a religion: a distinct view of human life and destiny. Greek drama is religious, for it gives 'man in his relations, surrounded by a kindred universe in which he fills his allotted place. He knows the meaning and issue of his life, and does not voyage without a chart.' If Shakespeare were the Christian dramatist that he is often taken to be, he would necessarily have—as he does not—a comparable sense of steady forces 'dominating and transcending' human affairs. Thus Santayana argues that Shakespeare, for all his genius, does not give us 'all that the highest poet could give'. The case is argued with skill, and with an attentiveness to the arguments that might be mobilized against it.

The quality of Santayana's account of *Hamlet*, of Shelley, and of Dickens makes us regret that he did not address himself more often to the work of specific writers. 'Hamlet' is the best essay of the three: there are disproportions in the argument (the ancillary characters being insufficiently considered), but nowhere else does Santayana give such evidence of close attention, of full and feeling response, to the central detail of a work. The hiatuses and inconsistencies in the play are expertly set out, yet his perception that Shakespeare has imperfectly assimilated an old plot does not lead him, as it led T. S. Eliot, to brand the play 'an artistic failure', still less to dwindle it to 'the feeling of a son towards a guilty mother'. He argues a more flexible and interesting case: that the dislocations in the plot have psychological appositeness:

In Hamlet's personality incoherent sentiments, due, in a genetic sense, to the imperfect recasting of a grotesque old story, are made attributable ideally to his habit of acting out a mood irresponsibly

> and of giving a mock expression to every successive intuition... Thus the least digested elements in the fable come, by a happy turn, to constitute its profoundest suggestion.[1]

Santayana's belief that the romantic mind is necessarily incoherent, and the art that expresses it always disorganized, is open to criticism, especially since he classed Shakespeare in all his phases as more or less of a romantic, and failed to perceive real structure in any of his plays. But such a view is relevant to the study of *Hamlet*, and enables Santayana to make the necessary criticisms of the play while accounting for the esteem in which it is held. It is a more persuasive approach than labelling Hamlet a sick adolescent and dismissing the play's perennial appeal as a sign of the childishness of men. The breadth and finesse of Santayana's view, his ability to synthesize various insights, mean that he can judge Hamlet's irrationality—'he acts without reflection, as he reflects without acting...[and] eternally pursues the good in a way especially designed never to attain it'—can judge it, while justifying the intensity of his own interest in him. He is one of the few critics able to focus on the 'Prince' without transforming him into a manikin of his own invention, and to discuss his 'philosophy' in a way that really illumines the play from which it has been abstracted. By the end he can say (what he has demonstrated) that 'here is no necessary human tragedy', while keeping his admiration entire: 'There is no richer or more exquisite monument to the failure of emotional goodwill, and of intelligence inclined to embroider rather than to build. So absolute a feat of imagination cannot be...estimated by any standard of which it does not itself furnish the suggestion and type.'

Santayana argues a similar case in his defence of Shelley, but with less success. He sets out unerringly Shelley's deficiencies: his egotism and invincible obtuseness, his inability to learn from experience, the small relevance of his utopian dreams to the actual conditions of human life; and has no difficulty in showing that his poetry is unintelligent in the

[1] Hamlet, vol. I.

same ways. But the attempt to see these weaknesses as the conditions of Shelley's poetic strength is not so convincing. We are made so aware of Shelley's estrangement from reality, of the 'moral incompetence' of his 'moral intensity', that any vindication of them becomes very difficult:

> He [Shelley] was thirsting to destroy kings, priests, soldiers, parents, and heads of colleges—to destroy them, I mean, in their official capacity; and the exhibition of their vileness in all its diabolical purity might serve to remove scruples in the half-hearted. We, whom the nineteenth century has left so tender to historical rights and historical beauties, may wonder that a poet, an impassioned lover of the beautiful, could have been such a leveller, and such a vandal in his theoretical destructiveness. But...he had, and knew he had, the seeds of a far lovelier order in his own soul; there he found the plan or memory of a perfect commonwealth of nature ready to rise at once on the ruins of this sad world, and to make regret for it impossible.[1]

Now there is no doubt that *Shelley* 'knew' he had the 'plan' of 'a far lovelier order in his own soul', an order 'ready to rise at once on the ruins' of this one; the essay makes beautifully clear the psychology of such certitude. But did Santayana believe that it was 'ready to rise', and can we? It was because Shelley was entrenched in this certitude that he could legislate for humanity in pure ignorance and disdain of its actual constitution and needs: 'With a sort of tyranny of which he does not suspect the possible cruelty, he would impose his ideals of love and equality upon all creatures; he would make enthusiasts of clowns and doves of vultures.' Since intelligence, by Santayana's own definition, is quickness in seeing things as they are, Shelley's tenacious failure to understand reality would seem a sign of stupidity. But, says Santayana, he was stupid only by Matthew Arnold's and the world's standards; actually, his obtuseness was the condition of a rarer excellence: it left him free to create an imaginary world undeformed by compromise with the 'perversities' of real life. It is a world, Santayana adds, that the vital spirit within many of us 'would gladly live in if it could have its

[1] Shelley, vol. I.

way'—except of course that it can't, actual life involving adaptation to existent things. Shelley's poetry is thus praised for contradicting reality and providing a refuge from it. Yet according to the criteria set out in 'The Elements and Function of Poetry', and in other of Santayana's works, such poetry, however delightful, remains meretricious: 'The highest ideality is the comprehension of the real', and poetry, where its appeal is to adequate minds, portrays 'the ideals of experience and destiny'. Santayana's Platonic idealism and his sense of fact—his sensibility and his intelligence, as it were—go different ways in the essay and involve him in a self-contradiction. There result confusions in the argument; and disingenuousness even, as in the presentment of Arnold. We might say that he supplies the most deadly rebuttal of his own defence, and that his analysis of Shelley's revolutionary principles leaves them without a leg to stand on.

The tribute to Dickens is a fine one. So much is said in so little, with such ease and such perspicacity. If, having none of Dickens's novels to hand, we wished to represent succinctly some of the chief elements of his genius, we would surely choose this essay:

> The sleepy fat boy in *Pickwick* looks foolish; but in himself he is no more foolish, nor less solidly self-justified, than a pumpkin lying on the ground. Toots seems ridiculous; and we laugh heartily at his incoherence, his beautiful waistcoats, and his extreme modesty; but when did anybody more obviously grow into what he is because he couldn't grow otherwise? So with Mr Pickwick, and Sam Weller, and Mrs Gamp, and Micawber, and all the rest of this wonderful gallery; they are ridiculous only by accident, and in a context in which they never intended to appear. If Oedipus and Lear and Cleopatra do not seem ridiculous, it is only because tragic reflection has taken them out of the context in which, in real life, they would have figured. If we saw them as facts, and not as emanations of a poet's dream, we should laugh at them till doomsday; what grotesque presumption, what silly whims, what mad contradictions of the simplest realities![1]

Here is no beery patronage of Dickens as a master of the wilfully grotesque, but exact appreciation of the naturalness and

[1] Dickens, vol. I.

the truth of his comedy; that it comes not to elude life but to reveal it. Dickens plays off our pompous notions of other people and ourselves against the blunt reality, involves us in our common humanity. Possessed of a 'capacity for vast sympathetic participation in the daily life of mankind', free of the least taint of priggishness or of arrogance, he could contemplate average, friendly, ramshackle existence and celebrate it as 'a golden mediocrity'. This tribute to the saturation and humanity of Dickens's art is the more effective for being accompanied by so absolute a sense of its deficiencies: that it is 'intellectually...provincial and poor', insensible to 'the greater themes of human imagination', devoid, in particular, of religious feeling: 'Churches, in his novels, are vague, desolate places where one has ghastly experiences, and where only the pew-opener is human'. Like Henry James, in his study of Hawthorne, Santayana enumerates the missing 'items of high civilization'. The criticism is valuable for being clear-cut, and arrestingly un-English; it induces us, as Santayana's writings so often do, to try and relate our responses to adequate standards. But when Santayana claims that Dickens was a 'waif', 'utterly disinherited', with 'no *ideas* on any subject', we perceive that he is simplifying: that Dickens's work can be more manifold and searching than the terms of his appraisal allow. Does *Dombey and Son*, or *Little Dorrit*, or *Hard Times*, or *Great Expectations* affect us as the work of a novelist without an idea on any subject? Does Santayana render for us the effect of *their* art? The criticism of F. R. Leavis, for one, has shown how much of structure there can be in Dickens's best novels, with what fullness they enact large and central human experience. But Santayana's critique is valuable because it illuminates important aspects of Dickens's genius, and even where we find the appraisal inadequate we are stimulated into making clear to ourselves the grounds of our dissatisfaction. Santayana, in fact, like any good critic, sends us back to the work he criticizes.

In 'The Function of Criticism at the Present Time', Matthew Arnold observes: 'how little of mind, or anything so worthy and quickening as mind, comes into the motives which alone, in general, impel great masses of men'. It is Santayana's distinction that, feeling the truth of this with the force he does, he yet holds absolute for the life of intelligence, for the creation of thought that is clear and alive: 'we cannot cease to think and still continue to know'; 'a habitual indulgence in the inarticulate is a sure sign of the philosopher who has not learned to think, the poet who has not learned to write... the impression that has not learned to express itself'. This conviction that the profundity of feeling 'is to be measured by its justifying relations', not by its intensity, and that intelligence is 'the highest form of vitality', accounts for the centrality, the resource and reasonableness of his criticism; his disinclination to retreat into vehement affirmation or yea-saying of any kind. He never tries to coerce us into seeing as he does: the appeal is always to the facts and ideal possibilities of the case, to the espousal of them for the truth's sake and not for his. We are encouraged to view our prepossessions with a certain dispassionateness, to become aware of their origin and conditions and thus avoid that hatred of all ideas not making for 'the habitual goal of our thought'. Yet the ultimate ideal remains always the same: 'perfection of form' and 'harmony in strength'. It is because Santayana works with such intelligence and style to vindicate this ideal that he takes his place among those writers who shape our thought, as well as question it.

Literature

PLATONIC LOVE IN SOME ITALIAN POETS

When the fruits of philosophic reflection, condensed into some phrase, pass into the common language of men, there does not and there cannot accompany them any just appreciation of their meaning or of the long experience and travail of soul from which they have arisen. Few doctrines have suffered more by popularization than the intuitions of Plato. The public sees in Platonic sayings little more than phrases employed by unpractical minds to cloak the emptiness of their yearnings. Finding these fragments of an obsolete speech put to bad uses, we are apt to ignore and despise them, much as a modern peasant might despise the fragment of a frieze or a metope which he found built into his cottage wall. It is not only the works of plastic art that moulder and disintegrate to furnish materials for the barbarous masons of a later age: the great edifices of reason also crumble, their plan is lost, and their fragments, picked where they happen to lie, become the materials of a feebler thought. In common speech we find such bits of ancient wisdom embedded; they prove the intelligence of some ancestor of ours, but are no evidence of our own. When used in ignorance of their meaning, they become misplaced flourishes, lapses into mystery in the business-like plainness of our thought.

Yet there is one man, the archaeologist, to whom nothing is so interesting as just these stones which a practical builder would have rejected. He forgives the ignorance and barbarism that placed them where they are; he is absorbed in studying their sculptured surface and delighted if his fancy can pass from them to the idea of the majestic whole to which they once belonged. So, in the presence of a much-abused philosophic phrase, we may be interested in reconstructing the experience which once gave it meaning and form. Words are at least the tombs of ideas, and the most conventional formulas of poets or theologians are still good subjects for the archaeologist of passion. He may find a treasure there; or at any rate he may hope to be rewarded for his labour by the ideal restoration of some once beautiful temple of Athena.

Something of this kind is what we may now attempt to do with regard to one or two Platonic ideas, ideas which, under the often ironical title of Platonic love, are constantly referred to and seldom understood. These ideas may be defined as the transformation of the appreciation of beautiful things into the worship of an ideal beauty and the transformation of the love of particular persons into the love of God. These mystical phrases may acquire a new and more human meaning if we understand, at least in part, how they first came to be spoken. We shall then not think of them merely as the reported sayings of Plato or Plotinus, Porphyry or Proclus; we shall not learn them by rote, as the unhappy student learns the enigmas, which, in the histories of philosophy, represent all that survives of the doctrine of a Thales or a Pythagoras. We shall have some notion of the ideas that once prompted such speech.

And we shall be the better able to reconstruct those conceptions inasmuch as the reflection by which they are bred has recurred often in the world—has recurred, very likely, in our own experience. We are often Platonists without knowing it. In some form or other Platonic ideas occur in all poetry of passion when it is seasoned with reflection. They are particularly characteristic of some Italian poets, scattered from the thirteenth to the sixteenth centuries. These poets had souls naturally Platonic; even when they had heard something of Plato they borrowed nothing from him. They repeated his phrases, when they did so, merely to throw the authority of an ancient philosopher over the spontaneous suggestions of their own minds. Their Platonism was all their own: it was Christian, medieval, and chivalrous, both in origin and expression. But it was all the more genuine for being a reincarnation rather than an imitation of the old wisdom.

Nothing, for example, could be a better object-lesson in Platonism than the well-known sentimental history of Dante.

There is no essential importance in the question whether Dante could have read anything of Plato or come indirectly under his influence. The Platonism of Dante is, in any case, quite his own. It is the expression of his inner experience moulded by the chivalry and theology of his time. He tells us the story himself very quaintly in the *Vita Nuova*.

At the age of nine he saw, at a wedding-feast in Florence, Beatrice, then a child of seven, who became, forthwith, the mistress of his thoughts. This precocious passion ruled his imagination for life, so that, when he brings to an end the account of the emotions she aroused in him by her life and death, he tells us that he determined to speak no more about her until he should be able to do so more worthily, and to say of her what had never been said of any woman. In the *Divine Comedy*, accordingly, where he fulfils this promise, she appears transfigured into a heavenly protectress and guide, whose gentle womanhood fades into an impersonation of theological wisdom. But this lifelong devotion of Dante to Beatrice was something purely mental and poetical; he never ventured to woo; he never once descended or sought to descend from the sphere of silent and distant adoration; his tenderness remained always tearful and dreamy, like that of a supersensitive child.

Yet, while his love of Beatrice was thus constant and religious, it was by no means exclusive. Dante took a wife as Beatrice herself had taken a husband; the temptations of youth, as well as the affection of married life, seem to have existed beneath this ideal love, not unrebuked by it, indeed, but certainly not disturbing it. Should we be surprised at this species of infidelity? Should we regard it as proof of the artificiality and hollowness of that so transcendental passion, and smile, as people have done in the case of Plato himself, at the thin disguise of philosophy that covers the most vulgar frailties of human nature? Or, should we say, with others, that Beatrice is a merely allegorical figure, and the love she is said to inspire nothing but a symbol for attachment to wisdom and virtue? These are old questions, and insoluble by any positive method, since they cannot be answered by the facts but only by our interpretation of them. Our solution can have little historical value, but it will serve to test our understanding of the metaphysics of feeling.

To guide us in this delicate business we may appeal to a friend of Dante, his fellow-poet Guido Cavalcanti, who will furnish us with another example of this same sort of idealization, and this same sort of inconstancy, expressed in a manner that will repay analysis. Guido Cavalcanti had a Beatrice of his own—something of the kind was then expected of every gentle knight and poet—and Guido's Beatrice was called Giovanna. Dante seems to acknowledge the parity of his friend's passion with his own by coupling the names of the two ladies, Monna Vanna and Monna Bice, in one or two of the sonnets he addresses to Guido. Now it came to pass that Guido, in the fervour of his devotion, at once chivalrous and religious, bethought him of making a pilgrimage to the tomb of Saint James the Apostle, at Compostela in Spain. Upon this journey—a journey beguiled, no doubt, by thoughts of the beautiful Giovanna he had left in Florence—he halted in the city of Toulouse. But at Toulouse, as chance would have it, there lived a lovely lady by the name of Mandetta, with whom it was impossible for the chivalrous pilgrim not to fall in love; for chivalry is nothing but a fine emblazoning of the original manly impulse to fight every man and love every woman. Now in an interesting sonnet Guido describes the conflict of these two affections, or perhaps we should rather say, their union.

> There is a lady in Toulouse so fair,
>   So young, so gentle, and so chastely gay,
> She doth a true and living likeness bear
>   In her sweet eyes to Love, whom I obey.

The word I have, to avoid confusion, here rendered by 'Love' is in the original 'la Donna mia', 'my Lady'; so that we have our poet falling in love with Mandetta on account of her striking resemblance to Giovanna. Is this inconstancy or only a more delicate and indirect homage? We shall see; for Guido goes on to represent his soul, according to his custom, as a being that dwells and moves about in the chambers of his heart; and speaking still of Mandetta, the lady of Toulouse, he continues:

> Within my heart my soul, when she appeared,
>   Was filled with longing and was fain to flee
> Out of my heart to her, yet was afeared
>   To tell the lady who my Love might be.
> She looked upon me with her quiet eyes,
>   And under their sweet ray my bosom burned,
> Cheered by Love's image, that within them lies.

So far we have still the familiar visible in the new and making its power; Mandetta is still nothing but a stimulus to reawaken the memory of Giovanna. But before the end there is trouble. The sting of the present attraction is felt in contrast to the eternal ideal. There is a necessity of sacrifice, and he cries, as the lady turns away her eyes:

> Alas! they shot an arrow as she turned,
> And with a death-wound from the piercing dart
> My soul came sighing back into my heart.

Perhaps this merely means that the lady was disdainful; had she been otherwise the poet might never have written sonnets about her, and surely not sonnets in which her charms were reduced to a Platonic reminiscence of a fairer ideal. But it is this turning away of the face of love, this ephemeral quality of its embodiments, that usually stimulates the imagination to the construction of a supersensible ideal in which all those evaporated impulses may meet again and rest in an adequate and permanent object. So that while Guido's 'death-wound' was perhaps in reality nothing but the rebuff offered him by a prospective mistress, yet the sting of it, in a mind of Platonic habit, served at once to enforce the distinction between the ideal beauty, so full of sweetness and heavenly charm, which had tempted the soul out of his heart on its brief adventure, and the particular and real object against which the soul was dashed, and from which it returned bruised and troubled to its inward solitude.

So the meditative Guido represents his experience: a new planet swam into his ken radiant with every grace and virtue; yet all the magic of that lady lay in her resemblance to the mysterious Giovanna, the double of Beatrice, the ideal of the poet's imagination. The soul, at first, went out eagerly to the new love as to an image and embodiment of the old, but was afraid, and justly, to mention the ideal in the presence of the reality. There is always danger in doing that; it breaks the spell and reduces us again to the old and patient loyalty to the unseen. The present thing being so like the ideal, we unhesitatingly pursue it: but we are quickly disappointed, and the soul returns sighing and mortally wounded, as the new object of passion fades away.

We may now understand somewhat better that strange combination of loyalty and disloyalty which we find in Dante. While the object of love is any particular thing, it excludes all others; but it includes all others as soon as it becomes a general ideal. All beauties attract by suggesting the ideal and then fail to satisfy by not fulfilling it. While Giovanna remained a woman, Guido, as his after life plainly showed, had no difficulty in forgetting her and in loving many others with a frank heart; but when Giovanna had become a name for the absolute ideal, that sovereign mistress could never be forgotten, and the thought of her subordinated every particular attachment and called the soul away from it. Compared with the ideal, every human perfection becomes a shadow and a deceit; every mortal passion leaves, as Keats has told us,

> A heart high-sorrowful and cloyed,
> A burning forehead and a parching tongue.

Such is the nature of idealization. Like the Venus of Apelles, in which all known beauties were combined, the ideal is the union of all we prize in all creatures; and the mind that has once felt the irresistible compulsion to create this ideal and to believe in it has become incapable of unreserved love of anything else. The absolute is a jealous god; it is a consuming fire that blasts the affections upon which it feeds. For this reason the soul of Guido, in his sonnet, is mortally wounded by the shaft of that beauty which has awakened a vehement longing for perfection without being able to satisfy it. All things become to the worshipper of the ideal so many signs and symbols of what he seeks; like the votary who, kneeling now before one image and now before another, lets his incense float by all with a certain abstracted impartiality, because his aspiration mounts through them equally to the invisible God they alike represent.

Another aspect of the same process is well described by Shakespeare, in whom Italian influences count for much, when he says to the person he has chosen as the object of his idealization:

> Thy bosom is endearèd with all hearts
>   Which I, by lacking, have supposèd dead,
> And there reigns love and all love's loving parts
>   And all those friends which I thought burièd.
> How many a holy and obsequious tear
>   Hath dear religious love stolen from mine eye
> As interest for the dead, which now appear
>   But things removed, which hidden in thee lie.
> Thou art the grave where buried love doth live
>   Hung with the trophies of my lovers gone,
> Who all their parts of me to thee did give:
>   That due of many now is thine alone.
> Their images I loved I view in thee,
> And thou, all they, hast all the all of me.

We need not, then, waste erudition in trying to prove whether Dante's Beatrice or Guido's Giovanna or anyone else who has been the subject of the greater poetry of love, was a symbol or a reality. To poets and philosophers real things are themselves symbols. The child of seven whom Dante saw at the Florentine feast was, if you will, a reality. As such she is profoundly unimportant. To say that Dante loved her then and ever after is another way of saying that she was a symbol to him. That is the way with childish loves. Neither the conscious spell of the senses nor the affinities of taste and character can then be powerful, but the sense of loneliness and the vague need of loving may easily conspire with the innocence of the eyes to fix upon a single image and to make it the imaginary goal of all those instincts which as yet do not know themselves.

When with time these instincts become explicit and select their respective objects, if the inmost heart still remains unsatisfied, as it must in all profound or imaginative natures, the name and memory of that vague early love may well subsist as a symbol for the perfect good yet unattained. It is intelligible that as time goes on that image, grown thus consciously symbolic, should become interchangeable with the abstract method of pursuing perfection—that Beatrice, that is, should become the same as sacred theology. Having recognized that she was to his childish fancy what the ideals of religion were to his mature imagination, Dante intentionally fused the two, as every poet intentionally fuses the general and the particular, the universal and the personal. Beatrice thenceforth appeared, as Plato wished that our loves should, as a manifestation of absolute beauty and as an avenue of divine grace. Dante merely added his Christian humility and tenderness to the insight of the pagan philosopher.

The tendency to impersonality, we see, is essential to the ideal. It could not fulfil its functions if it retained too many of the traits of any individual. A blind love, an unreasoning passion, is therefore inconsistent with the Platonic spirit, which is favourable rather to abstraction from persons and to admiration of qualities. These may, of course, be found in many individuals. Too much subjection to another personality makes the expression of our own impossible, and the ideal is nothing but a projection of the demands of our imagination. If the imagination is overpowered by too strong a fascination, by the absolute dominion of an alien influence, we form no ideal at all. We must master a passion before we can see its meaning.

For this reason, among others, we find so little Platonism in that poet in whom we might have expected to find most—I mean in Petrarch. Petrarch is musical, ingenious, learned, and passionate, but he is weak. His art is greater than his thought. In the quality of his mind there is nothing truly distinguished. The discipline of his long and hopeless love brings him little wisdom, little consolation. He is lachrymose and sentimental at the end as at the beginning, and his best dream of heaven, expressed, it is true, in entrancing verse, is only to hold his lady's hand and hear her voice. Sometimes, indeed, he repeats what he must have read and heard so often, and gives us his version of Plato in half a sonnet. Thus, for instance, speaking of his love for Laura, he says in one place:

> Hence comes the understanding of love's scope
> That seeking her to perfect good aspires,
> Accounting little what all flesh desires;
> And hence the spirit's happy pinions ope
> In flight impetuous to the heaven's choirs,
> Wherefore I walk already proud in hope.

If we are looking, however, for more direct expressions of the idealism of feeling, of love, and the sense of beauty passing into religion, we shall do well to turn to another Italian, not so great a poet as Petrarch by any means, but a far greater man—to Michael Angelo. Michael Angelo justly regarded himself as essentially a sculptor, and said even of painting that it was not his art; his verses are therefore both laboured and rough. Yet they have been too much neglected, for they breathe the same pathos of strength, the same agony in hope, as his Titanic designs.

Like every Italian of culture in those days, Michael Angelo was in the habit of addressing little pieces to his friends, and of casting his thoughts or his prayers into the mould of a sonnet or a madrigal. Verse has a greater naturalness and a wider range among the Latin peoples than among the English; poetry and prose are less differentiated. In French, Italian, and Spanish, as in Latin itself, elegance and neatness of expression suffice for verse. The reader passes without any sense of incongruity or anti-climax from passion to reflection, from sentiment to satire, from flights of fancy to homely details: the whole has a certain human sincerity and intelligibility which weld it together. As the Latin languages are not composed of two diverse elements, as English is of Latin and German, so the Latin mind does not have two spheres of sentiment, one vulgar and the other sublime. All changes are variations on a single key, which is the key of intelligence. We must not be surprised, therefore, to find now a message to a friend, now an artistic maxim, now a bit of dialectic, and now a confession of sin, taking the form of verse and filling out the fourteen lines of a sonnet. On the contrary, we must look to these familiar compositions for the most genuine evidence of a man's daily thoughts.

We find in Michael Angelo's poems a few recurring ideas, or rather the varied expression of a single half aesthetic, half religious creed. The soul, he tells us in effect, is by nature made for God and for the enjoyment of divine beauty. All true beauty leads to the idea of perfection; the effort toward perfection is the burden of all art, which labours, therefore, with a superhuman and insoluble problem. All love, also, that does not lead to the love of God and merge into that love, is a long and hopeless torment; while the light of love is already the light of heaven, the fire of love is already the fire of hell. These are the thoughts that perpetually recur, varied now with a pathetic reference to the poet's weariness and old age, now with an almost despairing appeal for divine mercy, often with a powerful and rugged description of the pangs of love, and with a pious acceptance of its discipline. The whole is intense, exalted, and tragic, haunted by something of that profound terror, of that magnificent strength, which we admire in the figures of the Sistine Chapel, those noble agonies of beings greater than any we find in this world.

What, we may ask, is all this tragedy about? What great sorrow, what great love, had Michael Angelo or his giants that they writhe so supernaturally? As those decorative youths are sprinkled over the Sistine vault, filled, we know not why, with we know not what emotion, so these scraps of verse, these sibylline leaves of Michael Angelo's, give us no reason for their passion. They tell no story; there seems to have been no story to tell. There is something impersonal and elusive about the subject and occasion of these poems. Attempts have been made to attribute them to discreditable passions, as also to a sentimental love for Vittoria Colonna. But the friendship with Vittoria Colonna was an incident of Michael Angelo's mature years; some of the sonnets and madrigals are addressed to her, but we cannot attribute to her influence the passion and sorrow that seem to permeate them all.

Perhaps there is less mystery in this than the curious would have us see in it. Perhaps the love and beauty, however base their primal incarnation, are really, as they think themselves, aspirations toward the Most High. In the long studies and weary journeys of the artist, in his mighty inspiration, in his intense love of the structural beauty of the human body, in his vicissitudes of fortune and his artistic disappointments, in his exalted piety, we may see quite enough explanation for the burden of his soul. It is not necessary to find vulgar causes for the extraordinary feelings of an extraordinary man. It suffices that life wore this aspect to him; that the great demands of his spirit so expressed themselves in the presence of his world. Here is a madrigal in which the Platonic theory of beauty is clearly stated:

> For faithful guide unto my labouring heart
> Beauty was given me at birth,
> To be my glass and lamp in either art.
> Who thinketh otherwise misknows her worth,
> For highest beauty only gives me light
> To carve and paint aright.
> Rash is the thought and vain
> That maketh beauty from the senses grow.
> She lifts to heaven hearts that truly know,
> But eyes grown dim with pain
> From mortal to immortal cannot go
> Nor without grace of God look up again.

And here is a sonnet, called by Mr Symonds 'The heavenly birth of love and beauty'. I borrow in part from his translation:

My love's life comes not from this heart of mine.
The love wherewith I love thee hath no heart,
Turned thither whither no fell thoughts incline
And erring human passion leaves no smart.
Love, from God's bosom when our souls did part,
Made me pure eye to see, thee light to shine,
And I must needs, half mortal though thou art,
In spite of sorrow know thee all divine.
As heat in fire, so must eternity
In beauty dwell; through thee my soul's endeavour
Mounts to the pattern and the source of thee;
And having found all heaven in thine eyes,
Beneath thy brows my burning spirit flies
There where I loved thee first to dwell for ever.

Something of this kind may also be found in the verses of Lorenzo de' Medici, who, like Michael Angelo, was a poet only incidentally, and even thought it necessary to apologize in a preface for having written about love. Many of his compositions are, indeed, trival enough, but his pipings will not seem vain to the severest philosopher when he finds them leading to strains like the following, where the thought rises to the purest sphere of tragedy and of religion:

As a lamp, burning through the waning night,
When the oil begins to fail that fed its fire
Flares up, and in its dying waxes bright
And mounts and spreads, the better to expire;
So in this pilgrimage and earthly flight
The ancient hope is spent that fed desire,
And if there burn within a greater light
'Tis that the vigil's end approacheth nigher.
Hence thy last insult, Fortune, cannot move,
Nor death's inverted torches give alarm;
I see the end of wrath and bitter moan.
My fair Medusa into sculptured stone
Turns me no more, my Siren cannot charm.
Heaven draws me up to its supernal love.

From such spontaneous meditation Lorenzo could even pass to verses officially religious; but in them too, beneath the threadbare metaphors of the pious muse and her mystical paradoxes, we may still feel the austerity and firmness of reason. The following stanzas, for instance, taken from his *Laude Spirituali*, assume a sublime meaning if we remember that the essence to which they are addressed, before being a celestial Monarch into whose visible presence any accident might usher us, was a general idea of what is good and an intransitive rational energy, indistinguishable from the truth of things.

O let this wretched life within me die
  That I may live in thee, my life indeed;
In thee alone, where dwells eternity,
  While hungry multitudes death's hunger feed.
I list within, and hark! Death's stealthy tread!
I look to thee, and nothing then is dead.

Then eyes may see a light invisible
  And ears may hear a voice without a sound,—
A voice and light not harsh, but tempered well,
  Which the mind wakens when the sense is drowned,
Till, wrapped within herself, the soul hath flown
To that last good which is her inmost own.

When, sweet and beauteous Master, on that day,
  Reviewing all my loves with aching heart,
  I take from each its bitter self away,
The remnant shall be thou, their better part.
This perfect sweetness be his single store
Who seeks the good; this faileth nevermore.

A thirst unquenchable is not beguiled
  By draught on draught of any running river
Whose fiery waters feed our pangs for ever,
  But by a living fountain undefiled.
O sacred well, I seek thee and were fain
To drink; so should I never thirst again.

Having before us these characteristic expressions of Platonic feeling, as it arose again in a Christian age, divorced from the accidental setting which Greek manners had given it, we may be better able to understand its essence. It is nothing else than the application to passion of that pursuit of something permanent in a world of change, of something absolute in a world of relativity, which was the essence of the Platonic philosophy. If we may give rein to the imagination in a matter which without imagination could not be understood at all, we may fancy Plato trying to comprehend the power which beauty exerted over his senses by applying to the objects of love that profound metaphysical distinction which he had learned to make in his dialectical studies—the distinction between the appearance to sense and the reality envisaged by the intellect, between the phenomenon and the ideal. The whole natural world had come to seem to him like a world of dreams. In dreams images succeed one another without other meaning than that which they derive from our strange power of recognition—a power which enables us somehow, among the most incongruous transformations and surroundings, to find again the objects of our waking life, and to name those absurd and unmannerly visions by the name of father or mother or by any other familiar name. As these resemblances to real things make up all the truth of our dream, and these recognitions all its meaning, so Plato thought that all the truth and meaning of earthly things was the reference they contained to a heavenly original. This heavenly original we remember and recognize even among the distortions, disappearances, and multiplications of its earthly copies.

This thought is easily applicable to the affections; indeed, it is not impossible that it was the natural transcendence of any deep glance into beauty, and the lessons in disillusion and idealism given by that natural metaphysician we call love, that first gave Plato the key to his general system. There is, at any rate, no sphere in which the supersensible is approached with so warm a feeling of its reality, in which the phenomenon is so transparent and so indifferent a symbol of something perfect and divine beyond. In love and beauty, if anywhere, even the common man thinks he has visitations from a better world, approaches to a lost happiness; a happiness never tasted by us in this world, and yet so natural, so expected, that we look for it at every turn of a corner, in every new face; we look for it with so much confidence, with so much depth of expectation, that we never quite overcome our disappointment that it is not found.

And it is not found—no, never—in spite of what we may think when we are first in love. Plato knew this well from his experience. He had had successful loves, or what the world calls such, but he could not fancy that these successes were more than provocations, more than hints of what the true good is. To have mistaken them for real happiness would have been to continue to dream. It would have shown as little comprehension of the heart's experience as the idiot shows of the experience of the senses when he is unable to put together impressions of his eyes and hands and to say, 'Here is a table; here is a stool'. It is by a parallel use of the understanding that we put together the impressions of the heart and the imagination and are able to say, 'Here is absolute beauty: here is God.' The impressions themselves have no permanence, no intelligible essence. As Plato said, they are never anything fixed but are always either becoming or ceasing to be what we think them. There must be, he tells us, an eternal and clearly definable object of which the visible appearances to us are the manifold semblance; now by one trait, now by another, the phantom before us lights up that vague and haunting idea, and makes us utter its name with a momentary sense of certitude and attainment.

Just so the individual beauties that charm our attention and enchain the soul have only a transitive existence; they are momentary visions, irrecoverable moods. Their object is unstable; we never can say what it is, it changes so quickly before our eyes. What is it that a mother loves in her child? Perhaps the babe not yet born, or the babe that grew long ago by her suffering and unrecognized care; perhaps the man to be or the youth that has been. What does a man love in a woman? The girl that is yet, perhaps, to be his, or the wife that once chose to give him her whole existence. Where, among all these glimpses, is the true object of love? It flies before us, it tempts us on, only to escape and turn to mock us from a new quarter. And yet nothing can concern us more or be more real to us than this mysterious good, since the pursuit of it gives our lives whatever they have of true earnestness and meaning, and the approach to it whatever they have of joy.

So far is this ideal, Plato would say, from being an illusion, that it is the source of the world, the power that keeps us in existence. But for it, we should be dead. A profound indifference, an initial torpor, would have kept us from ever opening our eyes, and we should have no world of business or pleasure, politics or science, to think about at all. We, and the whole universe, exist only by the passionate attempt to return to our perfection, by the radical need of losing ourselves again in God. That ineffable good is our natural possession; all we honour in this life is but the partial recovery of our birthright; every delightful thing is like a rift in the clouds through which we catch a glimpse of our native heaven. If that heaven seems so far away and the idea of it so dim and unreal, it is because we are so far from perfect, so much immersed in what is alien and destructive to the soul.

Thus the history of our loves is the record of our divine conversations, of our intercourse with heaven. It matters very little whether this history seems to us tragic or not. In one sense, all mortal loves are tragic because never is the creature we think we possess the true and final object of our love; this love must ultimately pass beyond that particular apparition, which is itself continually passing away and shifting all its lines and colours. As Heraclitus could never bathe twice in the same river, because its water had flowed away, so Plato could never look twice at the same face, for it had become another. But on the other hand the most unsuccessful passion cannot be a vain thing. More, perhaps, than if it had found an apparent satisfaction, it will reveal to us an object of infinite worth, and the flight of the soul, detached by it from the illusions of common life, will be more straight and steady toward the ultimate good.

Such, if we are not mistaken, is the lesson of Plato's experience and also of that of the Italian poets whom we have quoted. Is this experience something normal? Is it the rational outcome of our own lives? That is a question which each man must answer for himself. Our immediate object will have been attained if we have made more intelligible a tendency which is certainly very common among men, and not among the men least worthy of honour. It is the tendency to make our experience of love rational, as scientific thinking is a tendency to make rational our experience of the outer world. The theories of natural science are creations of human reason; they change with the growth of reason, and express the intellectual impulses of each nation and age. Theories about the highest good do the same; only being less applicable in practice, less controllable by experiment, they seldom attain the same distinctness and articulation. But there is nothing authoritative in those constructions of the intellect, nothing coercive except in so far as our own experience and reflection force us to accept them. Natural science is persuasive because it embodies the momentum of common sense and of the practical arts; it carries on their spontaneous processes by more refined but essentially similar methods. Moral science is persuasive under the same conditions, but these conditions are not so generally found in the minds of men. Their conscience is often superstitious and perfunctory; their imagination is usually either disordered or dull. There is little momentum in their lives which the moralist can rely upon to carry them onward toward rational ideals. Deprived of this support his theories fall to the ground; they must seem, to every man whose nature cannot elicit them from his own experience, empty verbiage and irrelevant dreams.

Nothing in the world of fact obliges us to agree with Michael Angelo when he says that eternity can no more be separated from beauty than heat from fire. Beauty is a thing we experience, a value we feel; but eternity is something problematical. It might well happen that beauty should exist for a while in our contemplation and that eternity should have nothing to do with it or with us. It might well happen that our affections, being the natural expression of our instincts in the family and in the state, should bind us for a while to the beings with whom life has associated us—a father, a lover, a child—and that these affections should gradually fade with the decay of our vitality, declining in the evening of life, and passing away when we surrender our breath, without leading us to any single and supreme good, to any eternal love. If, therefore, the thoughts and consolations we have been rehearsing have sounded to us extravagant or unnatural, we cannot justify them by attempting to prove the actual existence of their objects, by producing the absolute beauty or by showing where and how we may come face to face with God. We may well feel that beauty and love are clear and good enough without any such additional embodiments. We may take the world as it is, without feigning another, and study actual experience without postulating any that is hypothetical. We can welcome beauty for the pleasure it affords and love for the happiness it brings, without asking that these things should receive supernatural extensions.

But we should have studied Plato and his kindred poets to little purpose if we thought that by admitting all this we were rejecting more than the mythical element that was sometimes mixed with their ideal philosophy. Its essence is not touched by any acknowledgment of what seems true or probable in the realm of actual existence. Nothing is more characteristic of the Platonic mind than a complete indifference to the continuance of experience and an exclusive interest in its comprehension. If we wish to understand this classic attitude of reason, all we need do is to let reason herself instruct us. We do not need more data, but more mind. If we take the sights and the loves that our mortal limitations have allowed of, and surrender ourselves unreservedly to their natural eloquence; if we say to the spirit that stirs within them, 'Be thou me, impetuous one'; if we become, as Michael Angelo says he was, all eyes to see or all heart to feel, then the force of our spiritual vitality, the momentum of our imagination, will carry us beyond ourselves, beyond an interest in our personal existence or eventual emotions, into the presence of a divine beauty and an eternal truth—things impossible to realize in experience, although necessarily envisaged by thought.

As the senses that perceive, in the act of perceiving assert an absolute reality in their object, as the mind that looks before and after believes in the existence of a past and a future which cannot now be experienced, so the imagination and the heart behold, when they are left free to expand and express themselves, an absolute beauty and a perfect love. Intense contemplation disentangles the ideal from the idol of sense, and a purified will rests in it as in the true object of worship. These are the oracles of reason, the prophecies of those profounder spirits who in the world of nature are obedient unto death because they belong intrinsically to a world where death is impossible, and who can rise continually, by abstraction from personal sensibility, into identity with the eternal objects of rational life.

Such a religion must elude popular apprehension until it is translated into myths and cosmological dogmas. It is easier for men to fill out the life of the spirit by supplementing the facts of experience by other facts for which there is no evidence than it is for them to master the given facts and turn them to spiritual uses. Many can fight for a doubtful fact when they cannot perform a difficult idealization. They trust, as all men must, to what they can see; they believe in things as their faculties represent things to them. By the same right, however, the rationalizer of experience believes in his visions; he rests, like the meanest of us, in the present object of his thought. So long as we live at all we must trust in something, at least in the coherence and permanence of the visible world and in the value of the objects of our own desires. And if we live nobly, we are under the same necessity of believing in noble things. However unreal, therefore, these Platonic intuitions may seem to those of us whose interests lie in other quarters, we may rest assured that these very thoughts would dominate our minds and these eternal companionships would cheer our desolation, if we had wrestled as manfully with the same passions and passed through the transmuting fire of as great a love.

THE ABSENCE OF RELIGION IN SHAKESPEARE

We are accustomed to think of the universality of Shakespeare as not the least of his glories. No other poet has given so many-sided an expression to human nature, or rendered so many passions and moods with such an appropriate variety of style, sentiment, and accent. If, therefore, we were asked to select one monument of human civilization that should survive to some future age, or be transported to another planet to bear witness to the inhabitants there of what we have been upon earth, we should probably choose the works of Shakespeare. In them we recognize the truest portrait and best memorial of man. Yet the archaeologists of that future age, or the cosmographers of that other part of the heavens, after conscientious study of our Shakespearian autobiography, would misconceive our life in one important respect. They would hardly understand that man had had a religion.

There are, indeed, numerous exclamations and invocations in Shakespeare which we, who have other means of information, know to be evidences of current religious ideas. Shakespeare adopts these, as he adopts the rest of his vocabulary, from the society about him. But he seldom or never gives them their original value. When Iago says ''sblood', a commentator might add explanations which should involve the whole philosophy of Christian devotion; but this Christian sentiment is not in Iago's mind, nor in Shakespeare's, any more than the virtues of Heracles and his twelve labours are in the mind of every slave and pander that cries 'hercule' in the pages of Plautus and Terence. Oaths are the fossils of piety. The geologist recognizes in them the relics of a once active devotion, but they are now only counters and pebbles tossed about in the unconscious play of expression. The lighter and more constant their use, the less their meaning.

Only one degree more inward than this survival of a religious vocabulary in profane speech is the reference we often find in Shakespeare to religious institutions and traditions. There are monks, bishops, and cardinals; there is even mention of saints, although none is ever presented to us in person. The clergy, if they have any wisdom, have an earthly one. Friar Lawrence culls his herbs like a more benevolent Medea; and Cardinal Wolsey flings away ambition with a profoundly pagan despair; his robe and his integrity to heaven are cold comfort to him. Juliet goes to shrift to arrange her love affairs, and Ophelia should go to a nunnery to forget hers. Even the chastity of Isabella has little in it that would have been out of place in Iphigenia. The metaphysical Hamlet himself sees a 'true ghost', but so far reverts to the positivism that underlies Shakespeare's thinking as to speak soon after of that 'undiscovered country from whose bourn no traveller returns'.

There are only two or three short passages in the plays, and one sonnet, in which true religious feeling seems to break forth. The most beautiful of these passages is that in *Richard II*, which commemorates the death of Mowbray, Duke of Norfolk:

> Many a time hath banished Norfolk fought
> For Jesu Christ in glorious Christian field,
> Streaming the ensign of the Christian cross
> Against black Pagans, Turks, and Saracens;
> And, toiled with works of war, retired himself
> To Italy; and there, at Venice, gave
> His body to that pleasant country's earth,
> And his pure soul unto his captain Christ,
> Under whose colours he had fought so long.

This is tender and noble, and full of an indescribable chivalry and pathos, yet even here we find the spirit of war rather than that of religion, and a deeper sense of Italy than of heaven. More unmixed is the piety of Henry V after the battle of Agincourt:

> O God, thy arm was here;
> And not to us, but to thy arm alone,
> Ascribe we all! When, without stratagem,

But in plain shock and even play of battle,
Was ever known so great and little loss,
On one part and on the other? Take it, God,
For it is none but thine...
Come, go we in procession to the village,
And be it death proclaimèd through our host,
To boast of this, or take that praise from God,
Which is his only...
                    Do we all holy rites;
Let there be sung *Non nobis* and *Te Deum.*

This passage is certainly a true expression of religious feeling, and just the kind that we might expect from a dramatist. Religion appears here as a manifestation of human nature and as an expression of human passion. The passion, however, is not due to Shakespeare's imagination, but is essentially historical: the poet has simply not rejected, as he usually does, the religious element in the situation he reproduces.*

With this dramatic representation of piety we may couple another, of a more intimate kind, from the Sonnets:

Poor soul, the centre of my sinful earth,
Fooled by these rebel powers that thee array,
Why dost thou pine within and suffer dearth,
Painting thy outward walls so costly gay?
Why so large cost, having so short a lease,
Dost thou upon thy fading mansion spend?
Shall worms, inheritors of this excess,
Eat up thy charge? Is this thy body's end?
Then, soul, live thou upon thy servant's loss,
And let that pine to aggravate thy store;
Buy terms divine in selling hours of dross,
Within be fed, without be rich no more:
So shalt thou feed on death, that feeds on men,
And death once dead, there's no more dying then.

* 'And so aboute foure of the clocke in the afternoone, the kynge when he saw no apparaunce of enimies, caused the retreite to be blowen, and gathering his armie togither, gave thankes to almightie God for so happie a victorie, causing his prelates and chapleines to sing this psalm, *In exitu Israel de Egipto*, and commandyng everie man to kneele downe on the grounde at this verse; *Non nobis, Domine, non nobis, sed nomini tuo da gloriam.* Which done, he caused *Te Deum*, with certeine anthems, to be song, giving laud and praise to God, and not boasting of his owne force or anie humane power' (Holinshed).

This sonnet contains more than a natural religious emotion inspired by a single event. It contains reflection, and expresses a feeling not merely dramatically proper but rationally just. A mind that habitually ran into such thoughts would be philosophically pious; it would be spiritual. The Sonnets, as a whole, are spiritual; their passion is transmuted into discipline. Their love, which, whatever its nominal object, is hardly anything but love of beauty and youth in general, is made to triumph over time by a metaphysical transformation of the object into something eternal. At first this is the beauty of the race renewing itself by generation, then it is the description of beauty in the poet's verse, and finally it is the immortal soul enriched by the contemplation of that beauty. This noble theme is the more impressively rendered by being contrasted with another, with a vulgar love that by its nature refuses to be so transformed and transmuted. 'Two loves,' cries the poet, in a line that gives us the essence of the whole, 'Two loves I have—of comfort, and despair.'

In all this depth of experience, however, there is still wanting any religious image. The Sonnets are spiritual, but, with the doubtful exception of the one quoted above, they are not Christian. And, of course, a poet of Shakespeare's time could not have found any other mould than Christianity for his religion. In our day, with our wide and conscientious historical sympathies, it may be possible for us to find in other rites and doctrines than those of our ancestors an expression of some ultimate truth. But for Shakespeare, in the matter of religion, the choice lay between Christianity and nothing. He chose nothing; he chose to leave his heroes and himself in the presence of life and of death with no other philosophy than that which the profane world can suggest and understand.

This positivism, we need hardly say, was not due to any grossness or sluggishness in his imagination. Shakespeare could be idealistic when he dreamed, as he could be spiritual when he reflected. The spectacle of life did not pass before his eyes as a mere phantasmagoria. He seized upon its principles; he became wise. Nothing can exceed the ripeness of his seasoned judgment, or the occasional breadth, sadness, and terseness of his reflection. The author of *Hamlet* could not be without metaphysical aptitude; *Macbeth* could not have been written without a sort of sibylline inspiration, or the Sonnets without something of the Platonic mind. It is all the more remarkable, therefore, that we should have to search through all the works of Shakespeare to find half a dozen passages that have so much as a religious sound, and that even these passages, upon examination, should prove not to be the expression of any deep religious conception. If Shakespeare had been without metaphysical capacity, or without moral maturity, we could have explained his strange insensibility to religion; but as it is, we must marvel at his indifference and ask ourselves what can be the causes of it. For, even if we should not regard the absence of religion as an imperfection in his own thought, we must admit it to be an incompleteness in his portrayal of the thought of others. Positivism may be a virtue in a philosopher, but it is a vice in a dramatist, who has to render those human passions to which the religious imagination has always given a larger meaning and a richer depth.

Those greatest poets by whose side we are accustomed to put Shakespeare did not forgo this advantage. They gave us man with his piety and the world with its gods. Homer is the chief repository of the Greek religion, and Dante the faithful interpreter of the Catholic. Nature would have been inconceivable to them without the supernatural, or man without the influence and companionship of the gods. These poets live in a cosmos. In their minds, as in the mind of their age, the fragments of experience have fallen together into a perfect picture, like the bits of glass in a kaleidoscope. Their universe is a total. Reason and imagination have mastered it completely and peopled it. No chaos remains beyond, or, if it does, it is thought of with an involuntary shudder that soon passes into a healthy indifference. They have a theory of human life; they see man in his relations, surrounded by a kindred universe in which he fills his allotted place. He knows the meaning and issue of his life, and does not voyage without a chart.

Shakespeare's world, on the contrary, is only the world of human society. The cosmos eludes him; he does not seem to feel the need of framing that idea. He depicts human life in all its richness and variety, but leaves that life without a setting, and consequently without a meaning. If we asked him to tell us what is the significance of the passion and beauty he had so vividly displayed, and what is the outcome of it all, he could hardly answer in any other words than those he puts into the mouth of Macbeth:

> To-morrow, and to-morrow, and to-morrow,
> Creeps in this petty pace from day to day,
> To the last syllable of recorded time;
> And all our yesterdays have lighted fools
> The way to dusty death. Out, out, brief candle!
> Life's but a walking shadow, a poor player
> That struts and frets his hour upon the stage
> And then is heard no more: it is a tale
> Told by an idiot, full of sound and fury,
> Signifying nothing.

How differently would Homer or Dante have answered that question! Their tragedy would have been illumined by a sense of the divinity of life and beauty, or by a sense of the sanctity of suffering and death. Their faith had enveloped the world of experience in a world of imagination, in which the ideals of the reason, of the fancy, and of the heart had a natural expression. They had caught in the reality the hint of a lovelier fable—a fable in which that reality was completed and idealized, and made at once vaster in its extent and more intelligible in its principle. They had, as it were, dramatized the universe, and endowed it with the tragic unities. In contrast with such a luminous philosophy and so well-digested an experience, the silence of Shakespeare and his philosophical incoherence have something in them that is still heathen; something that makes us wonder whether the northern mind, even in him, did not remain morose and barbarous at its inmost core.

But before we allow ourselves such hasty and general

inferences, we may well stop to consider whether there is not some simpler answer to our question. An epic poet, we might say, naturally deals with cosmic themes. He needs the supernatural machinery because he depicts the movement of human affairs in their generality, as typified in the figures of heroes whose function it is to embody or to overcome elemental forces. Such a poet's world is fabulous, because his inspiration is impersonal. But the dramatist renders the concrete reality of life. He has no need of a superhuman setting for his pictures. Such a setting would destroy the vitality of his creations. His plots should involve only human actors and human motives: the *deus ex machina* has always been regarded as an interloper on his stage. The passions of man are his all-sufficient material; he should weave his whole fabric out of them.

To admit the truth of all this would not, however, solve our problem. The dramatist cannot be expected to put cosmogonies on the boards. Miracle plays become dramatic only when they become human. But the supernatural world, which the playwright does not bring before the footlights, may exist nevertheless in the minds of his characters and of his audience. He may refer to it, appeal to it, and imply it, in the actions and in the sentiments he attributes to his heroes. And if the comparison of Shakespeare with Homer or Dante on the score of religious inspiration is invalidated by the fact that he is a dramatist while they are epic poets, a comparison may yet be instituted between Shakespeare and other dramatists, from which his singular insensibility to religion will as readily appear.

Greek tragedy, as we know, is dominated by the idea of fate. Even when the gods do not appear in person, or where the service or neglect of them is not the moving cause of the whole play—as it is in the *Bacchae* and the *Hippolytus* of Euripides—still the deep conviction of the limits and conditions of human happiness underlies the fable. The will of man fulfils the decrees of Heaven. The hero manifests a higher force than his own, both in success and in failure. The fates guide the willing and drag the unwilling. There is no such fragmentary view of life as we have in our romantic drama, where accidents make the meaningless happiness or unhappiness of a supersensitive adventurer. Life is seen whole, although in miniature. Its boundaries and its principles are studied more than its incidents. The human, therefore, everywhere merges with the divine. Our mortality, being sharply defined and much insisted upon, draws the attention all the more to that eternity of nature and of law in which it is embosomed. Nor is the fact of superhuman control left for our reflection to discover; it is emphatically asserted in those oracles on which so much of the action commonly turns.

When the Greek religion was eclipsed by the Christian, the ancient way of conceiving the ultra-human relations of human life became obsolete. It was no longer possible to speak with sincerity of the oracles and gods, of Nemesis and ὕβρις. Yet for a long time it was not possible to speak in any other terms. The new ideas were without artistic definition, and literature was paralysed. But in the course of ages, when the imagination had had time and opportunity to develop a Christian art and a Christian philosophy, the dramatic poets were ready to deal with the new themes. Only their readiness in this respect surpassed their ability, at least their ability to please those who had any memory of the ancient perfection of the arts.

The miracle plays were the beginning. Their crudity was extreme and their levity of the frankest; but they had still, like the Greek plays, a religious excuse and a religious background. They were not without dramatic power, but their offences against taste and their demands upon faith were too great for them to survive the Renaissance. Such plays as the *Polyeucte* of Corneille and the *Devoción de la Cruz* of Calderón, with other Spanish plays that might be mentioned, are examples of Christian dramas by poets of culture; but as a whole we must say that Christianity, while it succeeded in expressing itself in painting and in architecture, failed to express itself in any adequate drama. Where Christianity was strong, the drama either disappeared or became secular; and it has never again dealt with cosmic themes successfully, except in such hands as those of Goethe and Wagner, men who either neglected Christianity altogether or used it only as an incidental ornament, having, as they say, transcended it in their philosophy.

The fact is, that art and reflection have never been able to unite perfectly the two elements of a civilization like ours, that draws its culture from one source and its religion from another. Modern taste has ever been, and still is, largely exotic, largely a revolution in favour of something ancient or foreign. The more cultivated a period has been, the more wholly it has reverted to antiquity for its inspiration. The existence of that completer world has haunted all minds struggling for self-expression, and interfered, perhaps, with the natural development of their genius. The old art which they could not disregard distracted them from the new ideal, and prevented them from embodying this ideal outwardly; while the same ideal, retaining their inward allegiance, made their revivals of ancient forms artificial and incomplete. The strange idea could thus gain admittance that art was not called to deal with everything; that its sphere was the world of polite conventions. The serious and the sacred things of life were to be left unexpressed and inarticulate; while the arts masqueraded in the forms of a pagan antiquity, to which a triviality was at the same time attributed which in fact it had not possessed. This unfortunate separation of experience and its artistic expression betrayed itself in the inadequacy of what was beautiful and the barbarism of what was sincere.

When such are the usual conditions of artistic creation, we need not wonder that Shakespeare, a poet of the Renaissance, should have confined his representation of life to its secular aspects, and that his readers after him should rather have marvelled at the variety of the things of which he showed an understanding than have taken note of the one thing he overlooked. To omit religion was after all to omit what was not felt to be congenial to a poet's mind. The poet was to trace for us the passionate and romantic embroideries of life; he was to be artful and humane, and above all he was to be delightful. The beauty and charm of things had nothing any longer to do with those painful mysteries and contentions which made the temper of the pious so acrid and sad. In Shakespeare's time and country, to be religious already began to mean to be Puritanical; and in the divorce between the fullness of life on the one hand and the depth and unity of faith on the other, there could be no doubt to which side a man of imaginative instincts would attach himself. A world of passion and beauty without a meaning must seem to him more interesting and worthy than a world of empty principle and dogma, meagre, fanatical, and false. It was beyond the power of synthesis possessed by that age and nation to find a principle of all passion and a religion of all life.

This power of synthesis is indeed so difficult and rare that the attempt to gain it is sometimes condemned as too philosophical, and as tending to embarrass the critical eye and creative imagination with futile theories. We might say, for instance, that the absence of religion in Shakespeare was a sign of his good sense; that a healthy instinct kept his attention within the sublunary world; and that he was in that respect superior to Homer and to Dante. For, while they allowed their wisdom to clothe itself in fanciful forms, he gave us his in its immediate truth, so that he embodied what they signified. The supernatural machinery of their poems was, we might say, an accidental incumbrance, a traditional means of expression, which they only half understood, and which made their representation of life indirect and partly unreal. Shakespeare, on the other hand, had reached his poetical majority and independence. He rendered human experience no longer through symbols, but by direct imaginative representation. What I have treated as a limitation in him would, then, appear as the maturity of his strength.

There is always a class of minds in whom the spectacle of history produces a certain apathy of reason. They flatter themselves that they can escape defeat by not attempting the highest tasks. We need not here stop to discuss what value as truth a philosophical synthesis may hope to attain, nor have we to protest against the aesthetic preference for the sketch and the episode over a reasoned and unified rendering of life. Suffice it to say that the human race hitherto, whenever it has reached a phase of comparatively high development and freedom, has formed a conception of its place in nature, no less than of the contents of its life; and that this conception has been the occasion of religious sentiments and practices; and further, that every art, whether literary or plastic, has drawn its favourite themes from this religious sphere. The poetic imagination has not commonly stopped short of the philosophical in representing a superhuman environment of man.

Shakespeare, however, is remarkable among the greater poets for being without a philosophy and without a religion. In his drama there is no fixed conception of any forces, natural or moral, dominating and transcending our mortal energies. Whether this characteristic be regarded as a merit or as a defect, its presence cannot be denied. Those who think it wise or possible to refrain from searching for general principles, and are satisfied with the successive empirical appearance of things, without any faith in their rational continuity or completeness, may well see in Shakespeare their natural prophet. For he, too, has been satisfied with the successive description of various passions and events. His world, like the earth before Columbus, extends in an indefinite plane which he is not tempted to explore.

Those of us, however, who believe in circumnavigation, and who think that both human reason and human imagination require a certain totality in our views, and who feel that the most important thing in life is the lesson of it, and its relation to its own ideal—we can hardly find in Shakespeare all that the highest poet could give. Fullness is not necessarily wholeness, and the most profuse wealth of characterization seems still inadequate as a picture of experience, if this picture is not somehow seen from above and reduced to a dramatic unity—to that unity of meaning that can suffuse its endless details with something of dignity, simplicity, and peace. This is the imaginative power found in several poets we have mentioned—the power that gives certain passages in Lucretius also their sublimity, as it gives sublimity to many passages in the Bible.

For what is required for theoretic wholeness is not this or that system but some system. Its value is not the value of truth, but that of victorious imagination. Unity of conception is an aesthetic merit no less than a logical demand. A fine sense of the dignity and pathos of life cannot be attained unless we conceive somehow its outcome and its relations. Without such a conception our emotions cannot be steadfast and enlightened. Without it the imagination cannot fulfil its essential function or achieve its supreme success. Shakespeare himself, had it not been for the time and place in which he lived, when religion and imagination blocked rather than helped each other, would perhaps have allowed more of a cosmic background to appear behind his crowded scenes. If the Christian in him was not the real man, at least the pagan would have spoken frankly. The material forces of nature, or their vague embodiment in some northern pantheon, would then have stood behind his heroes. The various movements of events would have appeared as incidents in a larger drama to which they had at least some symbolic relation. We should have been awed as well as saddened, and purified as well as pleased, by being made to feel the dependence of human accidents upon cosmic forces and their fated evolution. Then we should not have been able to say that Shakespeare was without a religion. For the effort of religion, says Goethe, is to adjust us to the inevitable; each religion in its way strives to bring about this consummation.

THE ELEMENTS AND FUNCTION OF POETRY

. . . If poetry in its higher reaches is more philosophical than history, because it presents the memorable types of men and things apart from unmeaning circumstances, so in its primary substance and texture poetry is more philosophical than prose because it is nearer to our immediate experience. Poetry breaks up the trite conceptions designated by current words into the sensuous qualities out of which those conceptions were originally put together. . .

The fullness and sensuousness of such effusions bring them nearer to our actual perceptions than common discourse could come; yet they may easily seem remote, overloaded, and obscure to those accustomed to think entirely in symbols, and never to be interrupted in the algebraic rapidity of their thinking by a moment's pause and examination of heart, nor ever to plunge for a moment into that torrent of sensation and imagery over which the bridge of prosaic associations habitually carries us safe and dry to some conventional act. How slight that bridge commonly is, how much an affair of trestles and wire, we can hardly conceive until we have trained ourselves to an extreme sharpness of introspection. But psychologists have discovered, what laymen generally will confess, that we hurry by the procession of our mental images as we do by the traffic of the street, intent on business, gladly forgetting the noise and movement of the scene, and looking only for the corner we would turn or the door we would enter. Yet in our alertest moment the depths of the soul are still dreaming; the real world stands drawn in bare outline against a background of chaos and unrest. Our logical thoughts dominate experience only as the parallels and meridians make a checkerboard of the sea. They guide our voyage without controlling the waves, which toss for ever in spite of our ability to ride over them to our chosen ends.

Sanity is a madness put to good uses; waking life is a dream controlled.

Out of the neglected riches of this dream the poet fetches his wares. He dips into the chaos that underlies the rational shell of the world and brings up some superfluous image, some emotion dropped by the way, and reattaches it to the present object; he reinstates things unnecessary, he emphasizes things ignored, he paints in again into the landscape the tints which the intellect has allowed to fade from it. If he seems sometimes to obscure a fact, it is only because he is restoring an experience. We may observe this process in the simplest cases. When Ossian, mentioning the sun, says it is round as the shield of his fathers, the expression is poetical. Why? Because he has added to the word sun, in itself sufficient and unequivocal, other words, unnecessary for practical clearness, but serving to restore the individuality of his perception and its associations in his mind. There is no square sun with which the sun he is speaking of could be confused; to stop and call it round is a luxury, a halting in the sensation for the love of its form. And to go on to tell us, what is wholly impertinent, that the shield of his fathers was round also, is to invite us to follow the chance wanderings of his fancy, to give us a little glimpse of the stuffing of his own brain, or, we might almost say, to turn over the pattern of his embroidery and show us the loose threads hanging out on the wrong side. Such an escapade disturbs and interrupts the true vision of the object, and a great poet, rising to a perfect conception of the sun and forgetting himself, would have disdained to make it; but it has a romantic and pathological interest, it restores an experience, and is in that measure poetical. We have been made to halt at the sensation, and to penetrate for a moment into its background of dream.

But it is not only thoughts or images that the poet draws in this way from the store of his experience, to clothe the bare form of conventional objects: he often adds to these objects a more subtle ornament, drawn from the same source. For the first element which the intellect rejects in forming its ideas of things is the emotion which accompanies the perception; and this emotion is the first thing the poet restores. He stops at the image, because he stops to enjoy. He wanders into the by-paths of association because the by-paths are delightful. The love of beauty which made him give measure and cadence to his words, the love of harmony which made him rhyme them, reappear in his imagination and make him select there also the material that is itself beautiful, or capable of assuming beautiful forms. The link that binds together the ideas, sometimes so wide apart, which his wit assimilates, is most often the link of emotion; they have in common some element of beauty or of horror.

The poet's art is to a great extent the art of intensifying emotions by assembling the scattered objects that naturally arouse them. He sees the affinities of things by seeing their common affinities with passion. As the guiding principle of practical thinking is some interest, so that only what is pertinent to that interest is selected by the attention; as the guiding principle of scientific thinking is some connection of things in time or space, or some identity of law; so in poetic thinking the guiding principle is often a mood or a quality of sentiment. By this union of disparate things having a common overtone of feeling, the feeling is itself evoked in all its strength; nay, it is often created for the first time, much as by a new mixture of old pigments Perugino could produce the unprecedented limpidity of his colour, or Titian the unprecedented glow of his. Poets can thus arouse sentiments finer than any which they have known, and in the act of composition become discoverers of new realms of delightfulness and grief. Expression is a misleading term which suggests that something previously known is rendered or imitated; whereas the expression is itself an original fact, the values of which are then referred to the thing expressed, much as the honours of a Chinese mandarin are attributed retroactively to his parents. So the charm which a poet, by his art of combining images and shades of emotion, casts over a scene or an action, is attached to the principal actor in it, who gets the benefit of the setting furnished him by a well-stocked mind.

The poet is himself subject to this illusion, and a great part of what is called poetry, although by no means the best part of it, consists in this sort of idealization by proxy. We dye the world of our own colour; by a pathetic fallacy, by a false projection of sentiment, we soak nature with our own feeling, and then celebrate her tender sympathy with our moral being. This aberration, as we see in the case of Wordsworth, is not inconsistent with a high development of both the faculties which it confuses—I mean vision and feeling. On the contrary, vision and feeling, when most abundant and original, most easily present themselves in this undivided form. There would be need of a force of intellect which poets rarely possess to rationalize their inspiration without diminishing its volume: and if, as is commonly the case, the energy of the dream and the passion in them is greater than that of the reason, and they cannot attain true propriety and supreme beauty in their works, they can, nevertheless, fill them with lovely images and a fine moral spirit.

The pouring forth of both perceptive and emotional elements in their mixed and indiscriminate form gives to this kind of imagination the directness and truth which sensuous poetry possesses on a lower level. The outer world bathed in the hues of human feeling, the inner world expressed in the forms of things,—that is the primitive condition of both before intelligence and the prosaic classification of objects have abstracted them and assigned them to their respective spheres. Such identifications, on which a certain kind of metaphysics prides itself also, are not discoveries of profound genius; they are exactly like the observation of Ossian that the sun is round and that the shield of his fathers was round too; they are disintegrations of conventional objects, so that the original associates of our perceptions reappear; then the thing and the emotion which chanced to be simultaneous are said to be one, and we return, unless a better principle of organization is substituted for the principle abandoned, to the chaos of a passive animal consciousness, where all is mixed together, projected together, and felt as an unutterable whole.

The pathetic fallacy is a return to that early habit of thought by which our ancestors peopled the world with benevolent and malevolent spirits; what they felt in the presence of objects they took to be a part of the objects themselves. In returning to this natural confusion, poetry does us a service in that she recalls and consecrates those phases of our experience which, as useless to the understanding of material reality, we are in danger of forgetting altogether. Therein is her vitality, for she pierces to the quick and shakes us out of our servile speech and imaginative poverty; she reminds us of all we have felt, she invites us even to dream a little, to nurse the wonderful spontaneous creations which at every waking moment we are snuffing out in our brain. And the indulgence is no mere momentary pleasure; much of its exuberance clings afterward to our ideas; we see the more and feel the more for that exercise; we are capable of finding greater entertainment in the common aspects of nature and life. When the veil of convention is once removed from our eyes by the poet, we are better able to dominate any particular experience and, as it were, to change its scale, now losing ourselves in its infinitesimal texture, now in its infinite ramifications.

If the function of poetry, however, did not go beyond this recovery of sensuous and imaginative freedom, at the expense of disrupting our useful habits of thought, we might be grateful to it for occasionally relieving our numbness, but we should have to admit that it was nothing but a relaxation; that spiritual discipline was not to be gained from it in any degree, but must be sought wholly in that intellectual system that builds the science of nature with the categories of prose. So conceived, poetry would deserve the judgment passed by Plato on all the arts of flattery and entertainment; it might be crowned as delightful, but must be either banished altogether as meretricious or at least confined to a few forms and occasions where it might do little harm. The judgment of Plato has been generally condemned by philosophers, although it is eminently rational, and justified by the simplest principles of morals. It has been adopted instead, although unwittingly, by the practical and secular part of mankind, who look upon artists and poets as inefficient and brain-sick people under whose spell it would be a serious calamity to fall, although they may be called in on feast days as an ornament and luxury together with the cooks, hairdressers, and florists.

Several circumstances, however, might suggest to us the possibility that the... great function of poetry, which we have not yet directly mentioned, is... to repair to the material of experience, seizing hold of the reality of sensation and fancy beneath the surface of conventional ideas, and then out of that living but indefinite material to build new structures, richer, finer, fitter to the primary tendencies of our nature, truer to the ultimate possibilities of the soul. Our descent into the elements of our being is then justified by our subsequent freer ascent toward its goal; we revert to sense only to find food for reason; we destroy conventions only to construct ideals.

Such analysis for the sake of creation is the essence of all great poetry. Science and common sense are themselves in their way poets of no mean order, since they take the material of experience and make out of it a clear, symmetrical, and beautiful world; the very propriety of this art, however, has made it common. Its figures have become mere rhetoric and its metaphors prose. Yet, even as it is, a scientific and mathematical vision has a higher beauty than the irrational poetry of sensation and impulse, which merely tickles the brain, like liquor, and plays upon our random, imaginative lusts. The imagination of a great poet, on the contrary, is as orderly as that of an astronomer, and as large; he has the naturalist's patience, the naturalist's love of detail and eye trained to see fine gradations and essential lines; he knows no hurry; he has no pose, no sense of originality; he finds his effects in his subject, and his subject in his inevitable world. Resembling the naturalist in all this, he differs from him in the balance of his interests; the poet has the concreter mind; his visible world wears all its colours and retains its indwelling passion and life. Instead of studying in experience its calculable elements, he studies its moral values, its beauty, the openings it offers to the soul: and the cosmos he constructs is accordingly an ideal theatre for the spirit in which its noblest potential drama is enacted and its destiny resolved.

The supreme function of poetry is only the consummation of the method by which words and imagery are transformed into verse. As verse breaks up the prosaic order of syllables and subjects them to a recognizable and pleasing measure, so poetry breaks up the whole prosaic picture of experience to introduce into it a rhythm more congenial and intelligible to the mind. And in both these cases the operation is essentially the same as that by which, in an intermediate sphere, the images rejected by practical thought, and the emotions ignored by it, are so marshalled as to fill the mind with a truer and intenser consciousness of its memorable experience. The poetry of fancy, of observation, and of passion moves on this intermediate level; the poetry of mere sound and virtuosity is confined to the lower sphere; and the highest is reserved for the poetry of the creative reason. But one principle is present throughout—the principle of beauty—the art of assimilating phenomena, whether words, images, emotions, or systems of ideas, to the deeper innate cravings of the mind.

Let us now dwell a little on this higher function of poetry and try to distinguish some of its phases.

The creation of characters is what many of us might at first be tempted to regard as the supreme triumph of the imagination. If we abstract, however, from our personal tastes and look at the matter in its human and logical relations, we shall see, I think, that the construction of characters is not the ultimate task of poetic fiction. A character can never be exhaustive of our materials: for it exists by its idiosyncrasy, by its contrast with other natures, by its development of one side, and one side only, of our native capacities. It is, therefore, not by characterization as such that the ultimate message can be rendered. The poet can put only a part of himself into any of his heroes, but he must put the whole into his noblest work. A character is accordingly only a fragmentary unity; fragmentary in respect to its origin—since it is conceived by enlargement, so to speak, of a part of our own being to the exclusion of the rest—and fragmentary in respect to the object it presents, since a character must live in an environment and be appreciated by contrast and by the sense of derivation. Not the character, but its effects and causes, is the truly interesting thing. Thus in master poets, like Homer and Dante, the characters, although well drawn, are subordinate to the total movement and meaning of the scene. There is indeed something pitiful, something comic, in any comprehended soul; souls, like other things, are only definable by their limitations. We feel instinctively that it would be insulting to speak of any man to his face as we should speak of him in his absence, even if what we say is in the way of praise: for absent he is a character understood, but present he is a force respected.

In the construction of ideal characters, then, the imagination is busy with material—particular actions and thoughts—which suggest their unification in persons; but the characters thus conceived can hardly be adequate to the profusion of our observations, nor exhaustive, when all personalities are taken together, of the interest of our lives. Characters are initially imbedded in life, as the gods themselves are originally imbedded in nature. Poetry must, therefore, to render all reality, render also the background of its figures, and the events that condition their acts. We must place them in that indispensable environment which the landscape furnishes to the eye and the social medium to the emotions.

The visible landscape is not a proper object for poetry. Its elements, and especially the emotional stimulation which it gives, may be suggested or expressed in verse; but landscape is not thereby represented in its proper form; it appears only as an element and associate of moral unities. Painting, architecture, and gardening, with the art of stage-setting, have the visible landscape for their object, and to those arts we may leave it. But there is a sort of landscape larger than the visible, which escapes the synthesis of the eye; it is present to that topographical sense by which we always live in the consciousness that there is a sea, that there are mountains, that the sky is above us, even when we do not see it, and that the tribes of men, with their different degrees of blamelessness, are scattered over the broad-backed earth. This cosmic landscape poetry alone can render, and it is no small part of the art to awaken the sense of it at the right moment, so that the object that occupies the centre of vision may be seen in its true lights, coloured by its wider associations, and dignified by its felt affinities to things permanent and great. As the Italian masters were wont not to paint their groups of saints about the Virgin without enlarging the canvas, so as to render a broad piece of sky, some mountains and rivers, and nearer, perhaps, some decorative pile; so the poet of larger mind envelops his characters in the atmosphere of nature and history, and keeps us constantly aware of the world in which they move.

The distinction of a poet—the dignity and humanity of his thought—can be measured by nothing, perhaps, so well as by the diameter of the world in which he lives; if he is supreme, his vision, like Dante's, always stretches to the stars. And Virgil, a supreme poet sometimes unjustly belittled, shows us the same thing in another form; his landscape is the Roman universe, his theme the sacred springs of Roman greatness in piety, constancy, and law. He has not written a line in forgetfulness that he was a Roman; he loves country life and its labours because he sees in it the origin and bulwark of civic greatness; he honours tradition because it gives perspective and momentum to the history that ensues; he invokes the gods, because they are symbols of the physical and moral forces by which Rome struggled to dominion.

Almost every classic poet has the topographical sense; he swarms with proper names and allusions to history and fable; if an epithet is to be thrown in anywhere to fill up the measure of a line, he chooses instinctively an appellation of place or family; his wine is not red, but Samian; his gorges are not deep, but are the gorges of Haemus; his songs are not sweet, but Pierian. We may deride their practice as conventional, but they could far more justly deride ours as insignificant.

Conventions do not arise without some reason, and genius will know how to rise above them by a fresh appreciation of their rightness, and will feel no temptation to overturn them in favour of personal whimsies. The ancients found poetry not so much in sensible accidents as in essential forms and noble associations; and this fact marks very clearly their superior education. They dominated the world as we no longer dominate it, and lived, as we are too distracted to live, in the presence of the rational and the important... We have learned to look for a symbolic meaning in detached episodes, and to accept the incidental emotions they cause, because of their violence and our absorption in them, as in some sense sacramental and representative of the whole. Thus the picture of an unmeaning passion, of a crime without an issue, does not appear to our romantic apprehension as the sorry farce it is, but rather as a true tragedy. Some have lost even the capacity to conceive of a true tragedy, because they have no idea of a cosmic order, of general laws of life, or of an impersonal religion. They measure the profundity of feeling by its intensity, not by its justifying relations; and in the radical disintegration of their spirit, the more they are devoured the more they fancy themselves fed. But the majority of us retain some sense of a meaning in our joys and sorrows, and even if we cannot pierce to their ultimate object, we feel that what absorbs us here and now has a merely borrowed or deputed power; that it is a symbol and foretaste of all reality speaking to the whole soul. At the same time our intelligence is too confused to give us any picture of that reality, and our will too feeble to marshal our disorganized loves into a religion consistent with itself and harmonious with the comprehended universe. A rational ideal eludes us, and we are the more inclined to plunge into mysticism.

Nevertheless, the function of poetry, like that of science, can only be fulfilled by the conception of harmonies that become clearer as they grow richer. As the chance note that comes to be supported by a melody becomes in that melody determinate and necessary, and as the melody, when woven into a harmony, is explicated in that harmony and fixed beyond recall; so the single emotion, the fortuitous dream, launched by the poet into the world of recognizable and immortal forms, looks in that world for its ideal supports and affinities. It must find them or else be blown back among the ghosts. The highest ideality is the comprehension of the real. Poetry is not at its best when it depicts a further possible experience, but when it initiates us, by feigning something which as an experience is impossible, into the meaning of the experience which we have actually had.

The highest example of this kind of poetry is religion; and although disfigured and misunderstood by the simplicity of men who believe in it without being capable of that imaginative interpretation of life in which its truth consists, yet this religion is even then often beneficent, because it colours life harmoniously with the ideal. Religion may falsely represent the ideal as a reality, but we must remember that the ideal, if not so represented, would be despised by the majority of men, who cannot understand that the value of things is moral, and who therefore attribute to what is moral a natural existence, thinking thus to vindicate its importance and value. But value lies in meaning, not in substance; in the ideal which things approach, not in the energy which they embody.

The highest poetry, then, is not that of the versifiers, but that of the prophets, or of such poets as interpret verbally the visions which the prophets have rendered in action and sentiment rather than in adequate words. That the intuitions of religion are poetical, and that in such intuitions poetry has its ultimate function, are truths of which both religion and poetry become more conscious the more they advance in refinement and profundity. A crude and superficial theology may confuse God with the thunder, the mountains, the heavenly bodies, or the whole universe; but when we pass from these easy identifications to a religion that has taken root in history and in the hearts of men, and has come to flower, we find its objects and its dogmas purely ideal, transparent expressions of moral experience and perfect counterparts of human needs. The evidence of history or of the senses is left far behind and never thought of; the evidence of the heart, the value of the idea, are alone regarded... In this same manner, where poetry rises from its elementary and detached expressions in rhythm, euphuism, characterization, and story-telling, and comes to the consciousness of its highest function, that of portraying the ideals of experience and destiny, then the poet becomes aware that he is essentially a prophet, and either devotes himself, like Homer or Dante, to the loving expression of the religion that exists, or like Lucretius or Wordsworth, to the heralding of one which he believes to be possible. Such poets are aware of their highest mission; others, whatever the energy of their genius, have not conceived their ultimate function as poets...

THE POETRY OF BARBARISM

1

It is an observation at first sight melancholy but in the end, perhaps, enlightening, that the earliest poets are the most ideal, and that primitive ages furnish the most heroic characters and have the clearest vision of a perfect life. The Homeric times must have been full of ignorance and suffering. In those little barbaric towns, in those camps and farms, in those shipyards, there must have been much insecurity and superstition. That age was singularly poor in all that concerns the convenience of life and the entertainment of the mind with arts and sciences. Yet it had a sense for civilization. That machinery of life which men were beginning to devise appealed to them as poetical; they knew its ultimate justification and studied its incipient processes with delight. The poetry of that simple and ignorant age was, accordingly, the sweetest and sanest that the world has known; the most faultless in taste, and the most even and lofty in inspiration. Without lacking variety and homeliness, it bathed all things human in the golden light of morning; it clothed sorrow in a kind of majesty, instinct with both self-control and heroic frankness. Nowhere else can we find so noble a rendering of human nature, so spontaneous a delight in life, so uncompromising a dedication to beauty, and such a gift of seeing beauty in everything. Homer, the first of poets, was also the best and the most poetical.

From this beginning, if we look down the history of Occidental literature, we see the power of idealization steadily decline. For while it finds here and there, as in Dante, a more spiritual theme and a subtler and riper intellect, it pays for that advantage by a more than equivalent loss in breadth, sanity, and happy vigour. And if ever imagination bursts out with a greater potency, as in Shakespeare (who excels the patriarch of poetry in depth of passion and vividness of characterization, and in those exquisite bubblings of poetry and humour in which English genius is at its best), yet Shakespeare also pays the price by a notable loss in taste, in sustained inspiration, in consecration, and in rationality. There is more or less rubbish in his greatest works. When we come down to our own day we find poets of hardly less natural endowment (for in endowment all ages are perhaps alike) and with vastly richer sources of inspiration; for they have many arts and literatures behind them, with the spectacle of a varied and agitated society, a world which is the living microcosm of its own history and presents in one picture many races, arts, and religions. Our poets have more wonderful tragedies of the imagination to depict than had Homer, whose world was innocent of any essential defeat, or Dante, who believed in the world's definitive redemption. Or, if perhaps their inspiration is comic, they have the pageant of medieval manners, with its picturesque artifices and passionate fancies, and the long comedy of modern social revolutions, so illusory in their aims and so productive in their aimlessness. They have, moreover, the new and marvellous conception which natural science has given us of the world and of the conditions of human progress.

With all these lessons of experience behind them, however, we find our contemporary poets incapable of any high wisdom, incapable of any imaginative rendering of human life and its meaning. Our poets are things of shreds and patches; they give us episodes and studies, a sketch of this curiosity, a glimpse of that romance; they have no total vision, no grasp of the whole reality, and consequently no capacity for a sane and steady idealization. The comparatively barbarous ages had a poetry of the ideal; they had visions of beauty, order, and perfection. This age of material elaboration has no sense for those things. Its fancy is retrospective, whimsical, and flickering; its ideals, when it has any, are negative and partial; its moral strength is a blind and miscellaneous vehemence. Its poetry, in a word, is the poetry of barbarism.

This poetry should be viewed in relation to the general moral crisis and imaginative disintegration of which it gives a verbal echo; then we shall avoid the injustice of passing it over as insignificant, no less than the imbecility of hailing it as essentially glorious and successful. We must remember that the imagination of our race has been subject to a double discipline. It has been formed partly in the school of classic literature and polity, and partly in the school of Christian piety. This duality of inspiration, this contradiction between the two accepted methods of rationalizing the world, has been a chief source of that incoherence, that romantic indistinctness and imperfection, which largely characterize the products of the modern arts. A man cannot serve two masters; yet the conditions have not been such as to allow him wholly to despise the one or wholly to obey the other. To be wholly pagan is impossible after the dissolution of that civilization which had seemed universal, and that empire which had believed itself eternal. To be wholly Christian is impossible for a similar reason, now that the illusion and cohesion of Christian ages is lost, and for the further reason that Christianity was itself fundamentally eclectic. Before it could succeed and dominate men even for a time, it was obliged to adjust itself to reality, to incorporate many elements of pagan wisdom, and to accommodate itself to many habits and passions at variance with its own ideal.

In these latter times, with the prodigious growth of material life in elaboration and of mental life in diffusion, there has supervened upon this old dualism a new faith in man's absolute power, a kind of return to the inexperience and self-assurance of youth. This new inspiration has made many minds indifferent to the two traditional disciplines; neither is seriously accepted by them, for the reason, excellent from their own point of view, that no discipline whatever is needed. The memory of ancient disillusions has faded with time. Ignorance of the past has bred contempt for the lessons which the past might teach. Men prefer to repeat the old experiment without knowing that they repeat it.

I say advisedly ignorance of the past, in spite of the unprecedented historical erudition of our time; for life is an art not to be learned by observation, and the most minute and comprehensive studies do not teach us what the spirit of man should have learned by its long living. We study the past as a dead object, as a ruin, not as an authority and as an experiment. One reason why history was less interesting to former ages was that they were less conscious of separation from the past. The perspective of time was less clear because the synthesis of experience was more complete. The mind does not easily discriminate the successive phases of an action in which it is still engaged; it does not arrange in a temporal series the elements of a single perception, but posits them all together as constituting a permanent and real object. Human nature and the life of the world were real and stable objects to the apprehension of our forefathers; the actors changed, but not the characters or the play. Men were then less studious of derivations because they were more conscious of identities. They thought of all reality as in a sense contemporary, and in considering the maxims of a philosopher or the style of a poet, they were not primarily concerned with settling his date and describing his environment. The standard by which they judged was eternal; the environment in which man found himself did not seem to them subject to any essential change.

To us the picturesque element in history is more striking because we feel ourselves the children of our own age only, an age which, being itself singular and revolutionary, tends to read its own character into the past, and to regard all other periods as no less fragmentary and effervescent than itself. The changing and the permanent elements are, indeed, everywhere present, and the bias of the observer may emphasize the one or the other as it will: the only question is whether we find the significance of things in their variations or in their similarities.

Now the habit of regarding the past as effete and as merely a stepping-stone to something present or future, is unfavourable to any true apprehension of that element in the past which was vital and which remains eternal. It is a habit of thought that destroys the sense of the moral identity of all ages, by virtue of its very insistence on the mechanical derivation of one age from another. Existences that cause one another exclude one another; each is alien to the rest inasmuch as it is the product of new and different conditions. Ideas that cause nothing unite all things by giving them a common point of reference and a single standard of value.

The classic and the Christian systems were both systems of ideas, attempts to seize the eternal morphology of reality and describe its unchanging constitution. The imagination was summoned thereby to contemplate the highest objects, and, the essence of things being thus described, their insignificant variations could retain little importance and the study of these variations might well seem superficial. Mechanical science, the science of causes, was accordingly neglected, while the science of values, with the arts that express these values, was exclusively pursued. The reverse has now occurred and the spirit of life, innocent of any rationalizing discipline and deprived of an authoritative and adequate method of expression, has relapsed into miscellaneous and shallow exuberance. Religion and art have become short-winded. They have forgotten the old maxim that we should copy in order to be copied and remember in order to be remembered. It is true that the multiplicity of these incompetent efforts seems to many a compensation for their ill success, or even a ground for asserting their absolute superiority. Incompetence, when it flatters the passions, can always find a greater incompetence to approve of it. Indeed, some people would have regarded the Tower of Babel as the best academy of eloquence on account of the variety of oratorical methods prevailing there.

It is thus that the imagination of our time has relapsed into barbarism. But discipline of the heart and fancy is always so rare a thing that the neglect of it need not be supposed to involve any very terrible or obvious loss. The triumphs of reason have been few and partial at any time, and perfect works of art are almost unknown. The failure of art and reason, because their principle is ignored, is therefore hardly more conspicuous than it was when their principle, although perhaps acknowledged, was misunderstood or disobeyed. Indeed, to one who fixes his eye on the ideal goal, the greatest art often seems the greatest failure, because it alone reminds him of what it should have been. Trivial stimulations coming from vulgar objects, on the contrary, by making us forget altogether the possibility of a deep satisfaction, often succeed in interesting and in winning applause. The pleasure they give us is so brief and superficial that the wave of essential disappointment which would ultimately drown it has not time to rise from the heart.

The poetry of barbarism is not without its charm. It can play with sense and passion the more readily and freely in that it does not aspire to subordinate them to a clear thought or a tenable attitude of the will. It can impart the transitive emotions which it expresses; it can find many partial harmonies of mood and fancy; it can, by virtue of its red-hot irrationality, utter wilder cries, surrender itself and us to more absolute passion, and heap up a more indiscriminate wealth of images than belong to poets of seasoned experience or of heavenly inspiration. Irrational stimulation may tire us in the end, but it excites us in the beginning; and how many conventional poets, tender and prolix, have there not been, who tire us now without ever having excited anybody? The power to stimulate is the beginning of greatness, and when the barbarous poet has genius, as he well may have, he stimulates all the more powerfully on account of the crudity of his methods and the recklessness of his emotions. The defects of such art—lack of distinction, absence of beauty, confusion of ideas, incapacity permanently to please—will hardly be felt by the contemporary public, if once its attention is arrested; for no poet is so undisciplined that he will not find many readers, if he finds readers at all, less disciplined than himself.

These considerations may perhaps be best enforced by applying them to two writers of great influence over the present generation who seem to illustrate them on different planes—Robert Browning and Walt Whitman. They are both analytic poets—poets who seek to reveal and express the elemental as opposed to the conventional; but the dissolution has progressed much farther in Whitman than in Browning, doubtless because Whitman began at a much lower stage of moral and intellectual organization; for the good will to be radical was present in both. The elements to which Browning reduces experience are still passions, characters, persons; Whitman carries the disintegration further and knows nothing but moods and particular images. The world of Browning is a world of history with civilization for its setting and with the conventional passions for its motive forces. The world of Whitman is innocent of these things and contains only far simpler and more chaotic elements. In him the barbarism is much more pronounced; it is, indeed, avowed, and the 'barbaric yawp' is sent 'over the roofs of the world' in full consciousness of its inarticulate character; but in Browning the barbarism is no less real though disguised by a literary and scientific language, since the passions of civilized life with which he deals are treated as so many 'barbaric yawps', complex indeed in their conditions, puffings of an intricate engine, but aimless in their vehemence and mere ebullitions of lustiness in adventurous and profoundly ungoverned souls.

Irrationality on this level is viewed by Browning with the same satisfaction with which, on a lower level, it is viewed by Whitman; and the admirers of each hail it as the secret of a new poetry which pierces to the quick and awakens the imagination to a new and genuine vitality. It is in the rebellion against discipline, in the abandonment of the ideals of classic and Christian tradition, that this rejuvenation is found. Both poets represent, therefore, and are admired for representing, what may be called the poetry of barbarism in the most accurate and descriptive sense of this word. For the barbarian is the man who regards his passions as their own excuse for being; who does not domesticate them either by understanding their cause or by conceiving their ideal goal. He is the man who does not know his derivations nor perceive his tendencies, but who merely feels and acts, valuing in his life its force and its filling, but being careless of its purpose and its form. His delight is in abundance and vehemence; his art, like his life, shows an exclusive respect for quantity and splendour of materials. His scorn for what is poorer and weaker than himself is only surpassed by his ignorance of what is higher.

2 WALT WHITMAN

The works of Walt Whitman offer an extreme illustration of this phase of genius, both by their form and by their substance. It was the singularity of his literary form—the challenge it threw to the conventions of verse and of language—that first gave Whitman notoriety: but this notoriety has become fame, because those incapacities and solecisms which glare at us from his pages are only the obverse of a profound inspiration and of a genuine courage. Even the idiosyncrasies of his style have a side which is not mere perversity or affectation; the order of his words, the procession of his images, reproduce the method of a rich, spontaneous, absolutely lazy fancy. In most poets such a natural order is modified by various governing motives—the thought, the metrical form, the echo of other poems in the memory. By Walt Whitman these conventional influences are resolutely banished. We find the swarms of men and objects rendered as they might strike the retina in a sort of waking dream. It is the most sincere possible confession of the lowest—I mean the most primitive—type of perception. All ancient poets are sophisticated in comparison and give proof of longer intellectual and moral training. Walt Whitman has gone back to the innocent style of Adam, when the animals filed before him one by one and he called each of them by its name.

In fact, the influences to which Walt Whitman was subject were as favourable as possible to the imaginary experiment of beginning the world over again. Liberalism and transcendentalism both harboured some illusions on that score; and they were in the air which our poet breathed. Moreover, he breathed this air in America, where the newness of the material environment made it easier to ignore the fatal antiquity of human nature. When he afterward became aware that there was or had been a world with a history, he studied that world with curiosity and spoke of it not without a certain shrewdness. But he still regarded it as a foreign world and imagined, as not a few Americans have done, that his own world was a fresh creation, not amenable to the same laws as the old. The difference in the conditions blinded him, in his merely sensuous apprehension, to the identity of the principles.

His parents were farmers in central Long Island and his early years were spent in that district. The family seems to have been not too prosperous and somewhat nomadic; Whitman himself drifted through boyhood without much guidance. We find him now at school, now helping the labourers at the farms, now wandering along the beaches of Long Island, finally at Brooklyn working in an apparently desultory way as a printer and sometimes as a writer for a local newspaper. He must have read or heard something, at this early period, of the English classics; his style often betrays the deep effect made upon him by the grandiloquence of the Bible, of Shakespeare, and of Milton. But his chief interest, if we may trust his account, was already in his own sensations. The aspects of nature, the forms and habits of animals, the sights of cities, the movement and talk of common people, were his constant delight. His mind was flooded with these images, keenly felt and afterward to be vividly rendered with bold strokes of realism and imagination.

Many poets have had this faculty to seize the elementary aspects of things, but none has had it so exclusively; with Whitman the surface is absolutely all and the underlying structure is without interest and almost without existence. He had had no education and his natural delight in imbibing sensations had not been trained to the uses of practical or theoretical intelligence. He basked in the sunshine of perception and wallowed in the stream of his own sensibility, as later at Camden in the shallows of his favourite brook. Even during the civil war, when he heard the drum-taps so clearly, he could only gaze at the picturesque and terrible aspects of the struggle, and linger among the wounded day after day with a canine devotion; he could not be aroused either to clear thought or to positive action. So also in his poems; a multiplicity of images pass before him and he yields himself to each in turn with absolute passivity. The world has no inside; it is a phantasmagoria of continuous visions, vivid, impressive, but monotonous and hard to distinguish in memory, like the waves of the sea or the decorations of some barbarous temple sublime only by the infinite aggregation of parts.

This abundance of detail without organization, this wealth of perception without intelligence and of imagination without taste, makes the singularity of Whitman's genius. Full of sympathy and receptivity, with a wonderful gift of graphic characterization and an occasional rare grandeur of diction, he fills us with a sense of the individuality and the universality of what he describes—it is a drop in itself, yet a drop in the ocean. The absence of any principle of selection or of a sustained style enables him to render aspects of things and of emotion which would have eluded a trained writer. He is, therefore, interesting even where he is grotesque or perverse. He has accomplished, by the sacrifice of almost every other good quality, something never so well done before. He has approached common life without bringing in his mind any higher standard by which to criticize it; he has seen it, not in contrast with an ideal, but as the expression of forces more indeterminate and elementary than itself; and the vulgar, in this cosmic setting, has appeared to him sublime.

There is clearly some analogy between a mass of images without structure and the notion of an absolute democracy. Whitman, inclined by his genius and habits to see life without relief or organization, believed that his inclination in this respect corresponded with the spirit of his age and country, and that nature and society, at least in the United States, were constituted after the fashion of his own mind. Being the poet of the average man, he wished all men to be specimens of that average, and being the poet of a fluid nature, he believed that nature was or should be a formless flux. This personal bias of

Whitman's was further encouraged by the actual absence of distinction in his immediate environment. Surrounded by ugly things and common people, he felt himself happy, ecstatic, overflowing with a kind of patriarchal love. He accordingly came to think that there was a spirit of the New World which he embodied, and which was in complete opposition to that of the Old, and that a literature upon novel principles was needed to express and strengthen this American spirit.

Democracy was not to be merely a constitutional device for the better government of given nations, not merely a movement for the material improvement of the lot of the poorer classes. It was to be a social and a moral democracy and to involve an actual equality among all men. Whatever kept them apart and made it impossible for them to be messmates together was to be discarded. The literature of democracy was to ignore all extraordinary gifts of genius or virtue, all distinction drawn even from great passions or romantic adventures. In Whitman's works, in which this new literature is foreshadowed, there is accordingly not a single character nor a single story. His only hero is Myself, the 'single separate person', endowed with the primary impulses, with health, and with sensitiveness to the elementary aspects of nature. The perfect man of the future, the prolific begetter of other perfect men, is to work with his hands, chanting the poems of some future Walt, some ideally democratic bard. Women are to have as nearly as possible the same character as men: the emphasis is to pass from family life and local ties to the friendship of comrades and the general brotherhood of man. Men are to be vigorous, comfortable, sentimental, and irresponsible.

This dream is, of course, unrealized and unrealizable, in America as elsewhere. Undeniably there are in America many suggestions of such a society and such a national character. But the growing complexity and fixity of institutions necessarily tend to obscure these traits of a primitive and crude democracy. What Whitman seized upon as the promise of the future was in reality the survival of the past. He sings the song of pioneers, but it is in the nature of the pioneer that the greater his success the quicker must be his transformation into something different. When Whitman made the initial and amorphous phase of society his ideal, he became the prophet of a lost cause. That cause was lost, not merely when wealth and intelligence began to take shape in the American Commonwealth, but it was lost at the very foundation of the world, when those laws of evolution were established which Whitman, like Rousseau, failed to understand. If we may trust Mr Herbert Spencer, these laws involve a passage from the homogeneous to the heterogeneous, and a constant progress at once in differentiation and in organization—all, in a word, that Whitman systematically deprecated or ignored. He is surely not the spokesman of the tendencies of his country, although he describes some aspects of its past and present condition: nor does he appeal to those whom he describes, but rather to the *dilettanti* he despises. He is regarded as representative chiefly by foreigners, who look for some grotesque expression of the genius of so young and prodigious a people.

Whitman, it is true, loved and comprehended men; but this love and comprehension had the same limits as his love and comprehension of nature. He observed truly and responded to his observation with genuine and pervasive emotion. A great gregariousness, an innocent tolerance of moral weakness, a genuine admiration for bodily health and strength, made him bubble over with affection for the generic human creature. Incapable of an ideal passion, he was full of the milk of human kindness. Yet, for all his acquaintance with the ways and thoughts of the common man of his choice, he did not truly understand him. For to understand people is to go much deeper than they go themselves; to penetrate to their characters and disentangle their inmost ideals. Whitman's insight into man did not go beyond a sensuous sympathy; it consisted in a vicarious satisfaction in their pleasures, and an instinctive love of their persons. It never approached a scientific or imaginative knowledge of their hearts.

Therefore Whitman failed radically in his dearest ambition: he can never be a poet of the people. For the people, like the early races whose poetry was ideal, are natural believers in perfection. They have no doubts about the absolute desirability of wealth and learning and power, none about the worth of pure goodness and pure love. Their chosen poets, if they have any, will be always those who have known how to paint these ideals in lively even if in gaudy colours. Nothing is farther from the common people than the corrupt desire to be primitive. They instinctively look toward a more exalted life, which they imagine to be full of distinction and pleasure, and the idea of that brighter existence fills them with hope or with envy or with humble admiration.

If the people are ever won over to hostility to such ideals, it is only because they are cheated by demagogues who tell them that if all the flowers of civilization were destroyed its fruits would become more abundant. A greater share of happiness, people think, would fall to their lot could they destroy everything beyond their own possible possessions. But they are made thus envious and ignoble only by a deception: what they really desire is an ideal good for themselves which they are told they may secure by depriving others of their pre-eminence. Their hope is always to enjoy perfect satisfaction themselves; and therefore a poet who loves the picturesque aspects of labour and vagrancy will hardly be the poet of the poor. He may have described their figure and occupation, in neither of which they are much interested; he will not have read their souls. They will prefer to him any sentimental story-teller, any sensational dramatist, any moralizing poet; for they are hero-worshippers by temperament, and are too wise or too unfortunate to be much enamoured of themselves or of the conditions of their existence.

Fortunately, the political theory that makes Whitman's principle of literary prophecy and criticism does not always inspire his chants, nor is it presented, even in his prose works, quite bare and unadorned. In 'Democratic Vistas' we find it clothed with something of the same poetic passion and lighted up with the same flashes of intuition which we admire in the poems. Even there the temperament is finer than the ideas and the poet wiser than the thinker. His ultimate appeal is really to something more primitive and general than any social aspirations, to something more elementary than an ideal of any kind. He speaks to those minds and to those moods in which sensuality is touched with mysticism. When the intellect is in abeyance, when we would 'turn and live with the animals, they are so placid and self-contained', when we are weary of conscience and of ambition, and would yield ourselves for a while to the dream of sense, Walt Whitman is a welcome companion. The images he arouses in us, fresh, full of light and health and of a kind of frankness and beauty, are prized all the more at such a time because they are not choice, but drawn perhaps from a hideous and sordid environment. For this circumstance makes them a better means of escape from convention and from that fatigue and despair which lurk not far beneath the surface of conventional life. In casting off with self-assurance and a sense of fresh vitality the distinctions of tradition and reason a man may feel, as he sinks back comfortably to a lower level of sense and instinct, that he is returning to nature or escaping into the infinite. Mysticism makes us proud and happy to renounce the work of intelligence, both in thought and in life, and persuades us that we become divine by remaining imperfectly human. Walt Whitman gives a new expression to this ancient and multiform tendency. He feels his own cosmic justification and he would lend the sanction of his inspiration to all loafers and holiday-makers. He would be the congenial patron of farmers and factory hands in their crude pleasures and pieties, as Pan was the patron of the shepherds of Arcadia: for he is sure that in spite of his hairiness and animality, the gods will acknowledge him as one of themselves and smile upon him from the serenity of Olympus.

3 ROBERT BROWNING

If we would do justice to Browning's work as a human document, and at the same time perceive its relation to the rational ideals of the imagination and to that poetry which passes into religion, we must keep, as in the case of Whitman, two things in mind. One is the genuineness of the achievement, the sterling quality of the vision and inspiration; these are their own justification when we approach them from below and regard them as manifesting a more direct or impassioned grasp of experience than is given to mildly blatant, convention-ridden minds. The other thing to remember is the short distance to which this comprehension is carried, its failure to approach any finality, or to achieve a recognition even of the traditional ideals of poetry and religion.

In the case of Walt Whitman such a failure will be generally felt; it is obvious that both his music and his philosophy are those of a barbarian, nay, almost of a savage. Accordingly there is need of dwelling rather on the veracity and simple dignity of his thought and art, on their expression of an order of ideas latent in all better experience. But in the case of Browning it is the success that is obvious to most people. Apart from a certain superficial grotesqueness to which we are soon accustomed, he easily arouses and engages the reader by the pithiness of his phrase, the volume of his passion, the vigour of his moral judgment, the liveliness of his historical fancy. It is obvious that we are in the presence of a great writer, of a great imaginative force, of a master in the expression of emotion. What is perhaps not so obvious, but no less true, is that we are in the presence of a barbaric genius, of a truncated imagination, of a thought and an art inchoate and ill digested, of a volcanic eruption that tosses itself quite blindly and ineffecually into the sky.

The points of comparison by which this becomes clear are perhaps not in everyone's mind, although they are merely the elements of traditional culture, aesthetic and moral. Yet even without reference to ultimate ideals, one may notice in

Browning many superficial signs of that deepest of all failures, the failure in rationality and the indifference to perfection. Such a sign is the turgid style, weighty without nobility, pointed without naturalness or precision. Another sign is the 'realism' of the personages, who, quite like men and women in actual life, are always displaying traits of character and never attaining character as a whole. Other hints might be found in the structure of the poems, where the dramatic substance does not achieve a dramatic form; in the metaphysical discussion, with its confused prolixity and absence of result; in the moral ideal, where all energies figure without their ultimate purposes; in the religion, which breaks off the expression of this life in the middle, and finds in that suspense an argument for immortality. In all this, and much more that might be recalled, a person coming to Browning with the habits of a cultivated mind might see evidence of some profound incapacity in the poet; but more careful reflection is necessary to understand the nature of this incapacity, its cause, and the peculiar accent which its presence gives to those ideas and impulses which Browning stimulates in us.

There is the more reason for developing this criticism (which might seem needlessly hostile and which time and posterity will doubtless make in their own quiet and decisive fashion) in that Browning did not keep within the sphere of drama and analysis, where he was strong, but allowed his own temperament and opinions to vitiate his representation of life, so that he sometimes turned the expression of a violent passion into the last word of what he thought a religion. He had a didactic vein, a habit of judging the spectacle he evoked and of loading the passions he depicted with his visible sympathy or scorn.

Now a chief support of Browning's popularity is that he is, for many, an initiator into the deeper mysteries of passion, a means of escaping from the moral poverty of their own lives and of feeling the rhythm and compulsion of the general striving. He figures, therefore, distinctly as a prophet, as a bearer of glad tidings, and it is easy for those who hail him as such to imagine that, knowing the labour of life so well, he must know something also of its fruits, and that in giving us the feeling of existence, he is also giving us its meaning. There is serious danger that a mind gathering from his pages the raw materials of truth, the unthreshed harvest of reality, may take him for a philosopher, for a rationalizer of what he describes. Awakening may be mistaken for enlightenment, and the galvanizing of torpid sensations and impulses for wisdom.

Against such fatuity reason should raise her voice. The vital and historic forces that produce illusions of this sort in large groups of men are indeed beyond the control of criticism. The ideas of passion are more vivid than those of memory, until they become memories in turn. They must be allowed to fight out their desperate battle against the laws of nature and reason. But it is worth while in the meantime, for the sake of the truth and of a just philosophy, to meet the varying though perpetual charlatanism of the world with a steady protest. As soon as Browning is proposed to us as a leader, as soon as we are asked to be not the occasional patrons of his art, but the pupils of his philosophy, we have a right to express the radical dissatisfaction which we must feel, if we are rational, with his whole attitude and temper of mind.

The great dramatists have seldom dealt with perfectly virtuous characters. The great poets have seldom represented mythologies that would bear scientific criticism. But by an instinct which constituted their greatness they have cast these mixed materials furnished by life into forms congenial to the specific principles of their art, and by this transformation they have made acceptable in the aesthetic sphere things that in the sphere of reality were evil or imperfect: in a word, their works have been beautiful as works of art. Or, if their genius exceeded that of the technical poet and rose to prophetic intuition, they have known how to create ideal characters, not possessed, perhaps, of every virtue accidentally needed in this world, but possessed of what is ideally better, of internal greatness and perfection. They have also known how to select and reconstruct their mythology so as to make it a true interpretation of moral life. When we read the maxims of Iago, Falstaff, or Hamlet, we are delighted if the thought strikes us as true, but we are not less delighted if it strikes us as false. These characters are not presented to us in order to enlarge our capacities of passion nor in order to justify themselves as processes of redemption; they are there, clothed in poetry and imbedded in plot, to entertain us with their imaginable feelings and their interesting errors. The poet, without being especially a philosopher, stands by virtue of his superlative genius on the plane of universal reason, far above the passionate experience which he overlooks and on which he reflects; and he raises us for the moment to his own level, to send us back again, if not better endowed for practical life, at least not unacquainted with speculation.

With Browning the case is essentially different. When his heroes are blinded by passion and warped by circumstance, as they almost always are, he does not describe the fact from the vantage-ground of the intellect and invite us to look at it from that point of view. On the contrary, his art is all self-expression or satire. For the most part his hero, like Whitman's, is himself; not appearing, as in the case of the American bard, *in puris naturalibus*, but masked in all sorts of historical and romantic finery. Sometimes, however, the personage, like Guido in *The Ring and the Book* or the 'frustrate ghosts' of other poems, is merely a Marsyas, shown flayed and quivering to the greater glory of the poet's ideal Apollo. The impulsive utterances and the crudities of most of the speakers are passionately adopted by the poet as his own. He thus perverts what might have been a triumph of imagination into a failure of reason.

This circumstance has much to do with the fact that Browning, in spite of his extraordinary gift for expressing emotion, has hardly produced works purely and unconditionally delightful. They not only portray passion, which is interesting, but they betray it, which is odious. His art was still in the service of the will. He had not attained, in studying the beauty of things, that detachment of the phenomenon, that love of the form for its own sake, which is the secret of contemplative satisfaction. Therefore, the lamentable accidents of his personality and opinions, in themselves no worse than those of other mortals, passed into his art. He did not seek to elude them: he had no free speculative faculty to dominate them by. Or, to put the same thing differently, he was too much in earnest in his fictions, he threw himself too unreservedly into his creations. His imagination, like the imagination we have in dreams, was merely a vent for personal preoccupations. His art was inspired by purposes less simple and universal than the ends of imagination itself. His play of mind consequently could not be free or pure. The creative impulse could not reach its goal or manifest in any notable degree its own organic ideal.

We may illustrate these assertions by considering Browning's treatment of the passion of love, a passion to which he gives great prominence and in which he finds the highest significance.

Love is depicted by Browning with truth, with vehemence, and with the constant conviction that it is the supreme thing in life. The great variety of occasions in which it appears in his pages and the different degrees of elaboration it receives, leave it always of the same quality—the quality of passion. It never sinks into sensuality; in spite of its frequent extreme crudeness, it is always, in Browning's hands, a passion of the imagination, it is always love. On the other hand it never rises into contemplation: mingled as it may be with friendship, with religion, or with various forms of natural tenderness, it always remains a passion; it always remains a personal impulse, a hypnotization, with another person for its object or its cause. Kept within these limits it is represented, in a series of powerful sketches, which are for most readers the gems of the Browning gallery, as the last word of experience, the highest phase of human life.

> The woman yonder, there's no use in life
> But just to obtain her! Heap earth's woes in one

And bear them—make a pile of all earth's joys
And spurn them, as they help or help not this;
Only, obtain her! [*In a Balcony*, 157–61]

When I do come, she will speak not, she will stand,
Either hand
On my shoulder, give her eyes the first embrace
Of my face,
Ere we rush, ere we extinguish sight and speech
Each on each...
O heart, O blood that freezes, blood that burns!
Earth's returns
For whole centuries of folly, noise, and sin!
Shut them in,
With their triumphs and their glories and the rest!
Love is best. [*Love among the Ruins*, 67–72, 79–84]

In the piece called *In a Gondola* the lady says to her lover:

Heart to heart
And lips to lips! Yet once more, ere we part,
Clasp me and make me thine, as mine thou art. [222–4]

And he, after being surprised and stabbed in her arms, replies:

It was ordained to be so, sweet!—and best
Comes now, beneath thine eyes, upon thy breast:
Still kiss me! Care not for the cowards; care
Only to put aside thy beauteous hair
My blood will hurt! The Three I do not scorn
To death, because they never lived, but I
Have lived indeed, and so—(yet one more kiss)—
can die. [225–31]

We are not allowed to regard these expressions as the cries of souls blinded by the agony of passion and lust. Browning unmistakably adopts them as expressing his own highest intuitions. He so much admires the strength of this weakness that he does not admit that it is a weakness at all. It is with the strut of self-satisfaction, with the sensation, almost, of muscular Christianity, that he boasts of it through the mouth of one of his heroes, who is explaining to his mistress the motive of his faithful services as a minister of the queen:

She thinks there was more cause
In love of power, high fame, pure loyalty?
Perhaps she fancies men wear out their lives
Chasing such shades...
I worked because I want you with my soul.

[*In a Balcony*, 174–8]

Readers of 'Platonic Love in some Italian Poets' need not be reminded here of the contrast which this method of understanding love offers to that adopted by the real masters of passion and imagination. They began with that crude emotion with which Browning ends; they lived it down, they exalted it by thought, they extracted the pure gold of it in a long purgation of discipline and suffering. The fierce paroxysm which for him is heaven, was for them the proof that heaven cannot be found on earth, that the value of experience is not in experience itself but in the ideals which it reveals. The intense voluminous emotion, the sudden, overwhelming self-surrender in which he rests was for them the starting-point of a life of rational worship, of an austere and impersonal religion, by which the fire of love, kindled for a moment by the sight of some creature, was put, as it were, into a censer, to burn incense before every image of the Highest Good. Thus love ceased to be a passion and became the energy of contemplation: it diffused over the universe, natural and ideal, that light of tenderness and that faculty of worship which the passion of love often is first to quicken in a man's breast.

Of this art, recommended by Plato and practised in the Christian Church by all adepts of the spiritual life, Browning knew absolutely nothing. About the object of love he had no misgivings. What could the object be except somebody or other? The important thing was to love intensely and to love often. He remained in the phenomenal sphere: he was a lover of experience; the ideal did not exist for him. No conception could be farther from his thought than the essential conception of any rational philosophy, namely, that feeling is to be treated as raw material for thought, and that the destiny of emotion is to pass into objects which shall contain all its value while losing all its formlessness. This transformation of sense and emotion into objects agreeable to the intellect, into clear ideas and beautiful things, is the natural work of reason; when it has been accomplished very imperfectly, or not at all, we have a barbarous mind, a mind full of chaotic sensations, objectless passions, and undigested ideas. Such a mind Browning's was, to a degree remarkable in one with so rich a heritage of civilization.

The nineteenth century, as we have already said, has nourished the hope of abolishing the past as a force while it studies it as an object; and Browning, with his fondness for a historical stage-setting and for the gossip of history, rebelled equally against the pagan and the Christian discipline. The 'Soul' which he trusted in was the barbarous soul, the 'Spontaneous Me' of his half-brother Whitman. It was a restless personal impulse, conscious of obscure depths within itself which it fancied to be infinite, and of a certain vague sympathy with wind and cloud and with the universal mutation. It was the soul that might have animated Attila and Alaric when they came down into Italy, a soul not incurious of the tawdriness and corruption of the strange civilization it beheld, but incapable of understanding its original spirit; a soul maintaining in the presence of that noble, unappreciated ruin all its own lordliness and energy, and all its native vulgarity.

Browning, who had not had the education traditional in his own country, used to say that Italy had been his university. But it was a school for which he was ill prepared, and he did not sit under its best teachers. For the superficial ferment, the worldly passions, and the crimes of the Italian Renaissance he had a keen interest and intelligence. But Italy has been always a civilized country, and beneath the trappings and suits of civilization which at that particular time it flaunted so gaily, it preserved a civilized heart to which Browning's insight could never penetrate. There subsisted in the best minds a trained imagination and a cogent ideal of virtue. Italy had a religion, and that religion permeated all its life, and was the background without which even its secular art and secular passions would not be truly intelligible. The most commanding and representative, the deepest and most appealing of Italian natures are permeated with this religious inspiration. A Saint Francis, a Dante, a Michael Angelo, breathe hardly anything else. Yet for Browning these men and what they represented may be said not to have existed. He saw, he studied, and he painted a decapitated Italy. His vision could not mount so high as her head.

One of the elements of that higher tradition which Browning was not prepared to imbibe was the idealization of love. The passion he represents is lava hot from the crater, in no way moulded, smelted, or refined. He had no thought of subjugating impulses into the harmony of reason. He did not master life, but was mastered by it. Accordingly the love he describes has no wings; it issues in nothing. His lovers 'extinguish sight and speech, each on each'; sense, as he says elsewhere, drowning soul. The man in the gondola may well boast that he can die; it is the only thing he can properly do. Death is the only solution of a love that is tied to its individual object and inseparable from the alloy of passion and illusion within itself. Browning's hero, because he has loved intensely, says that he has lived; he would be right, if the significance of life were to be measured by the intensity of the feeling it contained, and if intelligence were not the highest form of vitality. But had that hero known how to love better and had he had enough spirit to dominate his love, he might perhaps have been able to carry away the better part of it and to say that he could not die; for one half of himself and of his love would have been dead already and the other half would have been eternal, having fed—

> On death, that feeds on men,
> And death once dead, there's no more dying then.

The irrationality of the passions which Browning glorifies, making them the crown of life, is so gross that at times he cannot help perceiving it.

> How perplexed
> Grows belief! Well, this cold clay clod

Was man's heart:
Crumble it, and what comes next? Is it God?

[*In a Year*, 75–80]

Yes, he will tell us. These passions and follies, however desperate in themselves and however vain for the individual, are excellent as parts of the dispensation of Providence:

Be hate that fruit or love that fruit,
It forwards the general deed of man,
And each of the many helps to recruit
The life of the race by a general plan,
Each living his own to boot.

[*By the Fireside*, 246–50]

If we doubt, then, the value of our own experience, even perhaps of our experience of love, we may appeal to the interdependence of goods and evils in the world to assure ourselves that, in view of its consequences elsewhere, this experience was great and important after all. We need not stop to consider this supposed solution, which bristles with contradictions; it would not satisfy Browning himself, if he did not back it up with something more to his purpose, something nearer to warm and transitive feeling. The compensation for our defeats, the answer to our doubts, is not to be found merely in a proof of the essential necessity and perfection of the universe; that would be cold comfort, especially to so uncontemplative a mind. No: that answer, and compensation, are to come very soon and very vividly to every private bosom. There is another life, a series of other lives, for this to happen in. Death will come, and—

I shall thereupon
Take rest, ere I be gone
Once more on my adventure brave and new,
Fearless and unperplexed,
When I wage battle next,
What weapons to select, what armour to endue.

[*Rabbi Ben Ezra*, 79–84]

For sudden the worst turns the best to the brave,
The black minute's at end,
And the element's rage, the fiend-voices that rave,
Shall dwindle, shall blend,

Shall change, shall become first a peace out of pain,
Then a light, then thy breast,
O thou soul of my soul! I shall clasp thee again,
And with God be the rest! [*Prospice*, 21–8]

Into this conception of continued life Browning has put, as a collection of further passages might easily show, all the items furnished by fancy or tradition which at the moment satisfied his imagination—new adventures, reunion with friends, and even, after a severe strain and for a short while, a little peace and quiet. The gist of the matter is that we are to live indefinitely, that all our faults can be turned to good, all our unfinished business settled, and that therefore there is time for anything we like in this world and for all we need in the other. It is in spirit the direct opposite of the philosophic maxim of regarding the end, of taking care to leave a finished life and a perfect character behind us. It is the opposite, also, of the religious *memento mori*, of the warning that the time is short before we go to our account. According to Browning, there is no account: we have an infinite credit. With an unconscious and characteristic mixture of heathen instinct with Christian doctrine, he thinks of the other world as heaven, but of the life to be led there as of the life of nature.

Aristotle observes that we do not think the business of life worthy of the gods, to whom we can only attribute contemplation; if Browning had had the idea of perfecting and rationalizing this life rather than of continuing it indefinitely, he would have followed Aristotle and the Church in this matter. But he had no idea of anything eternal; and so he gave, as he would probably have said, a filling to the empty Christian immortality by making every man busy in it about many things. And to the irrational man, to the boy, it is no unpleasant idea to have an infinite number of days to live through, an infinite number of dinners to eat, with an infinity of fresh fights and new love-affairs, and no end of last rides together.

But it is a mere euphemism to call this perpetual vagrancy a development of the soul. A development means the unfolding of a definite nature, the gradual manifestation of a known idea. A series of phases, like the successive leaps of a waterfall, is no development. And Browning has no idea of an intelligible good which the phases of life might approach and with reference to which they might constitute a progress. His notion is simply that the game of life, the exhilaration of action, is inexhaustible. You may set up your tenpins again after you have bowled them over, and you may keep up the sport for ever. The point is to bring them down as often as possible with a master-stroke and a big bang. That will tend to invigorate in you that self-confidence which in this system passes for faith. But it is unmeaning to call such an exercise heaven, or to talk of being 'with God' in such a life, in any sense in which we are not with God already and under all circumstances. Our destiny would rather be, as Browning himself expresses it in a phrase which Attila or Alaric might have composed, 'bound dizzily to the wheel of change to slake the thirst of God'.

Such an optimism and such a doctrine of immortality can give no justification to experience which it does not already have in its detached parts. Indeed, those dogmas are not the basis of Browning's attitude, not conditions of his satisfaction in living, but rather overflowings of that satisfaction. The present life is presumably a fair average of the whole series of 'adventures brave and new' which fall to each man's share; were it not found delightful in itself, there would be no motive for imagining and asserting that it is reproduced *in infinitum*. So too if we did not think that the evil in experience is actually utilized and visibly swallowed up in its good effects, we should hardly venture to think that God could have regarded as a good something which has evil for its condition and which is for that reason profoundly sad and equivocal. But Browning's philosophy of life and habit of imagination do not require the support of any metaphysical theory. His temperament is perfectly self-sufficient and primary; what doctrines he has are suggested by it and are too loose to give it more than a hesitant expression; they are quite powerless to give it any justification which it might lack on its face.

It is the temperament, then, that speaks; we may brush aside as unsubstantial, and even as distorting, the web of arguments and theories which it has spun out of itself. And what does the temperament say? That life is an adventure, not a discipline; that the exercise of energy is the absolute good, irrespective of motives or of consequences. These are the maxims of a frank barbarism; nothing could express better the lust of life, the dogged unwillingness to learn from experience, the contempt for rationality, the carelessness about perfection, the admiration for mere force, in which barbarism always betrays itself. The vague religion which seeks to justify this attitude is really only another outburst of the same irrational impulse.

In Browning this religion takes the name of Christianity, and identifies itself with one or two Christian ideas arbitrarily selected; but at heart it has far more affinity to the worship of Thor or of Odin than to the religion of the Cross. The zest of life becomes a cosmic emotion; we lump the whole together and cry, 'Hurrah for the Universe!' A faith which is thus a pure matter of lustiness and inebriation rises and falls, attracts or repels, with the ebb and flow of the mood from which it springs. It is invincible because unseizable; it is as safe from refutation as it is rebellious to embodiment. But it cannot enlighten or correct the passions on which it feeds. Like a servile priest, it flatters them in the name of Heaven. It cloaks irrationality in sanctimony; and its admiration for every bluff folly, being thus justified by a theory, becomes a positive fanaticism, eager to defend any wayward impulse.

Such barbarism of temper and thought could hardly, in a man of Browning's independence and spontaneity, be without its counterpart in his art. When a man's personal religion is passive, as Shakespeare's seems to have been, and is adopted without question or particular interest from the society around him, we may not observe any analogy between it and the free creations of that man's mind. Not so when the religion is created afresh by the private imagination; it is then merely one among many personal works of art, and will naturally bear a family likeness to the others. The same individual temperament, with its limitations and its bias, will appear in the art which has appeared in the religion. And such is the case of Browning. His limitations as a poet are the counterpart of his limitations as a moralist and theologian; only in the poet they are not so regrettable. Philosophy and religion are nothing if not ultimate; it is their business to deal with general principles and final aims. Now it is in the conception of things fundamental and ultimate that Browning is weak; he is strong in the conception of things immediate. The pulse of the emotion, the bobbing up of the thought, the streaming of the reverie—these he can note down with picturesque force or imagine with admirable fecundity.

Yet the limits of such excellence are narrow, for no man can safely go far without the guidance of reason. His long poems have no structure—for that name cannot be given to the singular mechanical division of *The Ring and the Book*. Even his short poems have no completeness, no limpidity. They are little torsos made broken so as to stimulate the reader to the restoration of their missing legs and arms. What is admirable in them is pregnancy of phrase, vividness of passion and sentiment, heaped-up scraps of observation, occasional flashes of light, occasional beauties of versification, —all like

> the quick sharp scratch
> And blue spurt of a lighted match.
>
> [*Meeting at Night*, 9–10]

There is never anything largely composed in the spirit of pure beauty, nothing devotedly finished, nothing simple and truly just. The poet's mind cannot reach equilibrium; at best he oscillates between opposed extravagances; his final word is still a *boutade*, still an explosion. He has no sustained nobility of style. He affects with the reader a confidential and vulgar manner, so as to be more sincere and to feel more at home. Even in the poems where the effort at impersonality is most successful, the dramatic disguise is usually thrown off in a preface, epilogue or parenthesis. The author likes to remind us of himself by some confidential wink or genial poke in the ribs, by some little interlarded sneer. We get in these tricks of manner a taste of that essential vulgarity, that indifference to purity and distinction, which is latent but pervasive in all the products of this mind. The same disdain of perfection which appears in his ethics appears here in his verse, and impairs its beauty by allowing it to remain too often obscure, affected, and grotesque.

Such a correspondence is natural: for the same powers of conception and expression are needed in fiction, which, if turned to reflection, would produce a good philosophy. Reason is necessary to the perception of high beauty. Discipline is indispensable to art. Work from which these qualities are absent must be barbaric; it can have no ideal form and must appeal to us only through the sensuousness and profusion of its materials. We are invited by it to lapse into a miscellaneous appreciativeness, into a subservience to every detached impression. And yet, if we would only reflect even on these disordered beauties, we should see that the principle by which they delight us is a principle by which an ideal, an image of perfection, is inevitably evoked. We can have no pleasure or pain, nor any preference whatsoever, without implicitly setting up a standard of excellence, an ideal of what would satisfy us there. To make these implicit ideals explicit, to catch their hint, to work out their theme, and express clearly to ourselves and to the world what they are demanding in the place of the actual—that is the labour of reason and the task of genius. The two cannot be divided. Clarification of ideas and disentanglement of values are as essential to aesthetic activity as to intelligence. A failure of reason is a failure of art and taste.

The limits of Browning's art, like the limits of Whitman's, can therefore be understood by considering his mental habit. Both poets had powerful imaginations, but the type of their imaginations was low. In Whitman imagination was limited to marshalling sensations in single file; the embroideries he made around that central line were simple and insignificant. His energy was concentrated on that somewhat animal form of contemplation, of which, for the rest, he was a great, perhaps an unequalled master. Browning rose above that level; with him sensation is usually in the background; he is not particularly a poet of the senses or of ocular vision. His favourite subject-matter is rather the stream of thought and feeling in the mind; he is the poet of soliloquy. Nature and life as they really are, rather than as they may appear to the ignorant and passionate participant in them, lie beyond his range. Even in his best dramas, like *A Blot in the 'Scutcheon* or *Colombe's Birthday*, the interest remains in the experience of the several persons as they explain it to us. The same is the case in *The Ring and the Book*, the conception of which, in twelve monstrous soliloquies, is a striking evidence of the poet's predilection for this form.

The method is, to penetrate by sympathy rather than to portray by intelligence. The most authoritative insight is not the poet's or the spectator's, aroused and enlightened by the spectacle, but the various heroes' own, in their moment of intensest passion. We therefore miss the tragic relief and exaltation, and come away instead with the uncomfortable feeling that an obstinate folly is apparently the most glorious and choiceworthy thing in the world. This is evidently the poet's own illusion, and those who do not happen to share it must feel that if life were really as irrational as he thinks it, it would be not only profoundly discouraging, which it often is, but profoundly disgusting, which it surely is not; for at least it reveals the ideal which it fails to attain.

This ideal Browning never disentangles. For him the crude experience is the only end, the endless struggle the only ideal, and the perturbed 'Soul' the only organon of truth. The arrest of his intelligence at this point, before it has envisaged any rational object, explains the arrest of his dramatic art at soliloquy. His immersion in the forms of self-consciousness prevents him from dramatizing the real relations of men and their thinkings to one another, to nature, and to destiny. For in order to do so he would have had to view his characters from above (as Cervantes did, for instance), and to see them not merely as they appeared to themselves, but as they appear to reason. This higher attitude, however, was not only beyond Browning's scope, it was positively contrary to his inspiration. Had he reached it, he would no longer have seen the universe through the 'Soul', but through the intellect, and he would not have been able to cry, 'How the world is made for each one of us!' On the contrary, the 'Soul' would have figured only in its true conditions, in all its ignorance and dependence, and also in its essential teachableness, a point against which Browning's barbaric wilfulness particularly rebelled. Rooted in his persuasion that the soul is essentially omnipotent and that to live hard can never be to live wrong, he remained fascinated by the march and method of self-consciousness, and never allowed himself to be weaned from that romantic fatuity by the energy of rational imagination, which prompts us not to regard our ideas as mere filling of a dream, but rather to build on them the conception of permanent objects and overruling principles, such as nature, society, and the other ideals of reason. A full-grown imagination deals with these things, which do not obey the laws of psychological progression, and cannot be described by the methods of soliloquy.

We thus see that Browning's sphere, though more subtle and complex than Whitman's, was still elementary. It lay far below the spheres of social and historical reality in which Shakespeare moved; far below the comprehensive and cosmic sphere of every great epic poet. Browning did not even reach the intellectual plane of such contemporary poets as Tennyson and Matthew Arnold, who, whatever may be thought of their powers, did not study consciousness for itself, but for the sake of its meaning and of the objects which it revealed. The best things that come into a man's consciousness are the things that take him out of it—the rational things that are independent of his personal perception and of his personal existence. These he approaches with his reason, and they, in the same measure, endow him with their immortality. But precisely these things—the objects of science and of the constructive imagination—Browning always saw askance, in the outskirts of his field of vision, for his eye was fixed and riveted on the soliloquizing Soul. And this Soul being, to his apprehension, irrational, did not give itself over to those permanent objects which might otherwise have occupied it, but ruminated on its own accidental emotions, on its love-affairs, and on its hopes of going on so ruminating for ever.

The pathology of the human mind—for the normal, too, is pathological when it is not referred to the ideal—the pathology of the human mind is a very interesting subject, demanding great gifts and great ingenuity in its treatment. Browning ministers to this interest, and possesses this ingenuity and these gifts. More than any other poet he keeps a kind of speculation alive in the now large body of sentimental, eager-minded people, who no longer can find in a definite religion a form and language for their imaginative life. That this service is greatly appreciated speaks well for the ineradicable tendency in man to study himself and his destiny. We do not deny the achievement when we point out its nature and limitations. It does not cease to be something because it is taken to be more than it is.

In every imaginative sphere the nineteenth century has been an era of chaos, as it has been an era of order and growing organization in the spheres of science and of industry. An ancient doctrine of the philosophers asserts that to chaos the world must ultimately return. And what is perhaps true of the cycles of cosmic change is certainly true of the revolutions of culture. Nothing lasts for ever: languages, arts, and religions disintegrate with time. Yet the perfecting of such forms is the only criterion of progress; the destruction of them the chief evidence of decay. Perhaps fate intends that we should have, in our imaginative decadence, the consolation of fancying that we are still progressing, and that the disintegration of religion and the arts is bringing us nearer to the protoplasm of sensation and passion. If energy and actuality are all that we care for, chaos is as good as order, and barbarism as good as discipline—better, perhaps, since impulse is not then restrained within any bounds of reason or beauty. But if the powers of the human mind are at any time adequate to the task of digesting experience, clearness and order inevitably supervene. The moulds of thought are imposed upon nature, and the conviction of a definite truth arises together with the vision of a supreme perfection. It is only at such periods that the human animal vindicates his title of rational. If such an epoch should return, people will no doubt retrace our present gropings with interest and see in them gradual approaches to their own achievement. Whitman and Browning might well figure then as representatives of our time. For the merit of being representative cannot be denied them. The mind of our age, like theirs, is choked with materials, emotional, and inconclusive. They merely aggravate our characteristics, and their success with us is due partly to their own absolute strength and partly to our common weakness. If once, however, this imaginative weakness could be overcome, and a form found for the crude matter of experience, men might look back from the height of a new religion and a new poetry upon the present troubles of the spirit; and perhaps even these things might then be pleasant to remember.

EMERSON

Those who knew Emerson, or who stood so near to his time and to his circle that they caught some echo of his personal influence, did not judge him merely as a poet or philosopher, nor identify his efficacy with that of his writings. His friends and neighbours, the congregations he preached to in his younger days, the audiences that afterward listened to his lectures, all agreed in a veneration for his person which had nothing to do with their understanding or acceptance of his opinions. They flocked to him and listened to his word, not so much for the sake of its absolute meaning as for the atmosphere of candour, purity, and serenity that hung about it, as about a sort of sacred music. They felt themselves in the presence of a rare and beautiful spirit, who was in communion with a higher world. More than the truth his teaching might express, they valued the sense it gave them of a truth that was inexpressible. They became aware, if we may say so, of the ultra-violet rays of his spectrum, of the inaudible highest notes of his gamut, too pure and thin for common ears.

This effect was by no means due to the possession on the part of Emerson of the secret of the universe, or even of a definite conception of ultimate truth. He was not a prophet who had once for all climbed his Sinai or his Tabor, and having there beheld the transfigured reality, descended again to make authoritative report of it to the world. Far from it. At bottom he had no doctrine at all. The deeper he went and the more he tried to grapple with fundamental conceptions, the vaguer and more elusive they became in his hands. Did he know what he meant by Spirit or the 'Over-Soul'? Could he say what he understood by the terms, so constantly on his lips, Nature, Law, God, Benefit, or Beauty? He could not, and the consciousness of that incapacity was so lively within him that he never attempted to give articulation to his philosophy. His finer instinct kept him from doing that violence to his inspiration.

The source of his power lay not in his doctrine, but in his temperament, and the rare quality of his wisdom was due less to his reason than to his imagination. Reality eluded him; he had neither diligence nor constancy enough to master and possess it; but his mind was open to all philosophic influences, from whatever quarter they might blow; the lessons of science and the hints of poetry worked themselves out in him to a free and personal religion. He differed from the plodding many, not in knowing things better, but in having more ways of knowing them. His grasp was not particularly firm, he was far from being, like a Plato or an Aristotle, past master in the art and the science of life. But his mind was endowed with unusual plasticity, with unusual spontaneity and liberty of movement—it was a fairyland of thoughts and fancies. He was like a young god making experiments in creation: he blotched the work, and always began again on a new and better plan. Every day he said, 'Let there be light', and every day the light was new. His sun, like that of Heraclitus, was different every morning.

What seemed, then, to the more earnest and less critical of his hearers a revelation from above was in truth rather an insurrection from beneath, a shaking loose from convention, a disintegration of the normal categories of reason in favour of various imaginative principles, on which the world might have been built, if it had been built differently. This gift of revolutionary thinking allowed new aspects, hints of wider laws, premonitions of unthought-of fundamental unities to spring constantly into view. But such visions were necessarily fleeting, because the human mind had long before settled its grammar, and discovered, after much groping and many defeats, the general forms in which experience will allow itself to be stated. These general forms are the principles of common sense and positive science, no less imaginative in their origin than those notions which we now call transcendental, but grown prosaic, like the metaphors of common speech, by dint of repetition.

Yet authority, even of this rational kind, sat lightly upon

Emerson. To reject tradition and think as one might have thought if no man had ever existed before was indeed the aspiration of the Transcendentalists, and although Emerson hardly regarded himself as a member of that school, he largely shared its tendency and passed for its spokesman. Without protesting against tradition, he smilingly eluded it in his thoughts, untamable in their quiet irresponsibility. He fled to his woods or to his 'pleachèd garden', to be the creator of his own worlds in solitude and freedom. No wonder that he brought thence to the tightly conventional minds of his contemporaries a breath as if from paradise. His simplicity in novelty, his profundity, his ingenuous ardour must have seemed to them something heavenly, and they may be excused if they thought they detected inspiration even in his occasional thin paradoxes and guileless whims. They were stifled with conscience and he brought them a breath of nature; they were surfeited with shallow controversies and he gave them poetic truth.

Imagination, indeed, is his single theme. As a preacher might under every text enforce the same lessons of the gospel, so Emerson traces in every sphere the same spiritual laws of experience—compensation, continuity, the self-expression of the Soul in the forms of nature and of society, until she finally recognizes herself in her own work and sees its beneficence and beauty. His constant refrain is the omnipotence of imaginative thought; its power first to make the world, then to understand it, and finally to rise above it. All nature is an embodiment of our native fancy, all history a drama in which the innate possibilities of the spirit are enacted and realized. While the conflict of life and the shocks of experience seem to bring us face to face with an alien and overwhelming power, reflection can humanize and rationalize that power by conceiving its laws; and with this recognition of the rationality of all things comes the sense of their beauty and order. The destruction which nature seems to prepare for our special hopes is thus seen to be the victory of our impersonal interests. To awaken in us this spiritual insight, an elevation of mind which is at once an act of comprehension and of worship, to substitute it for lower passions and more servile forms of intelligence—that is Emerson's constant effort. All his resources of illustration, observation, and rhetoric are used to deepen and clarify this sort of wisdom.

Such thought is essentially the same that is found in the German romantic or idealistic philosophers, with whom Emerson's affinity is remarkable, all the more as he seems to have borrowed little or nothing from their works. The critics of human nature, in the eighteenth century, had shown how much men's ideas depend on their predispositions, on the character of their senses and the habits of their intelligence. Seizing upon this thought and exaggerating it, the romantic philosophers attributed to the spirit of man the omnipotence which had belonged to God, and felt that in this way they were reasserting the supremacy of mind over matter and establishing it upon a safe and rational basis.

The Germans were great system-makers, and Emerson cannot rival them in the sustained effort of thought by which they sought to reinterpret every sphere of being according to their chosen principles. But he surpassed them in an instinctive sense of what he was doing. He never represented his poetry as science, nor countenanced the formation of a new sect that should nurse the sense of a private and mysterious illumination, and relight the faggots of passion and prejudice. He never tried to seek out and defend the book he had once planned on the law of compensation, foreseeing, we may well believe, the sophistries in which he would have been directly involved. He fortunately preferred a fresh statement on a fresh subject. A suggestion once given, the spirit once aroused to speculation, a glimpse once gained of some ideal harmony, he chose to descend again to common sense and to touch the earth for a moment before another flight. The faculty of idealization was itself what he valued. Philosophy for him was rather a moral energy flowering into sprightliness of thought than a body of serious and defensible doctrines. In practising transcendental speculation only in this poetic and sporadic fashion, Emerson retained its true value and avoided its greatest danger. He secured the freedom and fertility of his thought and did not allow one conception of law or one hint of harmony to sterilize the mind and prevent the subsequent birth within it of other ideas, no less just and imposing than their predecessors. For we are not dealing at all in such a philosophy with matters of facts or with such verifiable truths as exclude their opposites. We are dealing only with imagination, with the art of conception, and with the various forms in which reflection, like a poet, may compose and recompose human experience.

A certain disquiet mingled, however, in the minds of Emerson's contemporaries with the admiration they felt for his purity and genius. They saw that he had forsaken the doctrines of the Church; and they were not sure whether he held quite unequivocally any doctrine whatever. We may not all of us share the concern for orthodoxy which usually caused this puzzled alarm: we may understand that it was not Emerson's vocation to be definite and dogmatic in religion any more than in philosophy. Yet that disquiet will not, even for us, wholly disappear. It is produced by a defect which naturally accompanies imagination in all but the greatest minds. I mean disorganization. Emerson not only conceived things in new ways, but he seemed to think the new ways might cancel and supersede the old. His imagination was to invalidate the understanding. That inspiration which should come to fulfil seemed too often to come to destroy. If he was able so constantly to stimulate us to fresh thoughts, was it not because he demolished the labour of long ages of reflection? Was not the startling effect of much of his writing due to its contradiction of tradition and of common sense?

So long as he is a poet and in the enjoyment of his poetic licence, we can blame this play of mind only by a misunderstanding. It is possible to think otherwise than as common sense thinks; there are other categories beside those of science. When we employ them we enlarge our lives. We add to the world of fact any number of worlds of the imagination in which human nature and the eternal relations of ideas may be nobly expressed. So far our imaginative fertility is only a benefit: it surrounds us with the congenial and necessary radiation of art and religion. It manifests our moral vitality in the bosom of nature.

But sometimes imagination invades the sphere of understanding and seems to discredit its indispensable work. Common sense, we are allowed to infer, is a shallow affair: true insight changes all that. When so applied, poetic activity is not an unmixed good. It loosens our hold on fact and confuses our intelligence, so that we forget that intelligence has itself every prerogative of imagination, and has besides the sanction of practical validity. We are made to believe that since the understanding is something human and conditioned, something which might have been different, as the senses might have been different, and which we may yet, so to speak, get behind—therefore the understanding ought to be abandoned. We long for higher faculties, neglecting those we have; we yearn for intuition, closing our eyes upon experience. We become mystical.

Mysticism, as we have said, is the surrender of a category of thought because we divine its relativity. As every new category, however, must share this reproach, the mystic is obliged in the end to give them all up, the poetic and moral categories no less than the physical, so that the end of his purification is the atrophy of his whole nature, the emptying of his whole heart and mind to make room, as he thinks, for God. By attacking the authority of the understanding as the organon of knowledge, by substituting itself for it as the herald of a deeper truth, the imagination thus prepares its own destruction. For if the understanding is rejected because it cannot grasp the absolute, the imagination and all its works—art, dogma, worship—must presently be rejected for the same reason. Common sense and poetry must both go by the board, and conscience must follow after: for all these are human and relative. Mysticism will be satisfied only with the absolute, and as the absolute, by its very definition, is not representable by any specific faculty, it must be approached through the abandonment of all. The lights of life must be extinguished that the light of the absolute may shine, and the possession of everything in general must be secured by the surrender of everything in particular.

The same diffidence, however, the same constant renewal of sincerity which kept Emerson's flights of imagination near to experience, kept his mysticism also within bounds. A certain mystical tendency is pervasive with him, but there are only one or two subjects on which he dwells with enough constancy and energy of attention to make his mystical treatment of them pronounced. One of these is the question of the unity of all minds in the single soul of the universe, which is the same in all creatures; another is the question of evil and of its evaporation in the universal harmony of things. Both these ideas suggest themselves at certain turns in every man's experience, and might receive a rational formulation. But they are intricate subjects, obscured by many emotional prejudices, so that the labour, impartiality, and precision which would be needed to elucidate them are to be looked for in scholastic rather than in inspired thinkers, and in Emerson least of all. Before these problems he is alternately ingenuous and rhapsodical, and in both moods equally helpless. Individuals no doubt exist, he says to himself. But, ah! Napoleon is in every schoolboy. In every squatter in the western prairies we shall find an owner—

> Of Caesar's hand and Plato's brain,
> Of Lord Christ's heart, and Shakespeare's strain.

But how? we may ask. Potentially? Is it because any mind, were it given the right body and the right experience, were it made over, in a word, into another mind, would resemble that other mind to the point of identity? Or is it that our souls are already so largely similar that we are subject to many kindred promptings and share many ideals unrealizable in our particular circumstances? But then we should simply be saying that if what makes men different were removed, men would be indistinguishable, or that, in so far as they are now alike, they can understand one another by summoning up their respective experiences in the fancy. There would be no mysticism in that, but at the same time, alas, no eloquence, no paradox, and, if we must say the word, no nonsense.

On the question of evil, Emerson's position is of the same kind. There is evil, of course, he tells us. Experience is sad. There is a crack in everything that God has made. But, ah! the laws of the universe are sacred and beneficent. Without them nothing good could arise. All things, then, are in their right places and the universe is perfect above our querulous tears. Perfect? we may ask. But perfect from what point of view, in reference to what ideal? To its own? To that of a man who, renouncing himself and all naturally dear to him, ignoring the injustice, suffering, and impotence in the world, allows his will and his conscience to be hypnotized by the spectacle of a necessary evolution, and lulled into cruelty by the pomp and music of a tragic show? In that case the evil is not explained, it is forgotten; it is not cured, but condoned. We have surrendered the category of the better and the worse, the deepest foundation of life and reason; we have become mystics on the one subject on which, above all others, we ought to be men.

Two forces may be said to have carried Emerson in this mystical direction; one, that freedom of his imagination which we have already noted, and which kept him from the fear of self-contradiction; the other the habit of worship inherited from his clerical ancestors and enforced by his religious education. The spirit of conformity, the unction, the loyalty even unto death inspired by the religion of Jehovah, were dispositions acquired by too long a discipline and rooted in too many forms of speech, of thought, and of worship for a man like Emerson, who had felt their full force, ever to be able to lose them. The evolutions of his abstract opinions left that habit unchanged. Unless we keep this circumstance in mind, we shall not be able to understand the kind of elation and sacred joy, so characteristic of his eloquence, with which he propounds laws of nature and aspects of experience which, viewed in themselves, afford but an equivocal support to moral enthusiasm. An optimism so persistent and unclouded as his will seem at variance with the description he himself gives of human life, a description coloured by a poetic idealism, but hardly by an optimistic bias.

We must remember, therefore, that this optimism is a pious tradition, originally justified by the belief in a personal God and in a providential government of affairs for the ultimate and positive good of the elect, and that the habit of worship survived in Emerson as an instinct after those positive beliefs had faded into a recognition of 'spiritual laws'. We must remember that Calvinism had known how to combine an awe-struck devotion to the Supreme Being with no very roseate picture of the destinies of mankind, and [that] for more than two hundred years [it] had been breeding in the stock from which Emerson came a willingness to be, as the phrase is, 'damned for the glory of God'.

What wonder, then, that when, for the former inexorable dispensation of Providence, Emerson substituted his general spiritual and natural laws, he should not have felt the spirit of worship fail within him? On the contrary, his thought moved in the presence of moral harmonies which seemed to him truer, more beautiful, and more beneficent than those of the old theology. An independent philosopher would not have seen in those harmonies an object of worship or a sufficient basis for optimism. But he was not an independent philosopher, in spite of his belief in independence. He inherited the problems and the preoccupations of the theology from which he started, being in this respect like the German idealists, who, with all their pretence of absolute metaphysics, were in reality only giving elusive and abstract forms to traditional theology. Emerson, too, was not primarily a philosopher, but a Puritan mystic with a poetic fancy and a gift for observation and epigram, and he saw in the laws of nature, idealized by his imagination, only a more intelligible form of the divinity he had always recognized and adored. His was not a philosophy passing into a religion, but a religion expressing itself as a philosophy and veiled, as at its setting it descended the heavens, in various tints of poetry and science.

If we ask ourselves what was Emerson's relation to the scientific and religious movements of his time, and what place he may claim in the history of opinion, we must answer that he belonged very little to the past, very little to the present, and almost wholly to that abstract sphere into which mystical or philosophic aspiration has carried a few men in all ages. The religious tradition in which he was reared was that of Puritanism, but of a Puritanism which, retaining its moral intensity and metaphysical abstraction, had minimized its doctrinal expression and become Unitarian. Emerson was indeed the Psyche of Puritanism, 'the latest-born and fairest vision far' of all that 'faded hierarchy'. A Puritan whose religion was all poetry, a poet whose only pleasure was thought, he showed in his life and personality the meagreness, the constraint, the frigid and conscious consecration which belonged to his clerical ancestors, while his inmost impersonal spirit ranged abroad over the fields of history and nature, gathering what ideas it might, and singing its little snatches of inspired song.

The traditional element was thus rather an external and unessential contribution to Emerson's mind; he had the professional tinge, the decorum, the distinction of an old-fashioned divine; he had also the habit of writing sermons, and he had the national pride and hope of a religious people that felt itself providentially chosen to establish a free and godly commonwealth in a new world. For the rest, he separated himself from the ancient creed of the community with a sense rather of relief than of regret. A literal belief in Christian doctrines repelled him as unspiritual, as manifesting no understanding of the meaning which, as allegories, those doctrines might have to a philosophic and poetical spirit. Although as a clergyman he was at first in the habit of referring to the Bible and its lessons as to a supreme authority, he had no instinctive sympathy with the inspiration of either the Old or the New Testament; in Hafiz or Plutarch, in Plato or Shakespeare, he found more congenial stuff.

While he thus preferred to withdraw, without rancour and

without contempt, from the ancient fellowship of the Church, he assumed an attitude hardly less cool and deprecatory toward the enthusiasms of the new era. The national ideal of democracy and freedom had his entire sympathy; he allowed himself to be drawn into the movement against slavery; he took a curious and smiling interest in the discoveries of natural science and in the material progress of the age. But he could go no farther. His contemplative nature, his religious training, his dispersed reading, made him stand aside from the life of the world, even while he studied it with benevolent attention. His heart was fixed on eternal things, and he was in no sense a prophet for his age or country. He belonged by nature to that mystical company of devout souls that recognize no particular home and are dispersed throughout history, although not without intercommunication. He felt his affinity to the Hindus and the Persians, to the Platonists and the Stoics. Like them he remains 'a friend and aider of those who would live in the spirit'. If not a star of the first magnitude, he is certainly a fixed star in the firmament of philosophy. Alone as yet among Americans, he may be said to have won a place there, if not by the originality of his thought, at least by the originality and beauty of the expression he gave to thoughts that are old and imperishable.

HAMLET

The greater figures of fiction, as behoves things destined to last, have usually had an evolution and a history. Like the immortal gods, they have taken vague shape in the popular mind and in anonymous legends before receiving their most memorable form at the hand of some supreme poet. Perhaps no small part of Shakespeare's eminence is due to his having adopted plots and characters already current, already sanctioned by a certain proved vitality and power to charm. This conservatism is one of the many bonds by which art, when successful, clings to the life of the world and sucks in strength parasitically through its practical functions. Shakespeare's need of being a playwright before he was a poet, his concern to produce a popular play, won an audience for him in the beginning and still enables him to hold the boards. When creative genius neglects to ally itself in this way to some public interest it hardly gives birth to works of wide or perennial influence. Imagination needs a soil in history, tradition, or human institutions, else its random growths are not significant enough and, like trivial melodies, go immediately out of fashion. A great poem needs to be built up and remodelled on some given foundation with materials already at hand. Even in those fables which, like that of *Don Quixote*, may seem to be casual and original thoughts, we can usually detect a certain stage of experimentation with the idea, a certain novitiate and self-discovery on its part. The hero's character does not come out at first in its ultimate shape; but the shape it comes in, taking root and branching out in the mind into growths that had never been expected, becomes the germ of what is finally accepted and given out to the public. The true ideal of the most airy things is discoverable only by experimental methods, and there is nothing to which the approach is more blind and tentative than to the heart.

For this reason readers of *Hamlet* should not be surprised if this most psychological of tragedies should turn out to be a product of gradual accretions, or if its hero, most spontaneous and individual of characters, should be an afterthought and a discovery. Shakespeare followed a classic precept in this romantic drama: he allowed the plot to suggest the characters, and conceived their motives and psychological movement only as an underpinning and satiric deepening for their known actions. The play is an ordinary story with an extraordinary elaboration. Not only did Shakespeare, as his practice was, borrow an old plot, but he apparently worked over a first version of his own play and 'enlarged it to almost as much again as it was'. The personage of Hamlet, no less than the episodes of the piece, shows traces of this expansion. Some of Hamlet's actions and speeches seem anterior to his true character. They apparently remain over from the old melodrama and mark the points neglected by the poet and left untransmuted by his intuition.

These survivals of cruder methods, if survivals they be, give a touch of positive incoherence to Hamlet's character, otherwise sufficiently complex. His behaviour, for instance, before the praying King, and the reasons he gives there for sparing the villain, are apparently a remnant of bombast belonging to the old story, far more Christian and conventional in its motives than Shakespeare's is. So the grotesque bout with Laertes in Ophelia's grave is perhaps a bit of old rodomontade left unexpunged. The disconcerting mixture of comic and ignoble elements in several crucial passages may be due to the same circumstance, as, for example, when Hamlet says of the Ghost, 'Ah, ha, boy...Art there, truepenny?... You hear this fellow in the cellarage...Old mole, canst work in the earth so fast?' or when he crowns the heart-rending closet scene with a bad pun: 'Come, sir, to draw toward an end with you', as he draws out Polonius's body. These passages may contain remnants of that conventional farce which, as some think, was inherited by Elizabethan drama from the Middle Ages, when piety and obscenity, quaint simplicity and rant, could be jumbled together without offence. Yet this barbaric medley, surviving by chance or by inertia, is the occasion for the creation of a spirit that shall justify it and shall express therein its own profound discord. The historical accidents that make these patches in the play are embodied and personified in a mind that can cover them all by its own complexity and dislocation. Each of these blots thus becomes a beauty, each of these accidents a piece of profound characterization. In Hamlet's personality incoherent sentiments, due, in a genetic sense, to the imperfect recasting of a grotesque old story, are made attributable ideally to his habit of acting out a mood irresponsibly and of giving a mock expression to every successive intuition. Thus his false rhetoric before the praying King becomes characteristic, and may be taken to betray an inveterate vacillation which seizes on verbal excuses and plays with unreal sentiments in order to put off the moment of action. So at Ophelia's grave he may be said to exhibit his ingrained histrionic habit, his incapacity to control the inner dialogue or dream in his own mind, which continually carries him into fits of speech and action, sometimes incongruous with one another but always ingenious and fetched from the depths of a distracted and tender heart. So, too, his sardonic humour and nonsensical verbiage at the most tragic junctures may justify themselves ideally and seem to be deeply inspired. These wild starts suggest a mind inwardly rent asunder, a delicate genius disordered, such as we now learn that Hamlet's was, a mind that with infinite sensibility possessed no mastery over itself nor over things. Thus the least digested elements in the fable come, by a happy turn, to constitute its profoundest suggestion.

The Middle Ages and the Renaissance into which they finally burst had at once a decrepit and a juvenile character. They looked back with rather a doting and indiscriminate respect on the confused past, while at the same time they bubbled over with all manner of native mischief and fancy. In Gothic drama, as in Gothic architecture, we find bits of savage or classic antiquity, incongruities, afterthoughts and accretions, old materials, precious or rude, built again into a new edifice. Yet these accepted and sanctified accidents made the charm and bewitching poetry of the work, for they have crystallized into a new style and a new structure; a historical junk-shop has become the temple of a new spirit. Its miscellaneous treasures, so heaped together, have acquired their own expression and pathos, and a certain unifying mystery has settled over the whole. The beauty and ideal import of a human work can thus come to resemble that of a landscape or of a living body; it can be felt instinctively by a certain assimilation as if to a mystical influence, without distinct discrimination of the elements involved.

Evidently the same thing happened to Shakespeare with his histrionic Prince that happened to Cervantes with his mad Knight: he fell in love with his hero. He caught in that figure, at first only grotesque and melodramatic, the suggestion of something noble, spiritual, and pathetic, and he devoted all his imaginative powers to developing that suggestion. He enriched the lines with all that reflection could furnish that was most pungent and poetical; he added the philosophic play of mind, gave free rein to soliloquy, insisted everywhere on what might seem keen and significant. At the same time he found pleasure in elaborating the story. He constructed, for instance, a young Hamlet, to stand behind the tragic hero, a witty, tender, and accomplished prince, to be overtaken by that cursed spite which he should prove incapable of turning aside. Here we have a piece of deliberate art. By numerous and well-chosen phrases scattered throughout the play, Shakespeare takes pains to evoke the image of a consummate and admirable nature, so that the charm and pathos of the tragedy which ruins it may be enhanced. In the young Hamlet we are asked to imagine the

> unmatched form and feature of blown youth.
>
> The courtier's, scholar's, soldier's, eye, tongue, sword;
> The expectancy and rose of the fair state,
> The glass of fashion, and the mould of form,
> The observed of all observers...!

We learn of his proficiency in fencing, his fondness for the stage, and his competence as a critic of it; he is attached enough to the university to prefer it to the court. He can adopt for a moment the affectations of clever people, and be enough of a prig 'to hold it baseness to write fair'; but he writes fair, nevertheless. His 'noble and most sovereign reason' pierces most things in the world, and among them philosophy (or, as we should say, science), of which he understands enough to see its limits. He knows how to humour and play with a fop no less than how to expose and transfix a flatterer, and he can be as contemptuous of foolish wordiness in a counsellor as he can be courteous to sincerity in a humble artist. For comradeship he has a natural sense and is willing to drink deep with an old acquaintance; but for true intimacy he chooses the poor scholar and devoted friend, unworldly because capable of understanding the world, and shows in this choice his princely freedom and elevation of mind. And lest the last crown and flower of generous youth should be wanting, Hamlet is, of course, in love. Yet he is not without a soberer and more settled affection than that expressed in his fancy for the fair Ophelia; his deepest sentiment is a great love and admiration for the King, his father. On this natural piety in the young Hamlet, his new tragic life is to be grafted. By striking rudely in this quarter fate strikes not merely at his filial affection, but at his intellectual peace and at his confidence in justice. The wound is mortal and saps his moral being.

The hero, so conceived, is presented to us by the instrumentality of that same plot which had originally suggested his character. The beloved father dies suddenly, and to the son's natural grief at this loss is added the scandal of his mother's hasty second marriage. A heavy mood, filled with vague sinister suspicions, falls upon Hamlet. Presently, the supernatural comes upon the scene. Hamlet sees his father's ghost. He receives audible and explicit tidings of his mother's adultery and the murder of his father.

We might say that to see—or if the spiritualistic reader prefers, to call up—a ghost is a first sign of Hamlet's moral dissolution. It would be easy to rationalize this part of the story, and explain the Ghost as a sort of symbol or allegory. Hamlet's character and situation were well conceived to base such a hallucination upon. His prophetic soul might easily have cheated him with such a counterfeit presentment of its own suspicions. But Shakespeare was evidently content to take the Ghost literally, and expected his audience naturally to do the same. Although not visible to the Queen on its final appearance, the Ghost is seen by Horatio and others on several occasions. The report it gives of its torments corresponds to the popular and orthodox conception of Purgatory, so that a Christian public might accept this Ghost as a possible wanderer from the other world. Had Shakespeare cared much about ghosts, or wished to give, as in *Macbeth*, a realistic picture of the shabby supernatural, Hamlet's Ghost might well have been a much less theological and conventional being. It might well have resembled somewhat more the shade of Achilles in the *Odyssey*, which is a beautiful idealization of the spirits actually evoked by necromancy in all ages, which are echoes of former existences in this world, witless, fretful, sad, and unseizable. But such shades were little cultivated in Shakespeare's day. The Church had no need for them, and wished to preserve its ideal conception of the other world from all empirical and pathological influences. Shakespeare's Ghost is accordingly wholly, though inconsistently, conventional. It is a Christian soul in Purgatory, which ought, in theological strictness, to be a holy and redeemed soul, a phase of penitential and spiritual experience; yet this soul fears to scent the morning air, trembles at the cock-crow, and instigates the revenging of crime by crime. That is, it is no Christian soul, but a heathen and pathological spectre. It speaks, as Hamlet justly feels, by the ambiguous authority of hell and heaven at once. This hybrid personage, however, like the other anomalies in the play, comes to have its expressive value. It unites in a single image various threads of superstition actually tangled in the public mind. Ostensibly an emissary from the other world, such as would be admissible by a slightly heterodox Christian fancy, the Ghost is at the same time an echo of popular fable and demonology, and withal a moral and dramatic symbol, a definite *point d'appui* for the hero's morbid impulses. If Hamlet had not been likely to imagine a Ghost, Shakespeare would hardly have created one. There is affinity and emotional congruity in the various mysteries gathered together in this scene—the night, the sea, the hidden crime, the hero's metaphysical melancholy, and the budding purpose in him to enact madness. Into this artful setting the Ghost falls naturally enough, and, under the scenic spell of its presence, we do not stop to ask which elements in that apparition are food for Hamlet's fancy, and which are rather its products and expression.

The first effect of the Ghost's revelation is characteristic of Hamlet's nature. He and the Ghost both insist on secrecy, as if too much had already been done. Hamlet induces his fellow-witnesses to swear to keep silence about the marvel they have seen; he checks a natural impulse to repeat the Ghost's story; and the Ghost itself, on its way to its subterranean torture-chamber, echoes Hamlet's demand—'Swear, Swear'—in hollow and melodramatic accents. Why this fear to divulge the truth? Why this unnecessary precaution and delay? Why this fantastic notion, at once imposing itself on the hero's mind, that there would be occasion for him to feign madness and put an antic disposition on? The simple truth is, that the play pre-exists and imposes itself here on the poet, who is reduced to paving the way as best he can for the foregone complications. Had Hamlet forthwith communicated his mission to his friends and rushed with them to the banquet hall where the King was at that moment carousing, had he instantly dispatched the usurper and proclaimed himself king in his stead, there would have been no occasion for four more acts and for so much heart-searching soliloquy. The given plot is the starting-point, and its irrationality at this juncture, by which the comic effects of a feigned madness were secured for the playwright, must be accepted as a fundamental datum on which incidents and characters are alike built up.

Those who have maintained that Hamlet is really mad have

had this partial justification for their paradox, that Hamlet is irrational. He acts without reflection, as he reflects without acting. At the basis of all his ingenuity and reasoning, of his nimble wit and varied fooling, lies this act of inexplicable folly, that he conceals his discovery, postpones his vengeance before questioning its propriety, and descends with no motive to a grotesque and pitiful piece of dissimulation. This unreason is not madness, because his intellect remains clear, his discourse sound and comprehensive; but it is a sort of passionate weakness and indirection in his will, which mocks its own ends, strikes fantastic attitudes, and invents elaborate schemes of action useless for his declared purposes. The psychology of Hamlet is like that which some German metaphysicians have attributed to their Spirit of the World, which is the prey to its own perversity and to what is called romantic irony, so that it eternally pursues the good in a way especially designed never to attain it. In Hamlet, as in them, beneath this histrionic duplicity and earnestness about the unreal, there is a very genuine pathos. Such brilliant futility is really helpless and sick at heart. The clouded will which plays with all these artifices of thought would fain break its way to light and self-knowledge through this magic circle of sophistication. It is the tragedy of a soul buzzing in the glass prison of a world which it can neither escape nor understand, in which it flutters about without direction, without clear hope, and yet with many a keen pang, many a dire imaginary problem, and much exquisite music.

This morbid indirection of Hamlet's, in the given situation, yields the rest of the play. Its theme is a hidden crime met by a fantastic and incapable virtue. The hero's reaction takes various forms: his soliloquies and reflections, his moody and artful treatment of other persons, his plans and spurts of action. In soliloquy Hamlet is much the same from the beginning to the end of the piece. His philosophy learns little from events and consequently makes little progress. When he has still nothing more portentous to disturb him than his father's death and his mother's marriage, he already wishes that his too, too solid flesh should melt, and that the Everlasting had not laid His canon against self-slaughter. The uses of this world seem to him even then wholly weary, flat, stale, and unprofitable. This remains his habitual sentiment whenever he looks within, but he can meantime be won over at any moment to shrewd and satirical observation of things external. If the funeral baked meats coldly furnish forth the marriage tables, it is, he tells us, but thrift; nor is his habit of mind at all changed when, at the point of highest tension in his adventures, he stops to consider how a king may go a progress through the guts of a beggar, nor when, in a lull that precedes the last spasm of his destiny, he versifies the same theme:

> Imperious Caesar, dead and turn'd to clay,
> Might stop a hole to keep the wind away;
> Oh, that the earth, which kept the world in awe,
> Should patch a wall to expel the winter's flaw!

This satirical humour, touching melancholy with the sting of absurdity, crops up everywhere. 'I am too much in the sun', he says, with a bitter and jocular obscurity. Polonius is 'at supper: not where he eats but where he is eaten; a certain convocation of politic worms are e'en at him.'

Reason in young men is an accomplishment rather than a vital function, and may be allowed to play pranks with respectable ideas and to seem capricious and even mad; but while enjoying this licence and turning, as it were, somersaults in the air, reason remains by nature the organ of truth, and seizes every opportunity which its game affords to prick some sanctified bubble and aim some home-thrust at the foibles of the world. This sort of youthful roguery has a fine sincerity about it; under the sparkle of paradox it shows a loyal heart and a tongue not yet suborned to the praising of familiar or necessary evils. Nevertheless such idealism is lame because it cannot conceive a better alternative to the things it criticizes. It stops at bickerings and lamentations which, although we cannot deny the ample warrant they have in experience, leave us disconcerted and in an unstable equilibrium, ready to revert, when imagination falters, to all our old platitudes and conventional judgments. Therefore, Hamlet's sad reflections have in the end the merit of humour rather than of wisdom. Their aptness is inconsequential. His sense for what is good and ideal is strong enough to raise him above worldliness and a gross optimism, but it is far too negative and poor to inspire creation in the imaginative sphere or better action in the world.

Hamlet's attitude towards the minor characters in the play is a source of perennial joy to spectators and readers. His words and manner to Polonius, Horatio, Rosencrantz, and Guildenstern, the players, the grave-diggers, the court messenger, are alike keen, kindly, witty, and noble. Since he is playing at madness he can allow his humour to be broader, his scorn franker, his fancy more wayward than they could well have been otherwise; yet in all mock disguises appears the same exquisite courtesy, even in that clever and cruel parrying of the King's treachery during the expedition to England. It is when we come to Hamlet's attitude towards the other chief figures—the Ghost, Ophelia, the Queen—that we observe a certain indistinctness and dispersion of mind, so that both the hero's character and the poet's intentions are, to say the least, less obvious. In the Ghost's presence Hamlet is overcome with feeling, in its absence with doubts. What he ostensibly wishes to have confirmed is the veracity of that witness, and the play-scene is arranged to obtain corroboration of this. Yet when that ostensible doubt is solved and the facts are beyond question, he is no more ready for action than before. He still feels a reluctance to kill the King, founded apparently no longer on doubts about his crime but on scruples or distaste in avenging it. The suspicious element in the Ghost was really less the testimony it gave than the behaviour it inspired, the mission of active vengeance which it seemed to lay on the kindly and meditative Prince. Such conduct was indeed conformable to tradition and barbarous practice, but it was opposed to the secret promptings of the hero's own mind. In his individual and free reflection he could find more grounds for suicide than for murder. When the Ghost appears there is room in Hamlet's heart only for filial affection, and horror at seeing his father in such a shape; but as the sensuous impression fades it passes into a doubtful and sinister obsession. Hamlet feels that he is leaving a duty unperformed and at the same time that he is being driven on by the devil. If his instinctive hesitation could have expressed itself theoretically he might perhaps have asked whether the treacherous murder of one innocent man could well be righted by more treachery and more murder, involving disaster to many innocent persons. Of course, neither a prosaic rationalism of this sort, nor foresight of what in that particular case was likely to ensue, could properly be expected in Hamlet; yet possibly some premonition of both existed in the poet's mind and gave Hamlet's hesitation that symbolic and moral import which we somehow feel it to possess. Conventional maxims, stock passions, and theological sanctions play very different roles in different people's lives. In the vulgar they may serve to cloak the absence of genuine principles and of a fixed purpose of any kind. In noble minds they may cheapen the genuine intuitions which they come to clothe, and cause these minds to fall short of that clearness and generosity which they would have shown if they had found free and untrammelled expression. So Hamlet's whole entanglement with the Ghost, and with the crude morality of vengeance which the plot imposes upon him, fails to bring his own soul to a right utterance, and this stifling of his better potential mind is no small part of his tragedy. Or is it only a fond critic's illusion that makes us read that better idea into what is a purely unconscious barbarism and a vacillation useful for theatrical purposes?

Towards his mother Hamlet maintains throughout the greater part of the play a wounded reserve appropriate to the situation. He speaks of her with sarcasm, but addresses her with curt respect. Only in the closet scene does he unbosom himself with a somewhat emphatic eloquence which shows touches of dignity and pathos; yet this scene, central as it is in the plot, hardly rises in power above the level of its neighbours. In comparison, for instance, the scenes with Ophelia are full of wonder and charm. There the poet's imagination flowers out, and Hamlet appears in all his originality and wild inspiration. Yet Ophelia and Hamlet's relation to her are incidental to the drama, while the Queen and her fate are essential to it. We may observe in general that Shakespeare's genius shines in the texture of his poems rather than in their structure, in imagery and happy strokes rather than in integrating ideas. His poetry plays about life like ivy about a house, and is more akin to landscape than to architecture. He feels no vocation to call the stones themselves to their ideal places and enchant the very substance and skeleton of the world. How blind to him, and to Hamlet, are all ultimate issues, and the sum total of things how unseizable! The heathen chaos enveloping everything is all the more sensible on account of the lovely natures which it engulfs. Ophelia, for instance, that slight and too flexible treble in the general dirge, turns it to favour and to prettiness. If she had been a casual ornamental figure, like Ariel, introduced only for its own sake, she would not have illustrated so well the main drift of the drama nor been herself so touching an apparition. She is closely bound up with the plot, and what is more important, with the emotion which it arouses; yet she is hardly necessary, and Hamlet's affection for her, though a real and congruent part of his experience, forms only an incidental and subordinate part of it. He loved Ophelia before the catastrophe came that unhinged his life; afterwards he remembers her, when he comes across her, as one might remember some tender episode of childhood. His feeling is sentiment rather than passion. He grows sentimental under the influence of her sensuous charm and of her innocence. 'Here's metal more attractive', he says in one place; and in another,

> Nymph, in thy orisons
> Be all my sins remember'd.

His love for her plays no part in his essential resolutions. She does not console him at all, even in his initial bereavement and first suspicions. The speeches in his first scene are not those of a man in love. His pleasure in Ophelia's presence, his interest in his own love, have been undone by enterprises of greater pith and moment. When face to face with her grief, he is not impelled to explain and appeal to her constancy and trust, or invite her to share his calamity. His impulse is merely to despair and throw the blame on the world at large. 'Get thee to a nunnery; why wouldst thou be a breeder of sinners?' There is doubtless a shade of jealousy in this cry, with a touch of tender solicitude to save and screen her from his own troubles. Yet the dominating sentiment is one of helpless regret. He is sorry, very sorry; but it does not occur to him that he can do anything or can find in Ophelia any resource or inspiration. His love, though sincere, seems to him now one of the frail treasures of his youth, blasted by destiny. It had never taken deep enough root in his soul to endure the blasts of fortune, and be, like his love for his father, one of the moving forces in his destiny itself.

Hamlet's positive and deliberate action is limited to two stratagems, one with the players, to catch the King's conscience, and one by which he makes Rosencrantz and Guildenstern suffer the fate prepared for himself in England. In both cases Hamlet betrays a sort of exuberance and wild delight. He feels the luxury of hitting home, the absolute joy of playing the game, without particular reference to the end in view. The speech in which he recounts his escape from shipboard and his counterfeiting the King's letter, positively bubbles over with high spirits and the sense of mastery. In the play scene, too, he is all vivacity and eager comments. He cannot suppress his tense excitement, and comes near defeating his plan by disclosing it prematurely. When the bubble has burst and his point is gained, he is incoherent in his exultation, in his relief at having discovered the worst, and his joy at having verified his expectations. If he acts seldom and with difficulty, it is not because he does not hugely enjoy action. Yet his delight is in the shimmer and movement of action rather than in its use; so that the weakness of his character appears just as much in his bursts of activity as in his long hesitations. He kills Polonius by accident, hoping that in a blind thrust through the arras he might turn out at last to have dispatched the King; and when, himself mortally wounded, he finally executes that long-meditated sentence, he can do so only by yielding to a sudden hysterical impulse. So consistently does unreason pursue him: an inexplicable crime is followed by a miraculous vision; that portent he meets by a senseless and too congenial pretence of madness; a successful stratagem confirms the King's guilt, but does not lead to exposure or punishment, rather to a passive reconciliation with him on Hamlet's part. Innocent persons meantime perish, and the end is a general but casual slaughter, amid treachery, misunderstandings, and ghastly confusions.

This picture of universal madness is relieved by the very finest and purest glints of wit, intelligence, and feeling. It is crammed with exquisite lines, and vivified by most interesting and moving characters in great variety, all drawn with masterly breadth, depth, and precision. Hamlet, in particular, as our analysis testifies, is more than a vivid dramatic figure, more than an unparalleled poetic vision. He lays bare the heart of a whole race, or, perhaps we should rather say, expresses a conflict to which every soul is more or less liable. There is a kind of initial earnestness in all life which in some people remains predominant; a certain soulfulness and idealism which the Germans attribute especially to themselves, but which they would probably recognize also in the deeper intuitions of English poetry. It is a mood proper to youth; and youth in a race (since there is no question of a shorter descent from Adam or his Darwinian rival) can only mean that at a given juncture sentiment, fancy, and dialectic have outrun external experience. Youth is far from implying less complexity than age or a meaner endowment, for youth, at least potentially, often has the advantage in these respects. Youth means only less complete adjustment of capacity to opportunity, of intelligence to practice and art. In a fertile mind such want of adjustment intensifies self-consciousness and, because so much that the mind is pregnant with remains unexpressed and untested, it produces a sense of vague profundity which is often an illusion. An unexpressed mind may be deep, but it is none the deeper for not exercising itself successfully on real things; and though it need not lack poetry or philosophy for being comparatively without experience, yet its poetry will tend to be irrelevant and fantastic, and its philosophy *a priori*. The former will show more airy richness than rational beauty, and the latter more ingenuity than wisdom. These characteristics, whether or not essential to the spirit of 'the North', are unmistakably present in Hamlet's person. They render his moral being 'dark, true, and tender'. He is strong in his integrity and purity of purpose, but lost in floating emotion, perplexed by want of concentration and of self-knowledge. Here is immense endowment and strange incompetence, constant perspicacity and general confusion, entire virtue in the intention, and complete disaster in the result. An apt pupil of philosophy, of politics, of art, of love, Hamlet is master in nothing. The solution eludes him for every riddle and even for every plain question; and his vast consciousness is ignorant of its own function.

Compare with such a mind what may be called by contrast the mind of the East or South, the mind of fatigued and long-indoctrinated races, disillusioned, distinct, malicious, for the most part unblushingly subservient to interest, passion, or superstition (for this temperament is too worn and sceptical to think rebellion worth while), yet in its reflective phase detached and contemplative, able occasionally to despise all entanglements, to dominate the will, and to look truth in the eye without blinking.

If Shakespeare had intended to make his drama allegorical of this contrast, he could not have hit upon a better theme and title: Hamlet the Dane! How that name evokes the image of virgin and barbarous heroes standing on the horizon of the world! Their experience upon descending among the nations must have been quite like Hamlet's on finding himself suddenly in a perverse world. They, too, must have been burdened with longing, scornful of corruption, touched yet puzzled by Christianity, attracted yet wounded by civilization. Although Shakespeare was troubled, of course, by no such thought of historic symbolism, and made Hamlet in all externals a prince of Queen Elizabeth's time, yet the assimilation would not on that account cease to be possible. It was at bottom no anachronism to give to a barbaric jewel an Elizabethan setting. The old Norseman's soul was uncontaminated by migration into a richer age and a milder air; in fact, the poet's nation had not, in spirit, outgrown or disowned its ancestry.

The ghost scenes in *Hamlet*—to return to them for a moment—are excellent examples of profound, ill-digested emotions breaking out fiercely against circumstances which are not well in hand, and which consequently are not met intelligently or successfully by the inspiration in question. This ghost is not like the deities that often appear in Greek tragedy, a *deus ex machina* coming to solve, in the light of serene thought and eternal interests, the tangled problems of the single life. On the contrary, this ghost is a party to the conflict, an instigator of sinister thoughts, a thing hatched in a nest of sorrows. Its scope is so exclusively personal that it may well seem the very coinage of the brain; yet it is ostensibly miraculous, noble, pathetic, veracious. It is at once a spectre and a suspicion, a physical marvel and an inward and authoritative voice. Our reason itself flits with this ghost through a night half mockery and half horror. We feel that not Hamlet the Dane but the human soul in its inmost depths is moonstruck and haunted. Poetry, in these wonderful scenes, does not entrance by presenting natural and heavenly harmonies so convincingly that the heart, too, begins to beat in unison with them; that might be the highest achievement of some classic poet. Here, when the deepest note is sounded, we can only cry, 'O Hamlet! thou hast cleft my heart in twain.' We wait to see the spectacle of things dissolved and exorcized. The fretted pipe has defied all earthly powers to play upon it, this too, too solid flesh has melted away, and the rest, as Hamlet says, is silence.

All this, however, is only half, and the less intentional half, of what comes before us in this unfathomable poem. The impression of utter gloom which the plot leaves when taken, so to speak, realistically, as if it were a picture of actual existences, is not the impression which it leaves when we take it as lyric poetry, as music, as an abstract representation of sundry moods and loyalties traversing a noble mind. The world which is here set before us may be grotesque and distracted; but we are not asked to be interested in that world. Had Hamlet himself been interested in it, he would have acted more rationally. It was not intelligence or courage that he lacked; it was practical conviction or sense for reality. Had he possessed this he would have turned his wits and sympathies towards improving the state of Denmark, as he turns them towards improving the players' art. In truth he cared nothing for the world; man pleased him not, no, nor woman, neither; and we may well abandon to its natural confusion a dream in which we do not believe. Had Hamlet tried to justify his temperament by expressing it in a philosophy, he would have been an idealist. He would have said that events were only occasions for exercising the spirit; they were nothing but imagined situations meant to elicit a certain play of mind. If a man's comments had been keen, if his heart had been tender, if his will had been upright and pure, the rest were nothing. The world might feign to be mad and put on an antic disposition; it was sane enough if it fulfilled its purpose and gave a man an opportunity to test his own mettle. Those idiocies and horrors which he lived among would have been in truth the flights of angels that bore him to his rest. At any rate, express it how we will, the sympathetic reader will instinctively feel that he should pass over lightly the experience which the play depicts and carry away from it only the moral feeling, the spiritual sentiment, which it calls forth in the characters. As the poet himself thought a violent and somewhat absurd fable not unworthy to support his richest verse and subtlest characterizations, so we must take the fabric of destiny, in this tragedy and in that, too, which we enact in the world, as it happens to be, and think the moral lights that flicker through it bright enough to redeem it.

We must remember that the modern mind, like the modern world, is compacted out of ruins, and that the fresh northern spirit, inducted into that Byzantine labyrinth which we call civilization, feels a marked discord between its genius and its culture. The latter is alien and imperfectly grafted on the living stem from which it must draw its sap. Hence the most radical and excruciating experience of the romantic mind comes from just such hereditary incoherence, just such perplexity and half-feigned madness, just such obsession by artifices, as Hamlet presents to us in a tragic miniature. The deep interest of this figure lies accordingly in its affinity to the situation in which every romantic spirit must in a measure find itself. There is no richer or more exquisite monument to the failure of emotional goodwill, and of intelligence inclined to embroider rather than to build. So absolute a feat of imagination cannot be ranked in comparison with other works, nor estimated by any standard of which it does not itself furnish the suggestion and type. It is rather to be studied and absorbed, to be made a part of our habitual landscape and mental furniture, lest we should miss much of what is deepest and rarest in human feeling. If we care to pass, however, from admiration of the masterpiece to reflection on the experience which it expresses, we see that here is no necessary human tragedy, no universal destiny or divine law. It is a picture of incidental unfitness, of a genius wasted for being plucked quite unripe from the sunny places of the world. In Hamlet our incoherent souls see their own image; in him romantic potentiality and romantic failure wears each its own feature. In him we see the gifts most congenial and appealing to us reduced to a pathetic impotence because of the disarray in which we are content to leave them.

THREE PHILOSOPHICAL POETS

INTRODUCTION

The sole advantage in possessing great works of literature lies in what they can help us to become. In themselves, as feats performed by their authors, they would have forfeited none of their truth or greatness if they had perished before our day. We can neither take away nor add to their past value or inherent dignity. It is only they, in so far as they are appropriate food and not poison for us, that can add to the present value and dignity of our minds. Foreign classics have to be retranslated and reinterpreted for each generation, to render their old naturalness in a natural way, and keep their perennial humanity living and capable of assimilation. Even native classics have to be reapprehended by every reader. It is this continual digestion of the substance supplied by the past that alone renders the insights of the past still potent in the present and for the future. Living criticism, genuine appreciation, is the interest we draw from year to year on the unrecoverable capital of human genius.

Regarded from this point of view, as substances to be digested, the poetic remains of Lucretius, Dante, and Goethe (though it is his *Faust* only that I shall speak of) afford rather a varied feast. In their doctrine and genius they may seem to be too much opposed to be at all convergent or combinable in their wisdom. Some, who know and care for one, perhaps, of these poets, may be disposed to doubt whether they have anything vital to learn from the other two. Yet...I venture to maintain that in what makes them great they are compatible; that without any vagueness or doubleness in one's criterion of taste one may admire enthusiastically the poetry of each in turn; and that one may accept the essential philosophy, the positive intuition, of each, without lack of definition or system in one's own thinking.

Indeed, the diversity of these three poets passes, if I may use the Hegelian dialect, into a unity of a higher kind. Each is typical of an age. Taken together they sum up all European philosophy. Lucretius adopts the most radical and the most correct of those cosmological systems which the genius of early Greece had devised. He sees the world to be one great edifice, one great machine, all its parts reacting upon one another, and growing out of one another in obedience to a general pervasive process or life. His poem describes the nature, that is, the birth and composition, of all things. It shows how they are compounded out of elements, and how these elements, which he thinks are atoms in perpetual motion, are being constantly redistributed, so that old things perish and new things arise. Into this view of the world he fits a view of human life as it ought to be led under such conditions. His materialism is completed by an aspiration towards freedom and quietness of spirit. Allowed to look once upon the wonderful spectacle, which is to repeat itself in the world for ever, we should look and admire, for tomorrow we die; we should eat, drink, and be merry, but moderately and with much art, lest we die miserably, and die today.

This is one complete system of philosophy—materialism in natural science, humanism in ethics. Such was the gist of all Greek philosophy before Socrates, of that philosophy which was truly Hellenic and corresponded with the movement which produced Greek manners, Greek government, and Greek art—a movement towards simplicity, autonomy, and reasonableness in everything, from dress to religion. Such is the gist also of what may be called the philosophy of the Renaissance, the reassertion of science and liberty in the modern world, by Bacon, by Spinoza, by the whole contemporary school that looks to science for its view of the facts, and to the happiness of men on earth for its ideal. This system is called naturalism; and of this Lucretius is the unrivalled poet.

Skip a thousand years and more, and a contrasting spectacle is before us. All minds, all institutions, are dominated by a religion that represents the soul as a pilgrim upon earth; the world is fallen and subject to the devil; pain and poverty are considered normal, happiness impossible here and to be hoped for only in a future life, provided the snares and pleasures of the present life have not entrapped us. Meantime a sort of Jacob's ladder stretches from the stone on which the wayfarer lays his head into the heaven he hopes for; and the angels he sees ascending and descending upon it are beautiful stories, wonderful theories, and comforting rites. Through these he partakes, even on earth, of what will be his heavenly existence. He partly understands his destiny; his own history and that of the world are transfigured before him and, without ceasing to be sad, become beautiful. The raptures of a perfect conformity with the will of God, and of union with Him, overtake him in his prayers. This is supernaturalism, a system represented in Christendom chiefly by the Catholic Church, but adopted also by the later pagans, and widespread in Asia from remote antiquity down to the present time. Little as the momentary temper of Europe and America may now incline to such a view, it is always possible for the individual, or for the race, to return to it. Its sources are in the solitude of the spirit and in the disparity, or the opposition, between what the spirit feels it is fitted to do and what, in this world, it is condemned to waste itself upon. The unmatched poet of this supernaturalism is Dante.

Skip again some five hundred years, and there is another change of scene. The Teutonic races that had previously conquered Europe have begun to dominate and understand themselves. They have become Protestants, or protesters against the Roman world. An infinite fountain of life seems to be unlocked within their bosom. They turn successively to the Bible, to learning, to patriotism, to industry, for new objects to love and fresh worlds to conquer; but they have too much vitality, or too little maturity, to rest in any of these things. A demon drives them on; and this demon, divine and immortal in its apparent waywardness, is their inmost self. It is their insatiable will, their radical courage. Nay, though this be a hard saying to the uninitiated, their will is the creator of all those objects by which it is sometimes amused, and sometimes baffled, but never tamed. Their will summons all opportunities and dangers out of nothing to feed its appetite for action; and in that ideal function lies their sole reality. Once attained, things are transcended. Like the episodes of a spent dream, they are to be smiled at and forgotten; the spirit that feigned and discarded them remains always strong and undefiled; it aches for new conquests over new fictions. This is romanticism. It is an attitude often found in English poetry, and characteristic of German philosophy. It was adopted by Emerson and ought to be sympathetic to Americans; for it expresses the self-trust of world-building youth, and mystical faith in will and action. The greatest monument to this romanticism is Goethe's *Faust*.

Can it be an accident that the most adequate and probably the most lasting exposition of these three schools of philosophy should have been made by poets? Are poets, at heart, in search of a philosophy? Or is philosophy, in the end, nothing but poetry? Let us consider the situation.

If we think of philosophy as an investigation into truth, or as reasoning upon truths supposed to be discovered, there is nothing in philosophy akin to poetry. There is nothing poetic about the works of Epicurus, or St Thomas Aquinas, or Kant; they are leafless forests. . . The reasonings and investigations of philosophy are arduous, and if poetry is to be linked with them, it can be artificially only, and with a bad grace. But the vision of philosophy is sublime. The order it reveals in the world is something beautiful, tragic, sympathetic to the mind, and just what every poet, on a small or on a large scale, is always trying to catch.

In philosophy itself investigation and reasoning are only preparatory and servile parts, means to an end. They terminate in insight, or what in the noblest sense of the word may be called *theory*, θεωρία—a steady contemplation of all things in their order and worth. Such contemplation is imaginative. No one can reach it who has not enlarged his mind and tamed his heart. A philosopher who attains it is, for the moment, a poet; and a poet who turns his practised and passionate imagination on the order of all things, or on anything in the light of the whole, is for that moment a philosopher.

Nevertheless, even if we grant that the philosopher, in his best moments, is a poet, we may suspect that the poet has his worst moments when he tries to be a philosopher, or rather, when he succeeds in being one. Philosophy is something reasoned and heavy; poetry something winged, flashing, inspired. Take almost any longish poem, and the parts of it are better than the whole. A poet is able to put together a few words, a cadence or two, a single interesting image. He renders in that way some moment of comparatively high tension, of comparatively keen sentiment. But at the next moment the tension is relaxed, the sentiment has faded, and what succeeds is usually incongruous with what went before, or at least inferior. The thought drifts away from what it had started to be. It is lost in the sands of versification. As man is now constituted, to be brief is almost a condition of being inspired.

Shall we say, then,—and I now broach an idea by which I set some store—that poetry is essentially short-winded, that what is poetic is necessarily intermittent in the writings of poets, that only the fleeting moment, the mood, the episode, can be rapturously felt, or rapturously rendered, while life as a whole, history, character, and destiny are objects unfit for imagination to dwell on, and repellent to poetic art? I cannot think so. If it be a fact, as it often is, that we find little things pleasing and great things arid and formless, and if we are better poets in a line than in an epic, that is simply due to lack of faculty on our part, lack of imagination and memory, and above all to lack of discipline.

This might be shown, I think, by psychological analysis, if we cared to rely on something so abstract and so debatable. For in what does the short-winded poet himself excel the common unimaginative person who talks or who stares? Is it that he thinks even less? Rather, I suppose, in that he feels more; in that his moment of intuition, though fleeting, has a vision, a scope, a symbolic something about it that renders it deep and expressive. Intensity, even momentary intensity, if it can be expressed at all, comports fullness and suggestion compressed into that intense moment. Yes, everything that comes to us at all must come to us at some time or other. It is always the fleeting moment in which we live. To this fleeting moment the philosopher, as well as the poet, is actually confined. Each must enrich it with his endless vistas, vistas necessarily focused, if they are to be disclosed at all, in the eye of the observer, here and now. What makes the difference between a moment of poetic insight and a vulgar moment is that the passions of the poetic moment have more perspective. Even the short-winded poet selects his words so that they have a magic momentum in them which carries us, we know not how, to mountain-tops of intuition. Is not the poetic quality of phrases and images due to their concentrating and liberating the confused promptings left in us by a long experience? When we feel the poetic thrill, is it not that we find sweep in the concise and depth in the clear, as we might find all the lights of the sea in the water of a jewel? And what is a philosophic thought but such an epitome?

If a short passage is poetical because it is pregnant with suggestion of a few things, which stretches our attention and makes us rapt and serious, how much more poetical ought a vision to be which was pregnant with all we care for? Focus a little experience, give some scope and depth to your feeling, and it grows imaginative; give it more scope and more depth, focus all experience within it, make it a philosopher's vision of the world, and it will grow imaginative in a superlative degree, and be supremely poetical. The difficulty, after having the experience to symbolize, lies only in having enough imagination to hold and suspend it in a thought; and further, to give this thought such verbal expression that others may be able to decipher it, and to be stirred by it as by a wind of suggestion sweeping the whole forest of their memories.

Poetry, then, is not poetical for being short-winded or incidental, but, on the contrary, for being comprehensive and having range. If too much matter renders it heavy, that is the fault of the poet's weak intellect, not of the outstretched world. A quicker eye, a more synthetic imagination, might grasp a larger subject with the same ease. The picture that would render this larger subject would not be flatter and feebler for its extent, but, on the contrary, deeper and stronger, since it would possess as much unity as the little one, with greater volume. As in a supreme dramatic crisis all our life seems to be focused in the present, and used in colouring our consciousness and shaping our decisions, so for each philosophic poet the whole world of man is gathered together; and he is never so much a poet as when, in a single cry, he summons all that has affinity to him in the universe, and salutes his ultimate destiny. It is the acme of life to understand life. The height of poetry is to speak the language of the gods...

CONCLUSION

...In Dante...we have a view of experience...in its totality...from above and, in a sense, from outside; but the external point of reference is moral, not physical, and what interests the poet is what experience is best, what processes lead to a supreme, self-justifying, indestructible sort of existence. Goethe is the poet of life; Lucretius the poet of nature; Dante the poet of salvation. Goethe gives us what is most fundamental—the turbid flux of sense, the cry of the heart, the first tentative notions of art and science, which magic or shrewdness might hit upon. Lucretius carries us one step farther. Our wisdom ceases to be impressionistic and casual. It rests on [an] understanding of things, so that what happiness remains to us does not deceive us, and we can possess it in dignity and peace. Knowledge of what is possible is the beginning of happiness. Dante, however, carries us much farther than that. He, too, has knowledge of what is possible and impossible. He has collected the precepts of old philosophers and saints, and the more recent examples patent in society around him, and by their help has distinguished the ambitions that may be wisely indulged in this life from those which it is madness to foster—the first being called virtue and piety and the second folly and sin. What makes such knowledge precious is not only that it sketches in general the scope and issue of life, but that it paints in the detail as well—the detail of what is possible no less than that (more familiar to tragic poets) of what is impossible.

Lucretius' notion, for instance, of what is positively worth while or attainable is very meagre: freedom from superstition, with so much natural science as may secure that freedom, friendship, and a few cheap and healthful animal pleasures. No love, no patriotism, no enterprise, no religion. So, too, in what is forbidden us, Lucretius sees only generalities—the folly of passion, the blight of superstition. Dante, on the contrary, sees the various pitfalls of life with intense distinctness; and seeing them clearly, and how fatal each is, he sees also why men fall into them, the dream that leads men astray, and the sweetness of those goods that are impossible. Feeling, even in what we must ultimately call evil, the soul of good that attracts us to it, he feels in good all its loveliness and variety. Where, except in Dante, can we find so many stars that differ from other stars in glory; so many delightful habitations for excellences; so many distinct beauties of form, accent, thought, and intention; so many delicacies and heroisms? Dante is the master of those who know by experience what is worth knowing by experience; he is the master of *distinction*.

Here, then, are our three poets and their messages: Goethe, with human life in its immediacy, treated romantically; Lucretius, with a vision of nature and of the limits of human life; Dante, with spiritual mastery of that life, and a perfect knowledge of good and evil.

You may stop at what stage you will, according to your sense of what is real and important; for what one man calls higher another man calls unreal; and what one man feels to be strength smells rank to another. In the end, we should not be satisfied with any one of our poets if we had to drop the other two. It is true that taken formally, and in respect to their type of philosophy and imagination, Dante is on a higher plane than Lucretius, and Lucretius on a higher plane than Goethe. But the plane on which a poet dwells is not everything; much depends on what he brings up with him to that level. Now there is a great deal, a very great deal, in Goethe that Lucretius does not know of. Not knowing of it, Lucretius cannot carry this fund of experience up to the intellectual and naturalistic level; he cannot transmute this abundant substance of Goethe's by his higher insight and clearer faith; he has not woven so much into his poem. So that while to see nature, as Lucretius sees it, is a greater feat than merely to live hard in a romantic fashion, and produces a purer and more exalted poem than Goethe's magical medley, yet this medley is full of images, passions, memories, and introspective wisdom that Lucretius could not have dreamed of. The intellect of Lucretius rises, but rises comparatively empty; his vision sees things as a whole, and in their right places, but sees very little of them; he is quite deaf to their intricacy, to their bird-like multiform little souls. These Goethe knows admirably; with these he makes a natural concert, all the more natural for being sometimes discordant, sometimes overloaded and dull. It is necessary to revert from Lucretius to Goethe to get at the volume of life.

So, too, if we rise from Lucretius to Dante, there is much left behind which we cannot afford to lose. Dante may seem at first sight to have a view of nature not less complete and clear than that of Lucretius; a view even more efficacious than materialism for fixing the limits of human destiny and marking the path to happiness. But there is an illusion here. Dante's idea of nature is not genuine; it is not sincerely put together out of reasoned observation. It is a view of nature intercepted by myths and worked out by dialectic. Consequently, he has no true idea either of the path to happiness or of its real conditions. His notion of nature is an inverted image of the moral world, cast like a gigantic shadow upon the sky. It is a mirage.

Now, while to know evil, and especially good, in all their forms and inward implications is a far greater thing than to know the natural conditions of good and evil, or their real distribution in space and time, yet the higher philosophy is not safe if the lower philosophy is wanting or is false. Of course it is not safe practically; but it is not safe even poetically. There is an attenuated texture and imagery in the *Divine Comedy*. The voice that sings it, from beginning to end, is a thin boy-treble, all wonder and naïveté. This art does not smack of life, but of somnambulism. The reason is that the intellect has been hypnotized by a legendary and verbal philosophy. It has been unmanned, curiously enough, by an excess of humanism; by the fond delusion that man and his moral nature are at the centre of the universe. Dante is always thinking of the divine order of history and of the spheres; he believes in controlling and chastening the individual soul; so that he seems to be a cosmic poet, and to have escaped the anthropocentric conceit of romanticism. But he has not escaped it. For, as we have seen, this golden cage in which his soul sings is artificial; it is constructed on purpose to satisfy and glorify human distinctions and human preferences. The bird is not in his native wilds; man is not in the bosom of nature. He is, in a moral sense, still at the centre of the universe; his ideal is the cause of everything. He is the appointed lord of the earth, the darling of heaven; and history is a brief and prearranged drama, with Judea and Rome for its chief theatre.

Some of these illusions are already abandoned; all are undermined. Sometimes, in moments when we are unnerved and uninspired, we may regret the ease with which Dante could reconcile himself to a world so imagined as to suit human fancy and flatter human will. We may envy Dante his ignorance of nature, which enabled him to suppose that he dominated it, as an infinite and exuberant nature cannot be dominated by any of its parts. In the end, however, knowledge is good for the imagination. Dante himself thought so; and his work proved that he was right, by infinitely excelling that of all ignorant contemporary poets. The illusion of knowledge is better than ignorance for a poet; but the reality of knowledge would be better than the illusion; it would stretch the mind over a vaster and more stimulating scene; it would concentrate the will upon a more attainable, distinct, and congenial happiness. The growth of what is known increases the scope of what may be imagined and hoped for. Throw open to the young poet the infinity of nature; let him feel the precariousness of life, the variety of purposes, civilizations, and religions even upon this little planet; let him trace the triumphs and follies of art and philosophy, and their perpetual resurrections—like that of the downcast Faust. If, under the stimulus of such a scene, he does not some day compose a natural comedy as much surpassing Dante's divine comedy in sublimity and richness as it will surpass it in truth, the fault will not lie with the subject, which is inviting and magnificent, but with the halting genius that cannot render that subject worthily...

SHELLEY: OR THE POETIC VALUE OF REVOLUTIONARY PRINCIPLES

It is possible to advocate anarchy in criticism as in politics, and there is perhaps nothing coercive to urge against a man who maintains that any work of art is good enough, intrinsically and incommensurably, if it pleased anybody at any time for any reason. In practice, however, the ideal of anarchy is unstable. Irrefutable by argument, it is readily overcome by nature. It melts away before the dogmatic operation of the anarchist's own will, as soon as he allows himself the least creative endeavour. In spite of the infinite variety of what is merely possible, human nature and will have a somewhat definite constitution, and only what is harmonious with their actual constitution can long maintain itself in the moral world. Hence it is a safe principle in the criticism of art that technical proficiency, and brilliancy of fancy or execution, cannot avail to establish a great reputation. They may dazzle for a moment, but they cannot absolve an artist from the need of having an important subject-matter and a sane humanity.

If this principle is accepted, however, it might seem that certain artists, and perhaps the greatest, might not fare well at our hands. How would Shelley, for instance, stand such a test? Everyone knows the judgment passed on Shelley by Matthew Arnold, a critic who evidently relied on this principle, even if he preferred to speak only in the name of his personal tact and literary experience. Shelley, Matthew Arnold said, was 'a beautiful and ineffectual angel, beating his wings in a luminous void in vain'. In consequence he declared that Shelley was not a classic, especially as his private circle had had an unsavoury morality, to be expressed only by the French word *sale*, and as, moreover, Shelley himself occasionally showed a distressing want of the sense of humour, which could only be called *bête*. These strictures, if a bit incoherent, are separately remarkably just. They unmask essential weaknesses not only in Shelley, but in all revolutionary people. The life of reason is a heritage and exists only through tradition. Half of it is an art, an adjustment to an alien reality, which only a long experience can teach: and even the other half, the inward inspiration and ideal of reason, must be also a common inheritance in the race, if people are to work together or so much as to understand one another. Now the misfortune of revolutionists is that they are disinherited, and their folly is that they wish to be disinherited even more than they are. Hence, in the midst of their passionate and even heroic idealisms, there is commonly a strange poverty in their minds, many an ugly turn in their lives, and an ostentatious vileness in their manners. They wish to be the leaders of mankind, but they are wretched representatives of humanity. In the concert of nature it is hard to keep in tune with oneself if one is out of tune with everything.

We should not then be yielding to any private bias, but simply noting the conditions under which art may exist and may be appreciated, if we accepted the classical principle of criticism and asserted that substance, sanity, and even a sort of pervasive wisdom are requisite for supreme works of art. On the other hand—who can honestly doubt it?—the rebels and individualists are the men of direct insight and vital hope. The poetry of Shelley in particular is typically poetical. It is poetry divinely inspired; and Shelley himself is perhaps no more ineffectual or more lacking in humour than an angel properly should be. Nor is his greatness all a matter of aesthetic abstraction and wild music. It is a fact of capital importance in the development of human genius that the great revolution in Christendom against Christianity, a revolution that began with the Renaissance and is not yet completed, should have found angels to herald it, no less than that other revolution did which began at Bethlehem; and that among these new angels there should have been one so winsome, pure, and rapturous as Shelley. How shall we reconcile these conflicting impressions? Shall we force ourselves to call the genius of Shelley second-rate because it was revolutionary, and shall we attribute all enthusiasm for him to literary affectation or political prejudice? Or shall we rather abandon the orthodox principle that an important subject-matter and a sane spirit are essential to great works? Or shall we look for a different issue out of our perplexity, by asking if the analysis and comprehension are not perhaps at fault which declare that these things are not present in Shelley's poetry? This last is the direction in which I conceive the truth to lie. A little consideration will show us that Shelley really has a great subject-matter: what ought to be; and that he has a real humanity—though it is humanity in the seed, humanity in its internal principle, rather than in those deformed expressions of it which can flourish in the world.

Shelley seems hardly to have been brought up; he grew up in the nursery among his young sisters, at school among the rude boys, without any affectionate guidance, without imbibing any religious or social tradition. If he received any formal training or correction, he instantly rejected it inwardly, set it down as unjust and absurd, and turned instead to sailing paper boats, to reading romances or to writing them, or to watching with delight the magic of chemical experiments. Thus the mind of Shelley was thoroughly disinherited; but not, like the minds of most revolutionists, by accident and through the niggardliness of fortune, for few revolutionists would be such if they were heirs to a baronetcy. Shelley's mind disinherited itself out of allegiance to itself, because it was too sensitive and too highly endowed for the world into which it had descended. It rejected ordinary education, because it was incapable of assimilating it. Education is suitable to those few animals whose faculties are not completely innate, animals that, like most men, may be perfected by experience because they are born with various imperfect alternative instincts rooted equally in their system. But most animals, and a few men, are not of this sort. They cannot be educated, because they are born complete. Full of predeterminate intuitions, they are without intelligence, which is the power of seeing things as they are. Endowed with a specific, unshakable faith, they are impervious to experience: and as they burst the womb they bring ready-made with them their final and only possible system of philosophy.

Shelley was one of these spokesmen of the *a priori*, one of these nurslings of the womb, like a bee or a butterfly; a dogmatic, inspired, perfect, and incorrigible creature. He was innocent and cruel, swift and wayward, illuminated and blind. Being a finished child of nature, not a joint product, like most of us, of nature, history, and society, he abounded miraculously in his own clear sense, but was obtuse to the droll, miscellaneous lessons of fortune. The cannonade of hard, inexplicable facts that knocks into most of us what little wisdom we have, left Shelley dazed and sore, perhaps, but uninstructed. When the storm was over, he began chirping again his own natural note. If the world continued to confine and obsess him, he hated the world, and gasped for freedom. Being incapable of understanding reality, he revelled in creating world after world in idea. For his nature was not merely predetermined and obdurate, it was also sensitive, vehement, and fertile. With the soul of a bird, he had the senses of a man-child; the instinct of the butterfly was united in him with the instinct of the brooding fowl and of the pelican. This winged spirit had a heart. It darted swiftly on its appointed course, neither expecting nor understanding opposition; but when it met opposition it did not merely flutter and collapse; it was inwardly outraged, it protested proudly against fate, it cried aloud for liberty and justice.

The consequence was that Shelley, having a nature preformed but at the same time tender, passionate, and moral, was exposed to early and continual suffering. When the world violated the ideal which lay so clear before his eyes, that violation filled him with horror. If to the irrepressible gushing of life from within we add the suffering and horror that continually checked it, we shall have in hand, I think, the chief elements of his genius.

Love of the ideal, passionate apprehension of what ought to be, has for its necessary counterpart condemnation of the actual, wherever the actual does not conform to that ideal. The spontaneous soul, the soul of the child, is naturally revolutionary; and when the revolution fails, the soul of the youth becomes naturally pessimistic. All moral life and moral judgment have this deeply romantic character; they venture to assert a private ideal in the face of an intractable and omnipotent world. Some moralists begin by feeling the attraction of untasted and ideal perfection. These, like Plato, excel in elevation, and they are apt to despise rather than to reform the world. Other moralists begin by a revolt against the actual, at some point where they find the actual particularly galling. These excel in sincerity; their purblind conscience is urgent, and they are reformers in intent and sometimes even in action. But the ideals they frame are fragmentary and shallow, often mere provisional vague watchwords, like liberty, equality, and fraternity; they possess no positive visions or plans for moral life as a whole, like Plato's *Republic*. The utopian or visionary moralists are often rather dazed by this wicked world; being well-intentioned but impotent, they often take comfort in fancying that the ideal they pine for is already actually embodied on earth, or is about to be embodied on earth in a decade or two, or at least is embodied eternally in a sphere immediately above the earth, to which we shall presently climb, and be happy for ever.

Lovers of the ideal who thus hastily believe in its reality are called idealists, and Shelley was an idealist in almost every sense of that hard-used word. He early became an idealist after Berkeley's fashion, in that he discredited the existence of matter and embraced a psychological or (as it was called) intellectual system of the universe. In his drama *Hellas* he puts this view with evident approval into the mouth of Ahasuerus:

> This Whole
> Of suns and worlds and men and beasts and flowers,
> With all the silent or tempestuous workings
> By which they have been, are, or cease to be,

Is but a vision;—all that it inherits
Are motes of a sick eye, bubbles and dreams.
Thought is its cradle and its grave; nor less
The future and the past are idle shadows
Of thought's eternal flight—they have no being:
Nought is but that which feels itself to be. [776–85]

But Shelley was even more deeply and constantly an idealist after the manner of Plato; for he regarded the good as a magnet (inexplicably not working for the moment) that draws all life and motion after it; and he looked on the types and ideals of things as on eternal realities that subsist, beautiful and untarnished, when the glimmerings that reveal them to our senses have died away. From the infinite potentialities of beauty in the abstract, articulate mind draws certain bright forms—the Platonic ideas—'the gathered rays which are reality', as Shelley called them: and it is the light of these ideals cast on objects of sense that lends to these objects some degree of reality and value, making out of them 'lovely apparitions, dim at first, then radiant... the progeny immortal of painting, sculpture, and rapt poesy'.

The only kind of idealism that Shelley had nothing to do with is the kind that prevails in some universities, that Hegelian idealism which teaches that perfect good is a vicious abstraction, and maintains that all the evil that has been, is, and ever shall be is indispensable to make the universe as good as it possibly could be. In this form, idealism is simply contempt for all ideals, and a hearty adoration of things as they are; and as such it appeals mightily to the powers that be, in Church and in State; but in that capacity it would have been as hateful to Shelley as the powers that be always were, and as the philosophy was that flattered them. For his moral feeling was based on suffering and horror at what is actual, no less than on love of a visioned good. His conscience was, to a most unusual degree, at once elevated and sincere. It was inspired in equal measure by prophecy and by indignation. He was carried away in turn by enthusiasm for what his ethereal and fertile fancy pictured as possible, and by detestation of the reality forced upon him instead. Hence that extraordinary moral fervour which is the soul of his poetry. His imagination is no playful undirected kaleidoscope; the images, often so tenuous and metaphysical, that crowd upon him, are all sparks thrown off at white heat, embodiments of a fervent, definite, unswerving inspiration. If we think that *The Cloud* and the *West Wind* and *The Witch of Atlas* are mere fireworks, poetic dust, a sort of *bataille des fleurs* in which we are pelted by a shower of images, we have not understood the passion that overflows in them, as any long-nursed passion may, in any of us, suddenly overflow in an unwonted profusion of words. This is a point at which Francis Thompson's understanding of Shelley, generally so perfect, seems to me to go astray. The universe, Thompson tells us, was Shelley's box of toys. 'He gets between the feet of the horses of the sun. He stands in the lap of patient Nature, and twines her loosened tresses after a hundred wilful fashions, to see how she will look nicest in his song.' This last is not, I think, Shelley's motive; it is not the truth about the spring of his genius. He undoubtedly shatters the world to bits, but only to build it nearer to the heart's desire, only to make out of its coloured fragments some more Elysian home for love, or some more dazzling symbol for that infinite beauty which is the need—the profound, aching, imperative need—of the human soul. This recreative impulse of the poet's is not wilful, as Thompson calls it: it is moral. Like the *Sensitive Plant*

> It loves even like Love,—its deep heart is full;
> It desires what it has not, the beautiful. [76–7]

The question for Shelley is not at all what will look nicest in his song; that is the preoccupation of mincing rhymesters, whose well is soon dry. Shelley's abundance has a more generous source; it springs from his passion for picturing what would be best, not in the picture, but in the world. Hence, when he feels he has pictured or divined it, he can exclaim:

> The joy, the triumph, the delight, the madness,
> The boundless, overflowing, bursting gladness,

The vaporous exultation, not to be confined!
Ha! Ha! the animation of delight,
Which wraps me like an atmosphere of light,
And bears me as a cloud is borne by its own wind!
[*Prometheus Unbound, Act IV*, 319–24]

To match this gift of bodying forth the ideal Shelley had his vehement sense of wrong; and as he seized upon and recast all images of beauty, to make them more perfectly beautiful, so, to vent his infinite horror of evil, he seized on all the worst images of crime or torture that he could find, and recast them so as to reach the quintessence of distilled badness. His pictures of war, famine, lust, and cruelty are, or seem, forced, although perhaps, as in *The Cenci*, he might urge that he had historical warrant for his descriptions, far better historical warrant, no doubt, than the beauty and happiness actually to be found in the world could give him for his *Skylark*, his *Epipsychidion*, or his *Prometheus*. But to exaggerate good is to vivify, to enhance our sense of moral coherence and beautiful naturalness; it is to render things more graceful, intelligible, and congenial to the spirit which they ought to serve. To aggravate evil, on the contrary, is to darken counsel—already dark enough—and the want of truth to nature in this pessimistic sort of exaggeration is not compensated for by any advantage. The violence and, to my feeling, the wantonness of these invectives—for they are invectives in intention and in effect—may have seemed justified to Shelley by his political purpose. He was thirsting to destroy kings, priests, soldiers, parents, and heads of colleges—to destroy them, I mean, in their official capacity; and the exhibition of their vileness in all its diabolical purity might serve to remove scruples in the half-hearted. We, whom the nineteenth century has left so tender to historical rights and historical beauties, may wonder that a poet, an impassioned lover of the beautiful, could have been such a leveller, and such a vandal in his theoretical destructiveness. But here the legacy of the eighteenth century was speaking in Shelley, as that of the nineteenth is speaking in us: and moreover, in his own person, the very fertility of imagination could be a cause of blindness to the past and its contingent sanctities. Shelley was not left standing aghast, like a Philistine, before the threatened destruction of all traditional order. He had, and knew he had, the seeds of a far lovelier order in his own soul; there he found the plan or memory of a perfect commonwealth of nature ready to rise at once on the ruins of this sad world, and to make regret for it impossible.

So much for what I take to be the double foundation of Shelley's genius, a vivid love of ideal good on the one hand, and on the other, what is complementary to that vivid love, much suffering and horror at the touch of actual evils. On this double foundation he based an opinion which had the greatest influence on his poetry, not merely on the subject-matter of it, but also on the exuberance and urgency of emotion which suffuses it. This opinion was that all that caused suffering and horror in the world could be readily destroyed: it was the belief in perfectibility.

An animal that has rigid instincts and an *a priori* mind is probably very imperfectly adapted to the world he comes into: his organs cannot be moulded by experience and use; unless they are fitted by some miraculous pre-established harmony, or by natural selection, to things as they are, they will never be reconciled with them, and an eternal war will ensue between what the animal needs, loves, and can understand and what the outer reality offers. So long as such a creature lives —and his life will be difficult and short—events will continually disconcert and puzzle him; everything will seem to him unaccountable, inexplicable, unnatural. He will not be able to conceive the real order and connection of things sympathetically, by assimilating his habits of thought to their habits of evolution. His faculties, being innate and unadaptable, will not allow him to correct his presumptions and axioms; he will never be able to make nature the standard of naturalness. What contradicts his private impulses will seem to him to contradict reason, beauty, and necessity. In this paradoxical situation he will probably take refuge in the conviction that what he finds to exist is an illusion, or at least not a fair sample of reality. Being so perverse, absurd, and repugnant, the given state of things must be, he will say, only accidental and temporary. He will be sure that his own *a priori* imagination is the mirror of all the eternal proprieties, and that as his mind can move only in one predetermined way, things cannot be prevented from moving in that same way save by some strange violence done to their nature. It would be easy, therefore, to set everything right again: nay, everything must be on the point of righting itself spontaneously. Wrong, of its very essence, must be in unstable equilibrium. The conflict between what such a man feels ought to exist and what he finds actually existing must, he will feel sure, end by a speedy revolution in things, and by the removal of all scandals; that it should end by the speedy removal of his own person, or by such a revolution in his demands as might reconcile him to existence, will never occur to him; or, if the thought occurs to him, it will seem too horrible to be true.

Such a creature cannot adapt himself to things by education, and consequently he cannot adapt things to himself by industry. His choice lies absolutely between victory and martyrdom. But at the very moment of martyrdom, martyrs, as is well known, usually feel assured of victory. The *a priori* spirit will therefore be always a prophet of victory, so long as it subsists at all. The vision of a better world at hand absorbed the Israelites in exile, St John the Baptist in the desert, and Christ on the cross. The martyred spirit always says to the world it leaves, 'This day thou shalt be with me in paradise.'

In just this way, Shelley believed in perfectibility. In his latest poems—in *Hellas*, in *Adonais*—he was perhaps a little inclined to remove the scene of perfectibility to a metaphysical region, as the Christian Church soon removed it to the other world. Indeed, an earth really made perfect is hardly distinguishable from a posthumous heaven: so profoundly must everything in it be changed, and so angel-like must everyone in it become. Shelley's earthly paradise, as described in *Prometheus* and in *Epipsychidion*, is too festival-like, too much of a mere culmination, not to be fugitive: it cries aloud to be translated into a changeless and metaphysical heaven, which to Shelley's mind could be nothing but the realm of Platonic ideas, where 'life, like a dome of many-coloured glass', no longer 'stains the white radiance of eternity'. But the age had been an age of revolution and, in spite of disappointments, retained its faith in revolution; and the young Shelley was not satisfied with a paradise removed to the intangible realms of poetry or of religion; he hoped, like the old Hebrews, for a paradise on earth. His notion was that eloquence could change the heart of man, and that love, kindled there by the force of reason and of example, would transform society. He believed, Mrs Shelley tells us, 'that mankind had only to will that there should be no evil, and there would be none'. And she adds: 'That man could be so perfectionized as to be able to expel evil from his own nature, and from the greater part of creation, was the cardinal point of his system.' This cosmic extension of the conversion of men reminds one of the cosmic extension of the Fall conceived by St Augustine; and in the *Prometheus* Shelley has allowed his fancy, half in symbol, half in glorious physical hyperbole, to carry the warm contagion of love into the very bowels of the earth, and even the moon, by reflection, to catch the light of love, and be alive again.

Shelley, we may safely say, did not understand the real constitution of nature. It was hidden from him by a cloud, all woven of shifting rainbows and bright tears. Only his emotional haste made it possible for him to entertain such opinions as he did entertain; or rather, it was inevitable that the mechanism of nature, as it is in its depths, should remain in his pictures only the most shadowy of backgrounds. His poetry is accordingly a part of the poetry of illusion; the poetry of truth, if we have the courage to hope for such a thing, is reserved for far different and yet unborn poets. But it is only fair to Shelley to remember that the moral being of mankind is as yet in its childhood; all poets play with images not understood; they touch on emotions sharply, at random, as in a dream; they suffer each successive vision, each poignant sentiment, to evaporate into nothing, or to leave behind only a heart vaguely softened and fatigued, a gentle languor, or a tearful hope. Every modern school of poets, once out of fashion, proves itself to have been sadly romantic and sentimental. None has done better than to spangle a confused sensuous pageant with some sparks of truth, or to give it some symbolic relation to moral experience. And this Shelley has done as well as anybody: all other poets also have been poets of illusion. The distinction of Shelley is that his illusions are so wonderfully fine, subtle, and palpitating; that they betray passions and mental habits so singularly generous and pure. And why? Because he did not believe in the necessity of what is vulgar, and did not pay that demoralizing respect to it under the title of fact or of custom, which it exacts from most of us. The past seemed to him no valid precedent, the present no final instance. As he believed in the imminence of an overturn that should make all things new, he was not checked by any divided allegiance, by any sense that he was straying into the vapid or fanciful, when he created what he justly calls 'Beautiful idealisms of moral excellence'.

That is what his poems are fundamentally—the *Skylark*, and *The Witch of Atlas*, and *The Sensitive Plant* no less than the grander pieces. He infused into his gossamer world the strength of his heroic conscience. He felt that what his imagination pictured was a true symbol of what human experience should and might pass into. Otherwise he would have been aware of playing with idle images; his poetry would have been mere millinery and his politics mere business; he would have been a worldling in art and in morals. The clear fire, the sustained breath, the fervent accent of his poetry are due to his faith in his philosophy. As Mrs Shelley expressed it, he 'had no care for any of his poems that did not emanate from the depths of his mind, and develop some high and abstruse truth'. Had his poetry not dealt with what was supreme in his own eyes, and dearest to his heart, it could never have been the exquisite and entrancing poetry that it is. It would not have had an adequate subject-matter, as, in spite of Matthew Arnold,

I think it had; for nothing can be empty that contains such a soul. An angel cannot be ineffectual if the standard of efficiency is moral; he is what all other things bring about, when they are effectual. And a void that is alive with the beating of luminous wings, and of a luminous heart, is quite sufficiently peopled. Shelley's mind was angelic not merely in its purity and fervour, but also in its moral authority, in its prophetic strain. What was conscience in his generation was life in him.

The mind of man is not merely a sensorium. His intelligence is not merely an instrument for adaptation. There is a germ within, a nucleus of force and organization, which can be unfolded, under favourable circumstances, into a perfection inwardly determined. Man's constitution is a fountain from which to draw an infinity of gushing music, not representing anything external, yet not unmeaning on that account, since it represents the capacities and passions latent in him from the beginning. These potentialities, however, are no oracles of truth. Being innate they are arbitrary; being *a priori* they are subjective; but they are good principles for fiction, for poetry, for morals, for religion. They are principles for the true expression of man, but not for the true description of the universe. When they are taken for the latter, fiction becomes deception, poetry illusion, morals fanaticism, and religion bad science. The orgy of delusion into which we are then plunged comes from supposing the *a priori* to be capable of controlling the actual, and the innate to be a standard for the true. That rich and definite endowment which might have made the distinction of the poet, then makes the narrowness of the philosopher. So Shelley, with a sort of tyranny of which he does not suspect the possible cruelty, would impose his ideal of love and equality upon all creatures; he would make enthusiasts of clowns and doves of vultures. In him, as in many people, too intense a need of loving excludes the capacity for intelligent sympathy. His feeling cannot accommodate itself to the inequalities of human nature: his good will is a geyser, and will not consent to grow cool, and to water the flat and vulgar reaches of life. Shelley is blind to the excellences of what he despises, as he is blind to the impossibility of realizing what he wants. His sympathies are narrow as his politics are visionary, so that there is a certain moral incompetence in his moral intensity. Yet his abstraction from half of life, or from nine-tenths of it, was perhaps necessary if silence and space were to be won in his mind for its own upwelling, ecstatic harmonies. The world we have always with us, but such spirits we have not always. And the spirit has fire enough within to make a second stellar universe.

An instance of Shelley's moral incompetence in moral intensity is to be found in his view of selfishness and evil. From the point of view of pure spirit, selfishness is quite absurd. As a contemporary of ours has put it: 'It is so evident that it is better to secure a greater good for *A* than a lesser good for *B* that it is hard to find any still more evident principle by which to prove this. And if *A* happens to be someone else, and *B* to be myself, that cannot affect the question.' It is very foolish not to love your neighbour as yourself, since his good is no less good than yours. Convince people of this—and who can resist such perfect logic?—and *presto*, all property in things has disappeared, all jealousy in love, and all rivalry in honour. How happy and secure everyone will suddenly be, and how much richer than in our mean, blind, competitive society! The word love—and we have just seen that love is a logical necessity—offers an easy and final solution to all moral and political problems. Shelley cannot imagine why this solution is not accepted, and why logic does not produce love. He can only wonder and grieve that it does not; and since selfishness and ill will seem to him quite gratuitous, his ire is aroused; he thinks them unnatural and monstrous. He could not in the least understand evil, even when he did it himself; all villainy seemed to him wanton, all lust frigid, all hatred insane. All was an abomination alike that was not the lovely spirit of love.

Now this is a very unintelligent view of evil; and if Shelley had had time to read Spinoza—an author with whom he would have found himself largely in sympathy—he might have learned that nothing is evil in itself, and that what is evil in things is not due to any accident in creation, nor to groundless malice in man. Evil is an inevitable aspect which things put on when they are struggling to preserve themselves in the same habitat, in which there is not room or matter enough for them to prosper equally side by side. Under these circumstances the partial success of any creature—say, the cancer microbe—is an evil from the point of view of those other creatures—say, men—to whom that success is a defeat. Shelley sometimes half perceived this inevitable tragedy. So he says of the fair lady in *The Sensitive Plant*:

> all killing insects and gnawing worms,
> And things of obscene and unlovely forms,
> She bore in a basket of Indian woof,
> Into the rough woods far aloof—
> In a basket of grasses and wild flowers full,
> The freshest her gentle hands could pull
> For the poor banished insects, whose intent,
> Although they did ill, was innocent. [155–62]

Now it is all very well to ask cancer microbes to be reasonable, and go feed on oak-leaves, if the oak-leaves do not object; oak-leaves might be poison for them, and in any case cancer microbes cannot listen to reason; they must go on propagating where they are, unless they are quickly and utterly exterminated. And fundamentally men are subject to the same fatality exactly; they cannot listen to reason unless they are reasonable; and it is unreasonable to expect that, being animals, they should be reasonable exclusively. Imagination is indeed at work in them, and makes them capable of sacrificing themselves for any idea that appeals to them, for their children, perhaps, or for their religion. But they are not more capable of sacrificing themselves to what does not interest them than the cancer microbes are of sacrificing themselves to men.

When Shelley marvels at the perversity of the world, he shows his ignorance of the world. The illusion he suffers from is constitutional, and such as larks and sensitive plants are possibly subject to in their way: what he is marvelling at is really that anything should exist at all [that is] not a creature of his own moral disposition. Consequently the more he misunderstands the world and bids it change its nature, the more he expresses his own nature: so that all is not vanity in his illusion, nor night in his blindness. The poet sees most clearly what his ideal is; he suffers no illusion in the expression of his own soul. His political utopias, his belief in the power of love, and his cryingly subjective and inconstant way of judging people are one side of the picture; the other is his lyrical power, wealth, and ecstasy. If he had understood universal nature, he would not have so glorified in his own. And his own nature was worth glorifying; it was, I think, the purest, tenderest, richest, most rational nature ever poured forth in verse. I have not read in any language such a full expression of the unadulterated instincts of the mind. The world of Shelley is that which the vital monad within many of us—I will not say within all, for who shall set bounds to the variations of human nature?—the world which the vital monad within many of us, I say, would gladly live in if it could have its way.

Matthew Arnold said that Shelley was not quite sane; and certainly he was not quite sane, if we place sanity in justness of external perception, adaptation to matter, and docility to the facts; but his lack of sanity was not due to any internal corruption; it was not even an internal eccentricity. He was like a child, like a Platonic soul just fallen from the Empyrean; and the child may be dazed, credulous, and fanciful; but he is not mad. On the contrary, his earnest playfulness, the constant distraction of his attention from observation to daydreams, is the sign of an inward order and fecundity appropriate to his age. If children did not see visions, good men would have nothing to work for. It is the soul of observant persons, like Matthew Arnold, that is apt not to be quite sane and whole inwardly, but somewhat warped by familiarity with the perversities of real things, and forced to misrepresent its true ideal, like a tree bent by too prevalent a wind. Half the fertility of such a soul is lost, and the other half is denaturalized. No doubt, in its sturdy deformity, the practical mind is an instructive and not unpleasing object, an excellent, if somewhat pathetic, expression of the climate in which it is condemned to grow, and of its dogged clinging to an ingrate soil; but it is a wretched expression of its innate possibilities. Shelley, on the contrary, is like a palm-tree in the desert or a star in the sky; he is perfect in the midst of the void. His obtuseness to things dynamic—to the material order—leaves his whole mind free to develop things aesthetic after their own kind; his abstraction permits purity, his playfulness makes room for creative freedom, his ethereal quality is only humanity having its way.

We perhaps do ourselves an injustice when we think that the heart of us is sordid; what is sordid is rather the situation that cramps or stifles the heart. In itself our generative principle is surely no less fertile and generous than the generative principle of crystals or flowers. As it can produce a more complex body, it is capable of producing a more complex mind; and the beauty and life of this mind, like that of the body, is all predetermined in the seed. Circumstances may suffer the organism to develop, or prevent it from doing so; they cannot change its plan without making it ugly and deformed. What Shelley's mind draws from the outside, its fund of images, is like what the germ of the body draws from the outside, its food—a mass of mere materials to transform and reorganize. With these images Shelley constructs a world determined by his native genius, as the seed organizes out of its food a predetermined system of nerves and muscles. Shelley's poetry shows us the perfect but naked body of human happiness. What clothes circumstances may compel most of us to add may be a necessary concession to climate, to custom, or to shame; they can hardly add a new vitality or any beauty comparable to that which they hide.

When the soul, as in Shelley's case, is all goodness, and when the world seems all illegitimacy and obstruction, we need not wonder that *freedom* should be regarded as a panacea. Even if freedom had not been the idol of Shelley's times, he would have made an idol of it for himself. 'I never could discern in him', says his friend Hogg, 'any more than two principles. The first was a strong, irrepressible love of liberty...

The second was an equally ardent love of toleration...and ...an intense abhorrence of persecution.' We all fancy nowadays that we believe in liberty and abhor persecution; but the liberty we approve of is usually only a variation in social compulsions, to make them less galling to our latest sentiments than the old compulsions would be if we retained them. Liberty of the press and liberty to vote do not greatly help us in living after our own mind, which is, I suppose, the only positive sort of liberty. From the point of view of a poet, there can be little essential freedom so long as he is forbidden to live with the people he likes, and compelled to live with the people he does not like. This, to Shelley, seemed the most galling of tyrannies; and free love was, to his feeling, the essence and test of freedom. Love must be spontaneous to be a spiritual bond in the beginning and it must remain spontaneous if it is to remain spiritual. To be bound by one's past is as great a tyranny to pure spirit as to be bound by the sin of Adam, or by the laws of Artaxerxes; and those of us who do not believe in the possibility of free love ought to declare frankly that we do not, at bottom, believe in the possibility of freedom.

> I never was attached to that great sect
> Whose doctrine is that each one should select,
> Out of the crowd, a mistress or a friend
> And all the rest, though fair and wise, commend
> To cold oblivion; though it is the code
> Of modern morals, and the beaten road
> Which those poor slaves with weary footsteps tread
> Who travel to their home among the dead
> By the broad highway of the world, and so
> With one chained friend, perhaps a jealous foe,
> The dreariest and the longest journey go.
> True love in this differs from gold and clay,
> That to divide is not to take away.
> Love is like understanding that grows bright
> Gazing on many truths...Narrow
> The heart that loves, the brain that contemplates,
> The life that wears, the spirit that creates
> One object and one form, and builds thereby
> A sepulchre for its eternity! [*Epipsychidion*, 149–63, 169–73]

The difficulties in reducing this charming theory of love to practice are well exemplified in Shelley's own life. He ran away with his first wife not because she inspired any uncontrollable passion, but because she declared she was a victim of domestic oppression and threw herself upon him for protection. Nevertheless, when he discovered that his best friend was making love to her, in spite of his free-love principles he was very seriously annoyed. When he presently abandoned her, feeling a spiritual affinity in another direction, she drowned herself in the Serpentine: and his second wife needed all her natural sweetness and all her inherited philosophy to reconcile her to the waves of Platonic enthusiasm for other ladies which periodically swept the too sensitive heart of her husband. Free love would not, then, secure freedom from complications; it would not remove the present occasion for jealousy, reproaches, tragedies, and the dragging of a lengthening chain. Freedom of spirit cannot be translated into freedom of action; you may amend laws, and customs, and social entanglements, but you will still have them; for this world is a lumbering mechanism and not, like love, a plastic dream. Wisdom is very old and therefore often ironical, and it has long taught that it is well for those who would live in the spirit to keep as clear as possible of the world: and that marriage, especially a free-love marriage, is a snare for poets. Let them endure to love freely, hopelessly, and infinitely, after the manner of Plato and Dante, and even of Goethe, when Goethe really loved: that exquisite sacrifice will improve their verse, and it will not kill them. Let them follow in the traces of Shelley when he wrote in his youth: 'I have been most of the night pacing a church-yard. I must now engage in scenes of strong interest...I expect to gratify some of this insatiable feeling in poetry...I slept with a loaded pistol and some poison last night, but did not die.' Happy man if he had been able to add, 'And did not marry!'

Last among the elements of Shelley's thought I may perhaps mention his atheism. Shelley called himself an atheist in his youth; his biographers and critics usually say that he was, or that he became, a pantheist. He was an atheist in the sense that he denied the orthodox conception of a deity who is a voluntary creator, a legislator, and a judge; but his aversion to Christianity was not founded on any sympathetic or imaginative knowledge of it; and a man who preferred the *Paradiso* of Dante to almost any other poem, and preferred it to the popular *Inferno* itself, could evidently be attracted by Christian ideas and sentiment the moment they were presented to him as expressions of moral truth rather than as gratuitous dogmas. A pantheist he was in the sense that he felt how fluid and vital this whole world is; but he seems to have had no tendency to conceive any conscious plan or logical necessity connecting the different parts of the whole; so that rather than a pantheist he might be called a panpsychist; especially as he did not subordinate morally the individual to the cosmos. He did not surrender the authority of moral ideals in the face of physical necessity, which is properly the essence of pantheism. He did the exact opposite; so much so that the chief characteristic of his philosophy is its Promethean spirit. He maintained that the basis of moral authority was internal, diffused among all individuals; that it was the natural love of the beautiful and the good wherever it might spring, and however fate might oppose it.

> To suffer...
> To forgive...
> To defy Power...
> To love and bear; to hope, till Hope creates
> From its own wreck the thing it contemplates;
> Neither to change, nor falter, nor repent;
> This...is to be
> Good, great and joyous, beautiful and free.
> [*Prometheus Unbound, Act* IV, 570–77]

Shelley was also removed from any ordinary atheism by his truly speculative sense for eternity. He was a thorough Platonist. All metaphysics perhaps is poetry, but Platonic metaphysics is good poetry, and to this class Shelley's belongs. For instance:

The pure spirit shall flow
Back to the burning fountain whence it came,
A portion of the Eternal, which must glow
Through time and change, unquenchably the same...
Peace, peace! he is not dead, he doth not sleep!
He hath awakened from the dream of life—
'Tis we who, lost in stormy visions, keep
With phantoms an unprofitable strife...
He is made one with Nature. There is heard
His voice in all her music, from the moan
Of thunder, to the song of night's sweet bird...
He is a portion of the loveliness
Which once he made more lovely...
The splendours of the firmament of time
May be eclipsed, but are extinguished not:
Like stars to their appointed height they climb,
And death is a low mist which cannot blot
The brightness it may veil. When lofty thought
Lifts a young heart above its mortal lair,
...the dead live there. [*Adonais*, 338 ff.]

Atheism or pantheism of this stamp cannot be taxed with being gross or materialistic; the trouble is rather that it is too hazy in its sublimity. The poet has not perceived the natural relation between facts and ideals so clearly or correctly as he has felt the moral relation between them. But his allegiance to the intuition which defies, for the sake of felt excellence, every form of idolatry or cowardice wearing the mask of religion—this allegiance is itself the purest religion; and it is capable of inspiring the sweetest and most absolute poetry. In daring to lay bare the truths of fate, the poet creates for himself the subtlest and most heroic harmonies; and he is comforted for the illusions he has lost by being made incapable of desiring them.

We have seen that Shelley, being unteachable, could never put together any just idea of the world: he merely collected images and emotions, and out of them made worlds of his own. His poetry accordingly does not well express history, nor human character, nor the constitution of nature. What he unrolls before us instead is, in a sense, fantastic; it is a series of landscapes, passions, and cataclysms such as never were on earth, and never will be. If you are seriously interested only in what belongs to earth you will not be seriously interested in Shelley. Literature, according to Matthew Arnold, should be criticism of life, and Shelley did not criticize life; so that his poetry had no solidity. But is life, we may ask, the same thing as the circumstances of life on earth? Is the spirit of life, that marks and judges those circumstances, itself nothing? Music is surely no description of the circumstances of life; yet it is relevant to life unmistakably, for it stimulates by means of a torrent of abstract movements and images the formal and emotional possibilities of living which lie in the spirit. By so doing music becomes a part of life, a congruous addition, a parallel life, as it were, to the vulgar one. I see no reason, in the analogies of the natural world, for supposing that the circumstances of human life are the only circumstances in which the spirit of life can disport itself. Even on this planet, there are sea-animals and air-animals, ephemeral beings and self-centred beings, as well as persons who can grow as old as Matthew Arnold, and be as fond as he was of classifying other people. And beyond this planet, and in the interstices of what our limited senses can perceive, there are probably many forms of life not criticized in any of the books which Matthew Arnold said we should read in order to know the best that has been thought and said in the world. The future, too, even among men, may contain, as Shelley puts it, many 'arts, though unimagined, yet to be'. The divination of poets cannot, of course, be expected to reveal any of these hidden regions as they actually exist or will exist; but what would be the advantage of revealing them? It could only be what the advantage of criticizing human life would be also, to improve subsequent life indirectly by turning it towards attainable goods, and is it not as important a thing to improve life directly and in the present, if one has the gift, by enriching rather than criticizing it? Besides, there is need of fixing the ideal by which criticism is to be guided. If you have no image of happiness or beauty or perfect goodness before you, how are you to judge what portions of life are important, and what rendering of them is appropriate?

Being a singer inwardly inspired, Shelley could picture the ideal goals of life, the ultimate joys of experience, better than a discursive critic or observer could have done. The circumstances of life are only the bases or instruments of life: the fruition of life is not in retrospect, not in description of the instruments, but in expression of the spirit itself, to which those instruments may prove useful; as music is not a criticism of violins, but a playing upon them. This expression need not resemble its ground. Experience is diversified by colours that are not produced by colours, sounds that are not conditioned by sounds, names that are not symbols for other names, fixed ideal objects that stand for ever-changing material processes. The mind is fundamentally lyrical, inventive, redundant. Its visions are its own offspring, hatched in the warmth of some favourable cosmic gale. The ambient weather may vary, and these visions be scattered; but the ideal world they pictured may some day be revealed again to some other poet similarly inspired; the possibility of restoring it, or something like it, is perpetual. It is precisely because Shelley's sense for things is so fluid, so illusive, that it opens to us emotionally what is a serious scientific probability; namely, that human life is not all life, nor the landscape of earth the only admired landscape in the universe; that the ancients who believed in gods and spirits were nearer the virtual truth (however anthropomorphically they may have expressed themselves) than any philosophy or religion that makes human affairs the centre and aim of the world. Such moral imagination is to be gained by sinking into oneself, rather than by observing remote happenings, because it is at its heart, not at its finger-tips, that the human soul touches matter, and is akin to whatever other centres of life may people the infinite.

For this reason the masters of spontaneity, the prophets, the inspired poets, the saints, the mystics, the musicians are welcome and most appealing companions. In their simplicity and abstraction from the world they come very near the heart.

They say little and help much. They do not picture life, but have life, and give it. So we may say, I think, of Shelley's magic universe what he said of Greece; if it

> Must be
> A wreck, yet shall its fragments re-assemble,
> And build themselves again impregnably
> In a diviner clime,
> To Amphionic music on some Cape sublime,
> Which frowns above the idle foam of Time.
>
> [*Hellas*, 1002–7]

'Frowns', says Shelley rhetorically, as if he thought that something timeless, something merely ideal, could be formidable, or could threaten existing things with any but an ideal defeat. Tremendous error! Eternal possibilities may indeed beckon; they may attract those who instinctively pursue them as a star may guide those who wish to reach the place over which it happens to shine. But an eternal possibility has no material power. It is only one of an infinity of other things equally possible intrinsically, yet most of them quite unrealizable in this world of blood and mire. The realm of eternal essences rains down no Jovian thunderbolts, but only a ghostly Uranian calm. There is no frown there; rather, a passive and universal welcome to any who may have in them the will and the power to climb. Whether anyone has the will depends on his material constitution, and whether he has the power depends on the firm texture of that constitution and on circumstances happening to be favourable to its operation. Otherwise what the rebel or the visionary hails as his ideal will be no picture of his destiny or of that of the world. It will be, and will always remain, merely a picture of his heart. This picture, indestructible in its ideal essence, will mirror also the hearts of those who may share, or may have shared, the nature of the poet who drew it. So purely ideal and so deeply human are the visions of Shelley. So truly does he deserve the epitaph which a clear-sighted friend wrote upon his tomb: *cor cordium*, the heart of hearts.

HINTS OF EGOTISM IN GOETHE

All transcendentalists are preoccupied with the self, but not all are egotists. Some regard as a sad disability this limitation of their knowledge to what they have created; they are humble, and almost ashamed to be human, and to possess a mind that must cut them off hopelessly from all reality. On the other hand there are many instinctive egotists who are not transcendentalists, either because their attention has not been called to this system, or because they discredit all speculation, or because they see clearly that the senses and the intellect, far from cutting us off from the real things that surround us, have the function of adjusting our action to them and informing our mind about them. Such an instinctive egotist does not allege that he creates the world by willing and thinking it, yet he is more interested in his own sensations, fancies, and preferences than in the other things in the world. The attention he bestows on things seems to him to bathe in light their truly interesting side. What he chiefly considers is his own experience—what he cared for first, what second, what he thinks today, what he will probably think tomorrow, what friends he has had, and how they have lost their charm, what religions he has believed in, and in general what contributions the universe has made to him and he to the universe. His interest in personality need not be confined to his own; he may have a dramatic imagination, and may assign their appropriate personality to all other people; every situation he hears of or invents may prompt him to conceive the thrilling passions and pungent thoughts of some *alter ego*, in whom latent sides of his own nature may be richly expressed. And impersonal things, too, may fascinate him, when he feels that they stir his genius fruitfully; and he will be the more ready to scatter his favours broadcast in that what concerns him is not any particular truth or person (things which might prove jealous and exclusive), but rather the exercise of his own powers of universal sympathy.

7-2

Something of this sort seems to appear in Goethe; and although his contact with philosophical egotism was but slight, and some of his wise maxims are incompatible with it, yet his romanticism, his feeling for development in everything, his private life, the nebulous character of his religion, and some of his most important works, like *Faust* and *Wilhelm Meister*, are all so full of the spirit of German philosophy, that it would be a pity not to draw some illustration for our subject from so pleasant a source.

There are hints of egotism in Goethe, but in Goethe there are hints of everything, and it would be easy to gather an imposing mass of evidence to the effect that he was not like the transcendentalists, but far superior to them. For one thing he was many-sided, not encyclopaedic; he went out to greet the variety of things, he did not pack them together. He did not even arrange the phases of his experience (as he did those of Faust) in an order supposed to be a progress, although, as the commentators on *Faust* inform us, not a progress in mere goodness. Hegel might have *understood* all these moral attitudes, and described them in a way not meant to appear satirical; but he would have criticized and demolished them, and declared them obsolete—all but the one at which he happened to stop. Goethe *loved* them all; he hated to outgrow them, and if involuntarily he did so, at least he still honoured feelings that he had lost. He kept his old age genial and green by that perennial love. In order to hold his head above water and be at peace in his own heart, he did not need to be a Christian, a pagan, or an epicurean; yet he lent himself unreservedly, in imagination, to Christianity, paganism, and sensuality—three things your transcendental egotist can never stomach: each in its way would impugn his self-sufficiency.

Nevertheless the sympathies of Goethe were only romantic or aesthetic; they were based on finding in others an interesting variation from himself, an exotic possibility, rather than an identity with himself in thought or in fate. Christianity was an atmosphere necessary to certain figures, that of Gretchen, for instance, who would have been frankly vulgar without it; paganism was a learned masque, in which one could be at once distinguished and emancipated; and sensuality was a sentimental and scientific licence in which the free mind might indulge in due season. The sympathy Goethe felt with things was that of a lordly observer, a traveller, a connoisseur, a philanderer; it was egotistical sympathy.

Nothing, for instance, was more romantic in Goethe than his classicism. His *Iphigenie* and his *Helena* and his whole view of antiquity were full of the pathos of distance. That pompous sweetness, that intense moderation, that moral somnambulism were too intentional; and Goethe felt it himself. In *Faust*, after Helen has evaporated, he makes the hero revisit his native mountains and revert to the thought of Gretchen. It is a wise home-coming, because that craze for classicism which Helen symbolized alienated the mind from real life and led only to hopeless imitations and lackadaisical poses. Gretchen's garden, even the *Walpurgisnacht*, was in truth more classical. This is only another way of saying that in the attempt to be Greek the truly classical was missed even by Goethe, since the truly classical is not foreign to anybody. It is precisely that part of tradition and art which does not alienate us from our own life or from nature, but reveals them in all their depth and nakedness, freed from the fashions and hypocrisies of time and place. The effort to reproduce the peculiarities of antiquity is a proof that we are not its natural heirs, that we do not continue antiquity instinctively. People can mimic only what they have not absorbed. They reconstruct and turn into an archaeological masquerade only what strikes them as outlandish. The genuine inheritors of a religion or an art never dream of reviving it; its antique accidents do not interest them, and its eternal substance they possess by nature.

The Germans are not in this position in regard to the ancients. Whether sympathetic like Goethe, or disparaging like Burckhardt, or both at once, like Hegel, they have seen in antiquity its local colour, its mannerisms, its documents, and above all its contrasts with the present. It was not so while the traditions of antiquity were still living and authoritative. But the moderns, and especially the Germans, have not a humble mind. They do not go to school with the Greeks unfeignedly, as if Greek wisdom might possibly be true wisdom, a pure expression of experience and reason, valid essentially for us. They prefer to take that wisdom for a phase of sentiment, of course outgrown, but still enabling them to reconstruct learnedly the image of a fascinating past. This is what they call giving vitality to classical studies, turning them into *Kulturgeschichte*. This is a vitality lent by the living to the dead, not one drawn by the young and immature from a perennial fountain. In truth classical studies were vital only so long as they were still authoritative morally and set the standard for letters and life. They became otiose and pedantic when they began to serve merely to recover a dead past in its trivial detail, and to make us grow sentimental over its remoteness, its beauty, and its ruins.

How much freer and surer was Goethe's hand when it touched the cord of romanticism! How perfectly he knew the heart of the romantic egotist! The romantic egotist sets no particular limits to the range of his interests and sympathies; his programme, indeed, is to absorb the whole world. He is no wounded and disappointed creature, like Byron, that takes to sulking and naughtiness because things taste bitter in his mouth. He finds good and evil equally digestible. The personal egotism of Byron or of Musset after all was humble; it knew how weak it was in the universe. But absolute egotism in Goethe, as in Emerson, summoned all nature to minister to the self: all nature, if not actually compelled to this service by a human creative fiat, could at least be won over to it by the engaging heroism of her favourite child. In his warm pantheistic way Goethe felt the swarming universal life about him; he had no thought of dragooning it all, as sectarians and nationalists would, into vindicating some particular creed or nation. Yet that fertile and impartial universe left each life free and in uncensored competition with every other life. Each creature might feed blamelessly on all the others and become, if it could, the focus and epitome of the world. The development of self was the only duty, if only the self was developed widely and securely enough, with insight, calmness, and godlike irresponsibility.

Goethe exhibited this principle in practice more plainly, perhaps, than in theory. His family, his friends, his feelings were so many stepping-stones in his moral career; he expanded as he left them behind. His love-affairs were means to the fuller realization of himself. Not that his love-affairs were sensual or his infidelities callous; far from it. They often stirred him deeply and unsealed the springs of poetry in his heart; that was precisely their function. Every tender passion opened before him a primrose path into which his inexorable genius led him to wander. If in passing he must tread down some flower, that was a great sorrow to him; but perhaps that very sorrow and his inevitable remorse were the most needful and precious elements in the experience. Every pathetic sweetheart in turn was a sort of Belgium to him; he violated her neutrality with a sigh; his heart bled for her innocent sufferings, and he never said afterwards in self-defence, like the German Chancellor, that she was no better than she should be. But he must press on. His beckoning destiny, the claims of his spiritual growth, compelled him to sacrifice her and to sacrifice his own lacerated feelings on the altar of duty to his infinite self. Indeed, so truly supreme was this vocation that universal nature too, he thought, was bound to do herself some violence in his behalf and to grant him an immortal life, that so noble a process of self-expansion might go on for ever.

Goethe's perfect insight into the ways of romantic egotism appears also in *Faust*, and not least in the latter parts of it, which are curiously prophetic. If the hero of that poem has a somewhat incoherent character, soft, wayward, emotional, yet at the same time stubborn and indomitable, that circumstance only renders him the fitter vehicle for absolute Will, a metaphysical entity whose business is to be vigorous and endlessly energetic while remaining perfectly plastic. Faust was at first a scholar, fervid and grubbing, but so confused and impatient that he gave up science for magic. Notwithstanding the shams of professional people which offended him, a private and candid science was possible, which might have brought him intellectual satisfaction; and the fact would not have escaped him if he had been a simple lover of truth. But absolute Will cannot be restricted to any single interest, much less to the pursuit of a frigid truth in which it cannot believe; for the Will would not be absolute if it recognized any truth which it had to discover; it can recognize and love only the truth that it makes. Its method of procedure, we are told, consists in first throwing out certain assumptions, such perhaps as that everything must have a cause or that life and progress must be everlasting; and the truth is then whatever conforms to these assumptions. But since evidently these assumptions might be utterly false, it is clear that what interests absolute Will is not truth at all, but only orthodoxy. A delightful illustration of this is given by Faust when, emulating Luther for a moment, he undertakes to translate the first verse of Saint John—that being the Gospel that impresses him most favourably. The point is not prosaically to discover what the Evangelist meant, but rather what he must and shall have meant. *The Word* will never do; *the Sense* would be somewhat better; but *In the beginning was Force* would have even more to recommend it. Suddenly, however, what absolute Will demands flashes upon him, and he writes down contentedly: *In the beginning was the Deed:*

> Auf einmal seh' ich Rat
> Und schreibe getrost: Im Anfang war die Tat!

Yet even in this exciting form, the life of thought cannot hold him long. He aches to escape from it; not that his knowledge of the sciences, as well as his magic, will not accompany him through life; he will not lose his acquired art nor his habit of reflection, and in this sense his career is really a progress, in that his experience accumulates; but the living interest is always something new. He turns to miscellaneous adventures, not excluding love; from that he passes to imperial politics, a sad mess, thence to sentimental classicism, rather an unreality, and finally to war, to public works, to trade, to piracy, to colonization, and to clearing his acquired estates of tiresome old natives, who insist on ringing church bells and are impervious to the new *Kultur*. These public enterprises he finds more satisfying, perhaps only because he dies in the midst of them.

Are these hints of romantic egotism in Goethe mere echoes of his youth and of the ambient philosophy, echoes which he would have rejected if confronted with them in an abstract and doctrinal form, as he rejected the system of Fichte? Would he not have judged Schopenhauer more kindly? Above all, what would he have thought of Nietzsche, his own wild disciple? No doubt he would have wished to buttress and qualify in a thousand ways that faith in absolute Will which they emphasized so exclusively, Schopenhauer in metaphysics and Nietzsche in morals. But the same faith was a deep element in his own genius, as in that of his country, and he would hardly have disowned it.

DICKENS

If Christendom should lose everything that is now in the melting-pot, human life would still remain amiable and quite adequately human. I draw this comforting assurance from the pages of Dickens. Who could not be happy in his world? Yet there is nothing essential to it which the most destructive revolution would be able to destroy. People would still be as different, as absurd, and as charming as are his characters; the springs of kindness and folly in their lives would not be dried up. Indeed, there is much in Dickens which communism, if it came, would only emphasize and render universal. Those schools, those poorhouses, those prisons, with those surviving shreds of family life in them, show us what in the coming age (with some sanitary improvements) would be the nursery and home of everybody. Everybody would be a waif, like Oliver Twist, like Smike, like Pip, and like David Copperfield; and amongst the agents and underlings of social government, to whom all these waifs would be entrusted, there would surely be a goodly sprinkling of Pecksniffs, Squeers's, and Fangs; whilst the Fagins would be everywhere commissioners of the people. Nor would there fail to be, in high places and in low, the occasional sparkle of some Pickwick or Cheeryble Brothers or Sam Weller or Mark Tapley; and the voluble Flora Finchings would be everywhere in evidence, and the strong-minded Betsey Trotwoods in office. There would also be, among the inefficient, many a Dora and Agnes and Little Emily—with her charm but without her tragedy, since this is one of the things which the promised social reform would happily render impossible; I mean, by removing all the disgrace of it. The only element in the world of Dickens which would become obsolete would be the setting, the atmosphere of material instrumentalities and arrangements, as travelling by coach is obsolete; but travelling by rail, by motor, or by airship will emotionally be much the same thing. It is worth noting how such instrumentalities, which absorb modern life, are admired and enjoyed by Dickens, as they were by Homer. The poets ought not to be afraid of them; they exercise the mind congenially, and can be played with joyfully. Consider the black ships and the chariots of Homer, the coaches and river-boats of Dickens, and the aeroplanes of today; to what would an unspoiled young mind turn with more interest? Dickens tells us little of English sports, but he shares the sporting nature of the Englishman, to whom the whole material world is a playing-field, the scene giving ample scope to his love of action, legality, and pleasant achievement. His art is to sport according to the rules of the game, and to do things for the sake of doing them, rather than for any ulterior motive.

It is remarkable, in spite of his ardent simplicity and openness of heart, how insensible Dickens was to the greater themes of the human imagination—religion, science, politics, art. He was a waif himself, and utterly disinherited. For example, the terrible heritage of contentious religions which fills the world seems not to exist for him. In this matter he was like a sensitive child, with a most religious disposition, but no religious ideas. Perhaps, properly speaking, he had no *ideas* on any subject; what he had was a vast sympathetic participation in the daily life of mankind; and what he saw of ancient institutions made him hate them, as needless sources of oppression, misery, selfishness, and rancour. His one political passion was philanthropy, genuine but felt only on its negative, reforming side; of positive utopias or enthusiasms we hear nothing. The political background of Christendom is only, so to speak, an old faded back-drop for his stage; a castle, a frigate, a gallows, and a large female angel with white wings standing above an orphan by an open grave—a decoration which has to serve for all the melodramas in his theatre, intellectually so provincial and poor. Common life as it is lived was varied and lovable enough for Dickens, if only the pests and cruelties could be removed from it. Suffering wounded him, but not vulgarity; whatever pleased his senses and whatever shocked them filled his mind alike with romantic wonder, with the endless delight of observation. Vulgarity—and what can we relish, if we recoil at vulgarity?—was innocent and amusing; in fact, for the humorist, it was the spice of life. There was more piety in being human than in being pious. In reviving Christmas, Dickens transformed it from the celebration of a metaphysical mystery into a feast of overflowing simple kindness and good cheer; the church bells were still there—in the orchestra; and the angels of Bethlehem were still there—painted on the back-curtain. Churches, in his novels, are vague, desolate places where one has ghastly experiences, and where only the pew-opener is human; and such religious and political conflicts as he depicts in *Barnaby Rudge* and in *A Tale of Two Cities* are street brawls and prison scenes and conspiracies in taverns, without any indication of the contrasts in mind or interests between the opposed parties. Nor had Dickens any lively sense for fine art, classical tradition, science, or even the manners and feelings of the upper classes in his own time and country: in his novels we may almost say there is no army, no navy, no Church, no sport, no distant travel, no daring adventure, no feeling for the watery wastes and the motley nations of the planet, and—luckily, with his notion of them—no lords and ladies. Even love of the traditional sort is hardly in Dickens's sphere—I mean the soldierly passion in which a rather rakish gallantry was sobered by devotion, and loyalty rested on pride. In Dickens love is sentimental or benevolent or merry or sneaking or canine; in his last book he was going to describe a love that was passionate and criminal; but love for him was never chivalrous, never poetical. What he paints most tragically is a quasi-paternal devotion in the old to the young, the love of Mr Peggotty for Little Emily, or of Solomon Gills for Walter Gay. A series of shabby little adventures, such as might absorb the interest of an average youth, were romantic enough for Dickens.

I say he was disinherited, but he inherited the most terrible negations. Religion lay on him like the weight of the atmosphere, sixteen pounds to the square inch, yet never noticed nor mentioned. He lived and wrote in the shadow of the most awful prohibitions. Hearts petrified by legality and falsified by worldliness offered, indeed, a good subject for a novelist, and Dickens availed himself of it to the extent of always contrasting natural goodness and happiness with whatever is morose; but his morose people were wicked, not virtuous in their own way; so that the protest of his temperament against his environment never took a radical form nor went back to first principles. He needed to feel, in his writing, that he was carrying the sympathies of every man with him. In him conscience was single, and he could not conceive how it could ever be divided in other men. He denounced scandals without exposing shams, and conformed willingly and scrupulously to the proprieties. Lady Dedlock's secret, for instance, he treats as if it were the sin of Adam, remote, mysterious, inexpiable. Mrs Dombey is not allowed to deceive her husband except by pretending to deceive him. The seduction of Little Emily is left out altogether, with the whole character of Steerforth, the development of which would have been so important in the moral experience of David Copperfield himself. But it is not public prejudice alone that plays the censor over Dickens's art; his own kindness and even weakness of heart act sometimes as marplots. The character of Miss Mowcher, for example, so brilliantly introduced, was evidently intended to be shady, and to play a very important part in the story; but its original in real life, which was recognized, had to be conciliated, and the sequel was omitted and patched up with an apology—itself admirable—for the poor dwarf. Such a sacrifice does honour to Dickens's heart; but artists should meditate on their works in time, and it is easy to remove any too great likeness in a portrait by a few touches making it more consistent than real people are apt to be; and in this case, if the little creature had been really guilty, how much more subtle and tragic her apology for herself might have been, like that of the bastard Edmund in *King Lear*! So, too, in *Dombey and Son*, Dickens could not bear to let Walter Gay turn out badly, as he had been meant to do, and to break his uncle's heart as well as the heroine's; he was accordingly transformed into a stage hero miraculously saved from shipwreck, and Florence was not allowed to reward the admirable Toots, as she should have done, with her trembling hand. But Dickens was no free artist; he had more genius than taste, a warm fancy not aided by a thorough understanding of complex characters. He worked under pressure, for money and applause, and often had to cheapen in execution what his inspiration had so vividly conceived.

What, then, is there left, if Dickens has all these limitations? In our romantic disgust we might be tempted to say, Nothing. But in fact almost everything is left, almost everything that counts in the daily life of mankind, or that by its presence or absence can determine whether life shall be worth living or not; because a simple good life is worth living, and an elaborate bad life is not. There remains in the first place eating and drinking; relished not bestially, but humanly, jovially, as the sane and exhilarating basis for everything else. This is a sound English beginning; but the immediate sequel, as the England of that day presented it to Dickens, is no less delightful. There is the ruddy glow of the hearth; the sparkle of glasses and brasses and well-scrubbed pewter; the savoury fumes of the hot punch, after the tingle of the wintry air; the coaching-scenes, the motley figures and absurd incidents of travel; the changing sights and joys of the road. And then, to balance this, the traffic of ports and cities, the hubbub of crowded streets, the luxury of shop windows and of palaces not to be entered; the procession of the passers-by, shabby or ludicrously genteel; the dingy look and musty smell of their lodgings; the labyrinth of back-alleys, courts, and mews, with their crying children, and scolding old women, and listless, half-drunken loiterers. These sights, like fables, have a sort of moral in them to which Dickens was very sensitive; the important airs of nobodies on great occasions, the sadness and preoccupation of the great as they hasten by in their mourning or on their pressing affairs; the sadly comic characters of the tavern; the diligence of shopkeepers, like squirrels turning in their cages; the children peeping out everywhere like grass in an untrodden street; the charm of humble things, the nobleness of humble people, the horror of crime, the ghastliness of vice, the deft hand and shining face of virtue passing through the midst of it all; and finally a fresh wind of indifference and change blowing across our troubles and clearing the most lurid sky.

I do not know whether it was Christian charity or naturalistic insight, or a mixture of both (for they are closely akin), that attracted Dickens particularly to the deformed, the half-witted, the abandoned, or those impeded or misunderstood by virtue of some singular inner consecration. The visible moral of these things, when brutal prejudice does not blind us to it, comes very near to true philosophy; one turn of the screw, one flash of reflection, and we have understood nature and human morality and the relation between them.

In his love of roads and wayfarers, of river-ports and wharves and the idle or sinister figures that lounge about them, Dickens was like Walt Whitman; and I think a second Dickens may any day appear in America, when it is possible in that land of hurry to reach the same degree of saturation, the same unquestioning pleasure in the familiar facts. The spirit of Dickens would be better able to do justice to America than was that of Walt Whitman; because America, although it may seem nothing but a noisy nebula to the impressionist, is not a nebula but a concourse of very distinct individual bodies, natural and social, each with its definite interests and story. Walt Whitman had a sort of transcendental philosophy which swallowed the universe whole, supposing there was a universal spirit in things identical with the absolute spirit that observed them; but Dickens was innocent of any such claptrap, and remained a true spirit in his own person. Kindly and clear-sighted, but self-identical and unequivocally human, he glided through the slums like one of his own little heroes, uncontaminated by their squalor and confusion, courageous and firm in his clear allegiances amid the flux of things, a pale angel at the Carnival, his heart aflame, his voice always flute-like in its tenderness and warning. This is the true relation of spirit to existence, not the other which confuses them; for this earth (I cannot speak for the universe at large) has no spirit of its own, but brings forth spirits only at certain points, in the hearts and brains of frail living creatures, who like insects flit through it, buzzing and gathering what sweets they can; and it is the spaces they traverse in this career, charged with their own moral burden, that they can report on or describe, not things rolling on to infinity in their vain tides. To be hypnotized by that flood would be a heathen idolatry. Accordingly Walt Whitman, in his comprehensive democratic vistas, could never see the trees for the wood, and remained incapable, for all his diffuse love of the human herd, of ever painting a character or telling a story; the very things in which Dickens was a master. It is this life of the individual, as it may be lived in a given nation, that determines the whole value of that nation to the poet, to the moralist, and to the judicious historian. But for the excellence of the typical single life, no nation deserves to be remembered more than the sands of the sea; and America will not be a success, if every American is a failure.

Dickens entered the theatre of this world by the stage door; the shabby little adventures of the actors in their private capacity replace for him the mock tragedies which they enact before a dreaming public. Mediocrity of circumstances and mediocrity of soul for ever return to the centre of his stage; a more wretched or a grander existence is sometimes broached, but the pendulum soon swings back, and we return, with the relief with which we put on our slippers after the most romantic excursion, to a golden mediocrity—to mutton and beer, and to love and babies in a suburban villa with one frowzy maid. Dickens is the poet of those acres of yellow brick streets which the traveller sees from the railway viaducts as he approaches London; they need a poet, and they deserve one, since a complete human life may very well be lived there. Their little excitements and sorrows, their hopes and humours are like those of the Wooden Midshipman in *Dombey and Son*;

but the sea is not far off, and the sky—Dickens never forgets it—is above all those brief troubles. He had a sentiment in the presence of this vast flatness of human fates, in spite of their individual pungency, which I think might well be the dominant sentiment of mankind in the future; a sense of happy freedom in littleness, an open-eyed reverence and religion without words. This universal human anonymity is like a sea, an infinite democratic desert, chock-full and yet the very image of emptiness, with nothing in it for the mind, except, as the Moslems say, the presence of Allah. Awe is the counterpart of humility—and this is perhaps religion enough. The atom in the universal vortex ought to be humble; he ought to see that, materially, he doesn't much matter, and that morally his loves are merely his own, without authority over the universe. He can admit without obloquy that he is what he is; and he can rejoice in his own being, and in that of all other things in so far as he can share it sympathetically. The apportionment of existence and of fortune is in Other Hands; his own portion is contentment, vision, love, and laughter.

Having humility, that most liberating of sentiments, having a true vision of human existence and joy in that vision, Dickens had in a superlative degree the gift of humour, of mimicry, of unrestrained farce. He was the perfect comedian. When people say Dickens exaggerates, it seems to me they can have no eyes and no ears. They probably have only *notions* of what things and people are; they accept them conventionally, at their diplomatic value. Their minds run on in the region of discourse, where there are masks only and no faces, ideas and no facts; they have little sense for those living grimaces that play from moment to moment upon the countenance of the world. The world is a perpetual caricature of itself; at every moment it is the mockery and the contradiction of what it is pretending to be. But as it nevertheless intends all the time to be something different and highly dignified, at the next moment it corrects and checks and tries to cover up the absurd thing it was; so that a conventional world, a world of masks, is superimposed on the reality, and passes in every sphere of human interest for the reality itself. Humour is the perception of this illusion, the fact allowed to pierce here and there through the convention, whilst the convention continues to be maintained, as if we had not observed its absurdity. Pure comedy is more radical, cruder, in a certain sense less human; because comedy throws the convention over altogether, revels for a moment in the fact, and brutally says to the notions of mankind, as if it slapped them in the face, There, take that! That's what you really are! At this the polite world pretends to laugh, not tolerantly as it does at humour, but a little angrily. It does not like to see itself by chance in the glass, without having had time to compose its features for demure self-contemplation. 'What a bad mirror,' it exclaims; 'it must be concave or convex; for surely I never looked like that. Mere caricature, farce, and horse play. Dickens exaggerates; *I* never was so sentimental as that; *I* never say anything so dreadful; *I* don't believe there were ever any people like Quilp, or Squeers, or Serjeant Buzfuz.' But the polite world is lying; there *are* such people; we are such people ourselves in our true moments, in our veritable impulses; but we are careful to stifle and to hide those moments from ourselves and from the world; to purse and pucker ourselves into the mask of our conventional personality; and so simpering, we profess that it is very coarse and inartistic of Dickens to undo our life's work for us in an instant, and remind us of what we are. And as to other people, though we may allow that considered superficially they are often absurd, we do not wish to dwell on their eccentricities, nor to mimic them. On the contrary, it is good manners to look away quickly, to suppress a smile, and to say to ourselves that the ludicrous figure in the street is not at all comic, but a dull ordinary Christian, and that it is foolish to give any importance to the fact that its hat has blown off, that it has slipped on an orange-peel and unintentionally sat on the pavement, that it has a pimple on its nose, that its one tooth projects over its lower lip, that it is angry with things in general, and that it is looking everywhere for the penny which it holds tightly in its hand. That may fairly represent the moral condition of most of us at most times; but we do not want to think of it; we do not want to see; we gloss the fact over; we console ourselves before we are grieved, and reassert our composure before we have laughed. We are afraid, ashamed, anxious to be spared. What displeases us in Dickens is that he does not spare us; he mimics things to the full; he dilates and exhausts and repeats; he wallows. He is too intent on the passing experience to look over his shoulder, and consider whether we have not already understood, and had enough. He is not thinking of us; he is obeying the impulse of the passion, the person, or the story he is enacting. This faculty, which renders him a consummate comedian, is just what alienated from him a later generation in which people of taste were aesthetes and virtuous people were higher snobs; they wanted a mincing art, and he gave them copious improvisation, they wanted analysis and development, and he gave them absolute comedy. I must confess, though the fault is mine and not his, that sometimes his absoluteness is too much for me. When I come to the death of Little Nell, or to What the Waves were always Saying, or even to the incorrigible perversities of the pretty Dora, I skip. I can't take my liquor neat in such draughts, and my inner man says to Dickens, Please don't. But then I am a coward in so many ways! There are so many things in this world that I skip, as I skip the undiluted Dickens! When I reach Dover on a rough day, I wait there until the Channel is smoother; am I not travelling for pleasure? But my prudence does not blind me to the admirable virtue of the sailors that cross in all weathers, nor even to the automatic determination of the sea-sick ladies, who might so easily have followed my example, if they were not the slaves of their railway tickets and of their labelled luggage. They are loyal to their tour, and I to my philosophy. Yet, as wrapped in my greatcoat and sure of a good dinner I pace the windy pier and soliloquize, I feel the superiority of the bluff tar, glad of breeze, stretching a firm arm to the unsteady passenger, and watching with a masterful thrill of emotion the home cliffs receding and the foreign coasts ahead. It is only courage (which Dickens had without knowing it) and universal kindness (which he knew he had) that are requisite to nerve us for a true vision of this world. And as some of us are cowards about crossing the Channel, and others about 'crossing the bar', so almost everybody is a coward about his own humanity. We do not consent to be absurd, though absurd we are. We have no fundamental humility. We do not wish the moments of our lives to be caught by a quick eye in their grotesque initiative, and to be pilloried in this way before our own eyes. For that reason we don't like Dickens, and don't like comedy, and don't like the truth. Dickens could don the comic mask with innocent courage; he could wear it with a grace, ease, and irresistible vivacity seldom given to men. We must go back for anything like it to the very greatest comic poets, to Shakespeare or to Aristophanes. Who else, for instance, could have penned this:

> 'It was all Mrs Bumble. She *would* do it', urged Mr Bumble; first looking round to ascertain that his partner had left the room.
>
> 'That is no excuse,' replied Mr Brownlow. 'You were present on the occasion of the destruction of these trinkets, and indeed are the more guilty of the two, in the eye of the law; for the law supposes that your wife acts under your direction.'
>
> 'If the law supposes that,' said Mr Bumble, squeezing his hat emphatically in both hands, 'the law is a ass, a idiot. If that's the eye of the law, the law is a bachelor; and the worst I wish the law is, that his eye may be opened by experience—by experience.'
>
> Laying great stress on the repetition of these two words, Mr Bumble fixed his hat on very tight, and putting his hands in his pockets, followed his helpmate downstairs.

This is high comedy; the irresistible, absurd, intense dream of the old fool, personifying the law in order to convince and punish it. I can understand that this sort of thing should not be common in English literature, nor much relished; because pure comedy is scornful, merciless, devastating, holding no door open to anything beyond. Cultivated English feeling winces at this brutality, although the common people love it in clowns and in puppet shows; and I think they are right. Dickens, who surely was tender enough, had so irresistible a comic genius that it carried him beyond the gentle humour which most Englishmen possess to the absolute grotesque reality. Squeers, for instance, when he sips the wretched dilution which he has prepared for his starved and shivering little pupils, smacks his lips and cries: 'Here's richness!' It is savage comedy; humour would come in if we understood (what Dickens does not tell us) that the little creatures were duly impressed and thought the thin liquid truly delicious. I suspect that English sensibility prefers the humour and wit of Hamlet to the pure comedy of Falstaff; and that even in Aristophanes it seeks consolation in the lyrical poetry for the flaying of human life in the comedy itself. Tastes are free; but we should not deny that in merciless and rollicking comedy life is caught in the act. The most grotesque creatures of Dickens are not exaggerations or mockeries of something other than themselves; they arise because nature generates them, like toadstools; they exist because they can't help it, as we all do. The fact that these perfectly self-justified beings are absurd appears only by comparison, and from outside; circumstances, or the expectations of other people, make them ridiculous and force them to contradict themselves; but in nature it is no crime to be exceptional. Often, but for the savagery of the average man, it would not even be a misfortune. The sleepy fat boy in *Pickwick* looks foolish; but in himself he is no more foolish, nor less solidly self-justified, than a pumpkin lying on the ground. Toots seems ridiculous; and we laugh heartily at his incoherence, his beautiful waistcoats, and his extreme modesty; but when did anybody more obviously grow into what he is because he couldn't grow otherwise? So with Mr Pickwick, and Sam Weller, and Mrs Gamp, and Micawber, and all the rest of this wonderful gallery; they are ridiculous only by accident, and in a context in which they never intended to appear. If Oedipus and Lear and Cleopatra do not seem ridiculous, it is only because tragic reflection has taken them out of the context in which, in real life, they would have figured. If we saw them as facts, and not as emanations of a poet's dream, we should laugh at them till doomsday; what grotesque presumption, what silly whims, what mad contradiction of the simplest realities! Yet we should not laugh at them without feeling how real their griefs were; as real and terrible as the griefs of children and of dreams. But facts, however serious inwardly, are always absurd outwardly; and the just critic of life sees both truths at once, as Cervantes did in *Don Quixote*. A pompous idealist who does not see the ridiculous in *all* things is the dupe of his sympathy and abstraction; and a clown who does not see that these ridiculous creatures are living quite in earnest is the dupe of his egotism. Dickens saw the absurdity, and understood the life; I think he was a good philosopher.

It is usual to compare Dickens with Thackeray, which is like comparing the grape with the gooseberry; there are obvious points of resemblance, and the gooseberry has some superior qualities of its own; but you can't make red wine of it. The wine of Dickens is of the richest, the purest, the sweetest, the most fortifying to the blood; there is distilled in it, with the perfection of comedy, the perfection of morals. I do not mean, of course, that Dickens appreciated all the values that human life has or might have; that is beyond any man. Even the greatest philosophers, such as Aristotle, have not always much imagination to conceive forms of happiness or folly other than those which their age or their temperament reveals to them; their insight runs only to discovering the *principle* of happiness, that it is spontaneous life of any sort harmonized with circumstances. The sympathies and imagination of Dickens, vivid in their sphere, were no less limited in range; and of course it was not his business to find philosophic formulas; nevertheless I call his the perfection of morals for two reasons: that he put the distinction between good and evil in the right place, and that he felt this distinction intensely. A moralist might have excellent judgment, he might see what sort of life is spontaneous in a given being and how far it may be harmonized with circumstances, yet his heart might remain cold, he might not suffer nor rejoice with the suffering or joy he foresaw. Humanitarians like Bentham and Mill, who talked about the greatest happiness of the greatest number, might conceivably be moral prigs in their own persons, and they might have been chilled to the bone in their theoretic love of mankind, if they had had the wit to imagine in what, as a matter of fact, the majority would place their happiness. Even if their theory had been correct (which I think it was in intention, though not in statement) they would then not have been perfect moralists, because their maxims would not have expressed their hearts. In expressing their hearts, they ought to have embraced one of those forms of 'idealism' by which men fortify themselves in their bitter passions or in their helpless commitments; for they do not wish mankind to be happy in its own way, but in theirs. Dickens was not one of those moralists who summon every man to do himself the greatest violence so that he may not offend them, nor defeat their ideals. Love of the good of others is something that shines in every page of Dickens with a truly celestial splendour. How entirely limpid is his sympathy with life—a sympathy uncontaminated by dogma or pedantry or snobbery or bias of any kind! How generous is this keen, light spirit, how pure this open heart! And yet, in spite of this extreme sensibility, not the least wobbling; no deviation from a just severity of judgment, from an uncompromising distinction between white and black. And this happens as it ought to happen; sympathy is not checked by a flatly contrary prejudice or commandment, by some categorical imperative irrelevant to human nature; the check, like the cheer, comes by tracing the course of spontaneous impulse amid circumstances that inexorably lead it to success or to failure. There is a bed to this stream, freely as the water may flow; when it comes to this precipice it must leap, when it runs over these pebbles it must sing, and when it spreads into that marsh it must become livid and malarial. The very sympathy with human impulse quickens in Dickens the sense of danger; his very joy in joy makes him stern to what kills it. How admirably drawn are his surly villains! No rhetorical vilification of them, as in a sermon; no exaggeration of their qualms or fears; rather a sense of how obvious and human all their courses seem from their own point of view; and yet no sentimental apology for them, no romantic worship of rebels in their madness or crime. The pity of it, the waste of it all, are seen not by a second vision but by the same original vision which revealed the lure and the drift of the passion. Vice is a monster here of such sorry mien that the longer we see it the more we deplore it; that other sort of vice which Pope found so seductive was perhaps only some innocent impulse artificially suppressed, and called a vice because it broke out inconveniently and displeased the company. True vice is human nature strangled by the suicide of attempting the impossible. Those so self-justified villains of Dickens never elude their fates. Bill Sikes is not let off, neither is Nancy; the oddly benevolent Magwitch does not escape from the net, nor does the unfortunate young Richard Carstone, victim of the Circumlocution Office. The horror and ugliness of their fall are rendered with the hand of a master; we see here, as in the world, that in spite of the romanticists it is not virtue to rush enthusiastically along any road. I think Dickens is one of the best friends mankind has ever had. He has held the mirror up to nature, and of its reflected fragments has composed a fresh world, where the men and women differ from real people only in that they live in a literary medium, so that all ages and places may know them. And they are worth knowing, just as one's neighbours are, for their picturesque characters and their pathetic fates. Their names should be in every child's mouth; they ought to be adopted members of every household. Their stories cause the merriest and the sweetest chimes to ring in the fancy, without confusing our moral judgment or alienating our interest from the motley commonplaces of daily life. In every English-speaking home, in the four quarters of the globe, parents and children will do well to read Dickens aloud of a winter's evening; they will love winter, and one another, and God the better for it. What a wreath that will be of ever-fresh holly, thick with bright berries, to hang to this poet's memory—the very crown he would have chosen!

A CONTRAST WITH SPANISH DRAMA

In classical Spanish drama the masks are few. The characters hardly have individual names. The lady in Calderón, for instance, if she is not Beatriz will be Leonor, and under either name so superlatively beautiful, young, chaste, eloquent, devoted, and resourceful, as to be indistinguishable from her namesakes in the other plays. The hero is always exaggeratedly in love, exaggeratedly chivalrous, and absolutely perfect, save for this heroic excess of sensitiveness and honour. The old father is always austere, unyielding, perverse, and sublime. All the maids in attendance possess the same roguishness, the same genius for intrigue and lightning mendacity; whilst the valet, whether called Crispin or Florin, is always a faithful soul and a coward, with the same quality of rather forced humour. No diversity from play to play save the diversity in the fable, in the angle at which the stock characters are exhibited and the occasion on which they versify; for they all versify in the same style, with the same inexhaustible facility, abundance, rhetorical finish, and lyric fire.

Why this monotony? Did Spanish life afford fewer contrasts, less individuality of character and idiom, than did the England of Shakespeare? Hardly: in Spain the soldier of fortune, the grandee, peasant, monk, or prelate, the rogue, beggar, and bandit were surely as highly characterized as anything to be then found in England; and Spanish women in their natural ardour of affection, in their ready speech and discretion, in their dignity and religious consecration, lent themselves rather better, one would think, to the making of heroines than did those comparatively cool and boy-like young ladies whom Shakespeare transmuted into tragic angels. I think we may go further and say positively that it was Spain rather than England that could have shown the spectacle of 'every man in his humour'.

Even in the days before Puritanism English character was English; it tended to silent independence and outward reserve, preferring to ignore its opposite rather than to challenge it. In pose and expression the Spaniard is naturally more theatrical and pungent; and his individuality itself is stiffer. No doubt, in society, he will simulate and dissimulate as an Englishman never would; but he is prompted to this un-English habit by the very fixity of his purposes; all his courtesy and loyalty are ironical, and inwardly he never yields an inch. He likes if possible to be statuesque; he likes to appeal to his own principles and character, and to say, 'Sir, whatever you may think of it, that is the sort of man I am.' He has that curious form of self-love which inclines to parade even its defects, as a mourner parades his grief. He admits readily that he is a sinner, and that he means to remain one; he composes his countenance proudly on that basis; whereas when English people say they are miserable sinners (which happens only in church) they feel perhaps that they are imperfect or unlucky, and they may even contemplate being somewhat different in future; but it never occurs to them to classify themselves as miserable sinners for good, with a certain pride in their class, deliberately putting on the mask of Satan or the cock's feather of Mephistopheles and saying to all concerned, 'See what a very devil I am!' The Englishman's sins are slips; he feels he was not himself on those occasions, and does not think it fair to be reminded of them. Though theology may sometimes have taught him that he is a sinner fundamentally, such is not his native conviction; the transcendental ego in him cannot admit any external standard to which it ought to have conformed. The Spaniard is metaphysically humbler, knowing himself to be a creature of accident and fate; yet he is dramatically more impudent, and respects himself more than he respects other people. He laughs at kings; and as amongst beggars it is etiquette to whine, and ostentatiously to call oneself blind, old, poor, crippled, hungry, and a brother of yours, so amongst avowed sinners it may become a point of pride to hold, as it were, the record as a liar, a thief, an assassin, or a harlot. These roles are disgraceful when one is reduced to them by force of circumstances or for some mean ulterior motive, but they recover their human dignity when one wears them as a chosen mask in the comedy of life. The pose, at that angle, redeems the folly, and the façade the building. Nor is this a lapse into sheer immorality; there is many a primitive or animal level of morality beneath the conventional code; and often crime and barbarism are as proud of themselves as virtue, and no less punctilious. If there is effrontery in such a rebellion, there may be also sincerity, courage, relief, profound truth to one's own nature. Hence the eloquence of romanticism. Passion and wilfulness (which romanticists think are above criticism) cannot be expected to understand that, if they merged and subsided into a harmony, the life distilled out of their several deaths would be infinitely more living and varied than any of them, and would be beautiful and perfect to boot; whereas the romantic chaos which they prolong by their obstinacy is the most hideous of hells. But avowed sinners and proud romanticists insist on preserving and on loving hell, because they insist on loving and preserving themselves.

It was not, then, moral variety that was lacking in Spain, always a romantic country, but only interest in moral variety. This lack of interest was itself an expression of romantic independence, intensity, and pride. The gentleman with his hand always on the hilt of his sword, lest some whiff from anywhere should wound his vanity, or the monk perpetually murmuring *memento mori*, closed his mind to every alien vista. Of course he knew that the world was full of motley characters: that was one of his reasons for holding it at arm's length. What were those miscellaneous follies to him but an offence or a danger? Why should he entertain his leisure in depicting or idealizing them? If some psychological zoologist cared to discant on the infinity of phenomena, natural or moral, well and good; but how should such things charm a man of honour, a Christian, or a poet? They might indeed be referred to on occasion, as fabulists make the animals speak, with a humorous and satirical intention, as a sort of warning and confirmation to us in our chosen path; but an appealing poet, for such tightly integrated minds, must illustrate and enforce their personal feelings. Moreover, although in words and under the spell of eloquence the Spaniard may often seem credulous and enthusiastic, he is disillusioned and cynical at heart; he does not credit the existence of motives or feelings better than those he has observed, or thinks he has observed. His preachers recommend religion chiefly by composing invectives against the world, and his political writers express sympathy with one foreign country only out of hatred for another, or perhaps for their own. The sphere of distrust and indifference begins for him very near home; he has little speculative sympathy with life at large; he is cruel to animals; he shrugs his shoulders at crime in high places; he feels little responsibility to the public, and has small faith in time and in work. This does not mean in the least that his character is weak or his morality lax within its natural range; his affections are firm, his sense of obligation deep, his delicacy of feeling often excessive; he is devoted to his family, and will put himself to any inconvenience to do a favour to a friend at the public expense. There are definite things to which his sentiments and habits have pledged him: beyond that horizon nothing speaks to his heart.

Such a people will not go to the play to be vaguely entertained, as if they were previously bored. They are not habitually bored; they are full to the brim of their characteristic passions and ideas. They require that the theatre should set forth these passions and ideas as brilliantly and convincingly as possible, in order to be confirmed in them, and to understand and develop them more clearly. Variety of plot and landscape they will relish, because nothing is easier for them than to imagine themselves born in the purple, or captive, or in love, or in a difficult dilemma of honour; and they will be deeply moved to see some constant spirit, like their own, buffeted by fortune, but even in the last extremity never shaken. The whole force of their dramatic art will lie in leading them to dream of themselves in a different, perhaps more glorious, position, in which their latent passions might be more splendidly expressed. These passions are intense and exceptionally definite; and this is the reason, I think, for the monotony of Spanish music, philosophy, and romantic drama. All eloquence, all issues, all sentiments, if they are not to seem vapid and trivial, must be such as each man can make his own, with a sense of enhanced vitality and moral glory. The lady, if he is to warm to her praises, must not be less divine than the one he loves, or might have loved; the hero must not fall short of what, under such circumstances, he himself would have wished to be. The language, too, must always be worthy of the theme: it cannot be too rapturous and eloquent. Unless his soul can be fired by the poet's words, and can sing them, as it were, in chorus, he will not care to listen to them. But he will not tire of the same cadences or the same images—stars, foam, feathers, flowers—if these symbols, better than any others, transport him into the ethereal atmosphere which it is his pleasure to breathe.

The Spanish nation boils the same peas for its dinner the whole year round; it has only one religion, if it has any; the pious part of it recites the same prayers fifty or one hundred and fifty times daily, almost in one breath; the gay and sentimental part never ceases to sing the same *jotas* and *malagueñas*. Such constancy is admirable. If a dish is cheap, nutritious, and savoury on Monday, it must be so on Tuesday, too; it was a ridiculous falsehood, though countenanced by some philosophers, which pretended that always to feel (or to eat) the same thing was equivalent to never feeling (or eating) anything. Nor does experience of a genuine good really have any tendency to turn it into an evil, or into an indifferent thing; at most, custom may lead people to take it for granted, and the thoughtless may forget its value, until, perhaps, they lose it. Of course, men and nations may slowly change their nature, and consequently their rational preferences; but at any assigned time a man must have some moral complexion, or if he has none, not much need be said about him.

But there is another point to be considered. Need human

nature's daily food be exclusively the Spanish pea? Might it not just as well be rice, or polenta, or even beef and bacon? Much as I admire my countrymen's stomachs for making a clear choice and for sticking to it, I rather pity them for the choice they have made. That hard yellow pea is decidedly heavy, flatulent, and indigestible. I am sure Pythagoras would not have approved of it; possibly it is the very bean he abhorred. Against the *jota* and the *malagueña* I can say nothing; I find in them I know not what infinite, never-failing thrill and inimitable power, the power which perfection of any kind always has; yet what are they in comparison to all the possibilities of human music? Enjoyment, which some people call criticism, is something aesthetic, spontaneous, and irresponsible; the aesthetic perfection of anything is incommensurable with that of anything else. But there is a responsible sort of criticism which is political and moral, and which turns on the human advantage of possessing or loving this or that sort of perfection. To cultivate some sorts may be useless or even hostile to the possible perfection of human life. Spanish religion, again, is certainly most human and most superhuman; but its mystic virtue to the devotee cannot alter the fact that, on a broad view, it appears to be a romantic *tour de force*, a desperate illusion, fostered by premature despair and by a total misunderstanding of nature and history. Finally, those lyrical ladies and entranced gentlemen of the Spanish drama are like filigree flowers upon golden stems; they belong to a fantastic ballet, to an exquisite dream, rather than to sane human society. The trouble is not that their types are few and constant, but that these types are eccentric, attenuated, and forced. They would not be monotonous if they were adequate to human nature. How vast, how kindly, how enveloping does the world of Shakespeare seem in comparison! We seem to be afloat again on the tide of time, in a young, green world; we are ready to tempt new fortunes, in the hope of reaching better things than we know. And this is the right spirit; because although the best, if it had been attained, would be all-sufficient, the best is not yet.

TRAGIC PHILOSOPHY

In comparing a passage from *Macbeth*[1] with one from the *Paradiso*, Mr T. S. Eliot tells us that poetically the two are equally good, but that the philosophy in Shakespeare is in-inferior. By what standard, I am tempted to ask, may the poetic value of different types of poetry in different languages be declared equal? By the equal satisfaction, perhaps, that fills the critic's mind? But the total allegiance of a mature person, his total joy in anything, can hardly be independent of his developed conscience and his sense for ultimate realities. He cannot be utterly enchanted by what he feels to be trivial or false. And if he is not utterly enchanted, how should he recognize the presence of the supremely beautiful? Two passages could hardly be pronounced equal in poetic force if the ultimate suggestions of the one were felt to be inferior to those of the other.

Admitting, then, that poetry expressing an inferior philosophy would to that extent be inferior poetry, we may ask this further question: In what respect other than truth may philosophies be called inferior or superior? Perhaps in being more or less poetical or religious, more or less inspired? Sometimes a philosophy may spring up imaginatively, and in that sense may be inspired rather than strictly reasoned or observed, as the myths of Plato are inspired; but nobody would call such inspired philosophy *superior* unless he felt it to spring from the total needs and total wisdom of the heart; and in that case he would certainly believe, or at least hope, that this superior philosophy was true. How then should the poetic expression of this inspired philosophy not be conspicuously superior as poetry, and more utterly enchanting, than the expression of any other philosophy?

[1] In fact from *King Lear*. See 'Shakespeare and the Stocism of Seneca' (T. S. Eliot, *Selected Essays* (London, 1932), pp. 136–7). Santayana would seem to have in mind as well a passage from Eliot's essay on *Dante*, where lines from the *Inferno* and from *Macbeth* are discussed in terms of the 'medium' (*Selected Essays*, p. 241).

Let me postpone generalities, and turn to the passages in question.

Lady Macbeth is dead. Macbeth foresees his own end. All the prophecies flattering his ambition have been fulfilled, and after the mounting horror of his triumph he stands at the brink of ruin. Surveying the whole in a supreme moment, he consents to his destiny.

> To-morrow, and to-morrow, and to-morrow,
> Creeps in this petty pace from day to day,
> To the last syllable of recorded time;
> And all our yesterdays have lighted fools
> The way to dusty death. Out, out, brief candle!
> Life's but a walking shadow, a poor player
> That struts and frets his hour upon the stage
> And then is heard no more: it is a tale
> Told by an idiot, full of sound and fury,
> Signifying nothing.

Mr Eliot says that this philosophy is derived from Seneca; and it is certain that in Seneca's tragedies, if not in his treatises, there is a pomp of diction, a violence of pose, and a suicidal despair not unlike the tone of this passage. But would Seneca ever have said that life signifies nothing? It signified for him the universal reign of law, of reason, of the will of God. Fate was inhuman, it was cruel, it excited and crushed every finite wish; yet there was something in man that shared that disdain for humanity, and triumphed in that ruthless march of order and necessity. Something superior, not inferior, Seneca would have said; something that not only raised the mind into sympathy with the truth of nature and the decrees of heaven, but that taught the blackest tragedy to sing in verse. The passions in foreseeing their defeat became prophets, in remembering it became poets; and they created the noblest beauties by defying and transcending death.

In Seneca this tragic philosophy, though magnificent, seems stilted and forced; it struts rhetorically like an army of hoplites treading down the green earth. He was the last of ancient tragedians, the most aged and withered in his titanic strength; but all his predecessors, from Homer down, had proclaimed the same tragic truths, softened but not concealed by their richer medium. Some of them, like Virgil, had rendered those truths even more poignant precisely by being more sensitive to the loveliness of perishable things. After all, the same inhuman power that crushes us, breeds us and feeds us; life and death are but two aspects of the same natural mutation, the same round of seed-time and harvest. And if all human passions must be fugitive, they need not all be unamiable: some are merry in their prime, and even smile at their own fading. An accident of ritual led the ancients to divide tragedy sharply from comedy; I think it has been a happy return to nature in modern dramatists and novelists to intermingle the two. Comic episodes abound in the most tragic experience, if only we have the wit to see them; and even the tragic parts are in reality relieved by all sorts of compensations that stimulate our sense of life and prompt us to high reflection. What greater pleasure than a tear that pays homage to something beautiful and deepens the sense of our own profundity?

Not every part of this classic philosophy re-echoes in the pessimism of Macbeth. Shakespeare was not expressing, like Seneca, a settled doctrine of his own or of his times. Like an honest miscellaneous dramatist, he was putting into the mouths of his different characters the sentiments that, for the moment, were suggested to him by their predicaments. Macbeth, who is superstitious and undecided, storms excessively when he storms; there is something feverish and wild in his starts of passion, as there is something delicate in his perceptions. Shakespeare could give rein in such a character to his own subtle fancy in diction and by-play, as well as in the main to the exaggerated rhetoric proper to a stage where everybody was expected to declaim, to argue, and to justify sophistically this or that extravagant impulse. So at this point in *Macbeth*, where Seneca would have unrolled the high maxims of orthodox Stoicism, Shakespeare gives us the humours of his distracted hero; a hero nonplussed, confounded, stultified in his own eyes, a dying gladiator, a blinded lion at bay. And yet intellectually—and this is the tragedy of it—Macbeth is divinely human, rational enough to pause and survey his own agony, and see how brutish, how insignificant, it is. He sees no escape, no alternative; he cannot rise morally above himself; his philosophy is that there is no philosophy, because, in fact, he is incapable of any.

Shakespeare was a professional actor, a professional dramatist; his greatness lay there, and in the gift of the gab: in that exuberance and joy in language which everybody had in that age, but he supremely. The Renaissance needed no mastering living religion, no mastering living philosophy. Life was gayer without them. Philosophy and religion were at best like travels and wars, matters for the adventurer to plunge into, or for the dramatist to describe; never in England or for Shakespeare central matters even in that capacity, but mere conventions or tricks of fancy or moods in individuals. Even in a Hamlet, a Prospero or a Jacques, in a Henry VI or an Isabella, the poet feels no inner loyalty to the convictions he rehearses; they are like the cap and bells of his fools; and possibly if he had been pressed by some tiresome friend to propound a personal philosophy, he might have found in his irritation nothing else to fall back upon than the animal despair of Macbeth. Fortunately we may presume that burgherly comfort and official orthodoxy saved him from being unreasonably pressed.

That which a mastering living philosophy or religion can be, we may see at once by turning to the passage from Dante. In the lowest circle of Paradise, that of the inconstant moon, dwells the spirit of Piccarda, a lady who, having once been a nun but having been carried off and married by force, when later she became a widow preferred to continue her life in the world rather than return to her convent. Dante asks her if those who dwell in this part of Heaven ever desire to go higher, so as to see more and to love more. And she replies, No: for the essence of religious love is union with the order of creation. Perfect happiness would be impossible, if we were not perfectly happy in what God has given us; and in his will is our peace.

> 'Frate, la nostra volontà quieta
> Virtù di carità, che fa volerne
> Sol quel ch'avemo, e d'altro non ci asseta.
> Se disiassimo esser più superne,
> Foran discordi li nostri disiri
> Dal voler di colui che qui ne cerne;
> Che vedrai non capere in questi giri,
> S'essere in caritate è qui *necesse*,
> E se la sua natura ben rimiri.
> Anzi è formale ad esto beato *esse*
> Tenersi, dentro alla divina voglia,
> Per ch'una fansi nostre voglie stesse.
> Sì che, come noi sem di soglia in soglia
> Per questo regno, a tutto il regno piace,
> Com' allo re ch'a suo voler ne invoglia.
> E la sua volontate è nostra pace:
> Ell'è quel mare al qual tutto si move
> Ciò ch'ella crea e che natura face.'
> Chiaro mi fu allor com' ogni dove
> In cielo è Paradiso, e sì la grazia
> Del sommo ben d'un modo non vi piove.

I questioned at the beginning whether the poetic value of unlike things could be pronounced equal: and if now I compare this whole passage with the passage from *Macbeth* I find that to my sense they are incommensurable. Both are notable passages, if that is all that was meant; but they belong to different poetic worlds, appealing to and developing different sides of the mind. And there is more than disparity between these two worlds; there is contrariety and hostility between them, inasmuch as each professes to include and to subordinate the other, and in so doing to annul its tragic dignity and moral finality. For the mood of Macbeth, religion and philosophy are insane vapours; for the mood of Dante, Macbeth is possessed by the devil. There is no possible common ground, no common criterion of truth, and no common criterion even of taste or beauty. We might at best say that both poets succeed in conveying what they wish to convey, and that in that sense their skill is equal: but I hardly think this is true in fact, because in Shakespeare the medium is rich and thick and more important than the idea; whereas in Dante the medium is as unvarying and simple as possible, and meant to be transparent. Even in this choice passage, there are stretches of pure scholastic reasoning, not poetical at all to our sensuous and romantic apprehension; yet the studious and rapt poet feels himself carried on those wings of logic into a paradise of truth, where choir answers choir, and everything is beautiful. A clear and transparent medium is admirable, when we love what we have to say; but when what we have to say is nothing previously definite, expressiveness depends on stirring the waters deeply, suggesting a thousand half-thoughts, and letting the very unutterableness of our passion become manifest in our disjointed words. The medium then becomes dominant: but can this be called success in expression? It is rather success in making an impression, if the reader is impressed; and this effect seems essentially incomparable with that of pure lucidity and tireless exact versification in one chosen form. To our insecure, distracted, impatient minds, the latter hardly seems poetry.

Voltaire said that Dante's reputation was safe, because nobody read him. Nowadays that is hardly true; all superior persons read him a little, or read a great deal about him. He sets tempting problems for professional critics and antiquarians, and he appeals to archaistic taste, that flies for refuge into the fourth dimension, to everything that seems pure and primitive. But as living poetry, as a mould and stimulus for honest feeling, is Dante for us at all comparable to Shakespeare? Shakespeare, in passages such as this from *Macbeth*, is orchestrated. He trills away into fancy: what was daylight a moment ago, suddenly becomes a candle: we are not thinking or reasoning, we are dreaming. He needs but to say 'all our yesterdays', and presently the tedium of childhood, the tedium of labour and illness, the vacancy of friendships lost, rise like vague ghosts before us, and fill us with a sense of the unreality of all that once seemed most real. When he mentions 'a poor player' we think at once of the poet himself, because our minds are biographical and our sympathies novelesque; we feel the misery and the lurid contrasts of a comedian's life; and the existence that just now seemed merely vain, now seems also tempestuous and bitter. And the rhythms help; the verse struts and bangs, holds our attention suspended, obliges our thoughts to become rhetorical, and brings our declamation round handsomely to a grand finale. We should hardly have found courage in ourselves for so much passion and theatricality; but we bless Shakespeare for enabling us still to indulge in such emotions, and to relieve ourselves of a weight that we hardly knew we were carrying.

Nothing of the sort in the Italian: the simplest language, the humble vernacular, made pungent and to us often obscure only by an excess of concision and familiarity, or by allusions to events then on everybody's tongue. Dante allows his personal fortunes and hatreds to crop out in many places, perhaps quickening the interest of the modern gossip-loving reader. Yet these are incidental indiscretions, which the poet's own conscience might have regarded as blemishes. His work as a whole, and in intention, is that of a consecrated mind. A single thread of thought guides him; the eye is focused on pure truth, on human wills illustrating the divine laws against which they profess to rebel; hell in the heart of earth, and earth enveloped in celestial harmonies. No occasion, as in modern edifying works, to avoid mentioning things unpleasant or to explain them away. Every detail is noted, not bashfully or apologetically but with zest; when anything is wicked, its wickedness is exhibited and proved for our instruction. We learn the scientific complexity of the moral world, all plain facts, demonstrable truths, principles undoubted and certified. Mastered and chastened by this divine dispensation, what need should we feel of verbal opulence or lurid rhetoric? Not one rare epithet, not one poetic plum; instead, a childlike intellectual delight in everything being exact, limpid, and duly named, and dovetailed perfectly into everything else. Each word, each rhyme, files dutifully by in procession, white verses, three abreast, like choristers, holding each his taper and each singing in turn his appointed note. But what sweetness in this endless fugue, what simple exactitude, what devout assurance; and how unanimously these humble voices, often harsh and untutored if taken singly, rise together into a soaring canticle! The poetry, you might say, of industrious children, careful to make no mistake, but having nothing of their own to say, or not daring to say it. And indeed Dante's mind is busy, learned, and intense; exact even in allegory, as in a sort of heraldry; yet this very minuteness and pedantry are the work of love. Never was heart more tender or subtle or passionate; only that its intensity is all turned towards metaphysical joys, and transferred to an inward spiritual heaven.

I doubt whether either the beauty or the weakness of such poetry can be understood without understanding the nature of religion, as neither religious people nor irreligious people are likely to do; not the irreligious, because of insensibility, and not the religious, because of delusion. Still, a disinterested student, say of the origins of Christianity, ought to understand. Religion is not essentially a supplement to common knowledge or natural affection on the same level as the latter: it is not essentially a part of rational life, adjusted however gropingly to cosmic or social influences, and expressing them and their effects. Religion is rather a second life, native to the soul, developed there independently of all evidence, like a waking dream: not like dreams coming in sleep and composed largely of distorted waking impressions, but an autonomous other life, such as we have also in music, in games, and in imaginative love. In religion the soul projects out of her own impulses, especially when these are thwarted, the conditions under which she will regard herself as living. If she needs salvation, she will posit a saviour; if the thought of death offends her, she will posit resurrection or even immortality; if she is troubled at the injustice of fortune, she will posit previous crimes or original sins of her own, to explain her misery. If in general she wishes to impose her will where she is impotent, she will utter that will in prayers or imprecations, and posit an invisible power inclined to listen, and able to help.

Now such an inner fountain of life and thought is evidently akin to poetic inspiration. As in poetry, so in religion, imagination evokes a more or less systematic invisible world in which the passions latent in the soul may work themselves out dramatically. Yet there are differences. The profane poet is by instinct a naturalist. He loves landscape, he loves love, he loves the humour and pathos of earthly existence. But the religious prophet loves none of these things. It is precisely because he does not love them that he cultivates in himself, and summons the world to cultivate, a second more satisfying life, more deeply rooted, as he imagines, in the nature of things. Earthly images therefore interest him only as symbols and metaphors, or as themes for denunciation. He is hardly a poet in the ordinary sense, except in so far as (like Milton, for instance) he may owe a double allegiance, and be a profane poet altogether when he is a poet at all. Religion is often professed and intellectually accepted without ever having flowered in the soul, or being suspected to have any kinship with poetry. It may have withered into a forced and angry metaphysics or semi-political party doctrine, poetically deplorable.

The opposite is the case in Dante, whose poetry is essentially religious, as his religion is essentially poetical. We are in the presence of an overpowering inspiration, become traditional, become also learned and quasi-scientific, but still kindled by moral passion and fertile in poetic ideas. The Hebrew prophets had begun by denouncing that which was and proclaiming that which should be; but that which should be could evidently never become actual without a miracle and a total revolution in the world; so that prophecy turned to eschatology and to expectation of a Messiah. At this point pagan streams of inspiration began to mingle with the Hebraic stream. Perhaps the Messiah had already come. Perhaps he was to be no conquering monarch, but a god in disguise. Perhaps he had been crucified, as the spirit is always crucified. Perhaps his kingdom was not of this world. Were there not reports that Jesus, who had been crucified, had been seen, risen from the dead? Would he not surely come again with glory in the clouds of heaven? Transfigured by this new spiritual faith, many current legends and maxims were ascribed to Jesus, and beautifully set down in the Gospels. The fathers worked out the theology. The saints repeated the miracles and explored all the phases of ascetic and mystical experience. Nothing remained but for Dante, with exquisite fidelity and minuteness, to paint a total picture of the Christian universe. The whole substance of that universe was poetry; only the details could threaten to become prosaic; but this danger was removed, in the more important places, by Dante's extraordinary sensitiveness. He had had a revelation of his own in childhood, interrupted later by the false glare of the world, but finally restored in the form of religious wisdom and consecration. The fresh dew of poetry and love trembled upon everything. Indeed, for our modern feeling the picture is too imaginative, too visionary, soaked too much in emotion. In spite of the stern historical details, when we rub our eyes and shake off the spell, the whole thing seems childishly unreal. We can understand why Mr Eliot feels this to be a 'superior' philosophy; but how can he fail to see that it is false?

Inspiration has a more intimate value than truth and one more unmistakably felt by a sensitive critic, since inspiration marks a sort of spring-tide in the life of some particular creature, whereas truth impassively maps the steady merciless stretches of creation at large. Inspiration has a kind of truth of its own, truth to the soul; and this sincerity in intuition, however private and special it might be, would never conflict with the truth of things, if inspiration were content to be innocently free and undogmatic, as in music or lyric poetry. The inmost vegetative impulses of life might then come to perfect flower, feeling and celebrating their own reality without pretending to describe or command reality beyond, or giving any hostages to fortune. But unfortunately animals cannot long imitate the lilies of the field. Where life is adventurous, combative and prophetic, inspiration must be so too. Ideas, however spontaneous, will then claim to be knowledge of ulterior facts, and will be in constant danger of being contradicted by the truth. Experience, from being lyrical, will become tragic; for what is tragedy but the conflict between inspiration and truth? From within or, as we may fancy, from above, some passionate hope takes shape in the mind. We fall in love or hear a voice from heaven; new energies seem to leap up within us; a new life begins crowding the old life out, or making it seem dreary or wicked. Even when inspiration is not moral, but merely poetical, it kindles a secret fire and an inner light that put vulgar sunshine to shame. Yet not for long, nor for ever; unless we passionately shut ourselves up in the *camera obscura* of our first inspiration, and fear the darkness of other lights. The more profound and voluminous that first inspiration was, the more complete at last will be our astonishment and despair. We shall cry with *Le Cid*:

> Percé jusques au fond du cœur
> D'une atteinte imprévue aussi bien que mortelle...
> Je demeure immobile, et mon âme abattue
> Cède au coup qui me tue.

Tragedy must end in death: for any immortality which the poet or his hero may otherwise believe in is irrelevant to the passion that has absorbed him. That passion, at least, dies, and all he cares for dies with it. The possibility of ulterior lives or alien interests destined in future to agitate the world makes no difference to this drama in this soul; and the mention of those irrelevant sequels to this ruin, and to this tragic acceptance of ruin, would tinkle with a ghastly mockery at this supreme moment, when a man is entering eternity, his measure taken, his heart revealed, and his pride entire.

These considerations may help us to understand why Shakespeare, although Christianity was at hand, and Seneca, although a Platonic philosophy was at hand, based like Christianity on moral inspiration, nevertheless stuck fast in a disillusioned philosophy which Mr Eliot thinks inferior. They stuck fast in the facts of life. They had to do so, whatever may have been their private religious convictions, because they were dramatists addressing the secular mind and concerned with the earthly career of passionate individuals, of inspired individuals, whose inspirations contradicted the truth and were shattered by it. This defeat, together with a proud and grandiloquent acceptance of it, is final for the tragic poet. His philosophy can build only on such knowledge of the world as the world can give. Even in the seventeenth century, when Christian orthodoxy was most severe, most intellectual, and most dominant, also most courtly and presentable to the worldly mind, Christianity was nevertheless strictly banished from the stage, except in a few expressly religious plays written for young ladies. Both Christian and pagan personages talked and felt throughout like thoroughly unregenerate mortals. To have allowed religion to shift the scenes, override the natural passions of men, and reverse the moral of the story, would have seemed an intolerable anticlimax.

Nor does even Dante, who calls his vision a comedy, really escape this tragic reality. Existence is indeed a comedy, in that it is a series of episodes, each blind and inconclusive, though often merry enough, but all having their justification beyond themselves, in a cosmic music which they help to make without knowing it. Nonetheless, the individual souls in Dante's hell and heaven speak the language of tragedy, either in desperate pride or in devout self-surrender. In either case, in eternity, they have no further hopes, fears, or ambitions. Their lives *there* are simply the full knowledge of what their lives had been *here*. If the *Divine Comedy* had not had in it this sublime note of recollection, if it had attempted to describe new adventures and fanciful Utopias succeeding one another *ad infinitum*, it would not have been divine at all, but only a romantic medley like the second part of *Faust*. In Dante the hurly-burly is rounded out into a moral tale, into a joyful tragedy, with that sense of finality, of eternity, which Christian eschatology had always preserved.

I can think of only one tragedy in which religion might well play a leading part, and that is the tragedy of religion itself. The point would be to show that a second life of pure inspiration, freely bred in the soul out of moral impulses, must sooner or later confront the cold truth. The illusions then surrendered would not lose their poetic value, since their source would remain alive in the soul; and the element of deception involved might disappear insensibly, as it did in paganism, yielding with a good grace to an impartial philosophy. Such a philosophy need not be in the least hostile to inspiration. There is inspiration wherever there is mind. The sensuous images and the categories of thought on which common knowledge relies are themselves poetic and wholly original in form, being products of a kind of inspiration in the animal organism. But they are controlled in their significance and application by experiment in the field of action. Higher fictions are more loosely controlled by the experience of the heart. They are less readily revived or communicated. They flare up into passionate prophecies, take themselves for revealed truths, and come more often to a tragic end.

The Theory of Art

THE SENSE OF BEAUTY

BEAUTY AND THE PERCEPTION OF FORM

The supposed disinterestedness of our love of beauty passes into another characteristic of it often regarded as essential—its universality. The pleasures of the senses have, it is said, no dogmatism in them; that anything gives me pleasure involves no assertion about its capacity to give pleasure to another. But when I judge a thing to be beautiful, my judgment means that the thing is beautiful in itself, or (what is the same thing more critically expressed) that it should seem so to everybody. The claim to universality is, according to this doctrine, the essence of the aesthetic; what makes the perception of beauty a judgment rather than a sensation. All aesthetic precepts would be impossible, and all criticism arbitrary and subjective, unless we admit a paradoxical universality in our judgment, the philosophical implications of which we may then go on to develop. But we are fortunately not required to enter the labyrinth into which this method leads; there is a much simpler and clearer way of studying such questions, which is to challenge and analyse the assertion before us and seek its basis in human nature. Before this is done, we should run the risk of expanding a natural misconception or inaccuracy of thought into an inveterate and pernicious prejudice by making it the centre of an elaborate construction.

That the claim of universality is such a natural inaccuracy will not be hard to show. There is notoriously no great agreement upon aesthetic matters; and such agreement as there is, is based upon similarity of origin, nature, and circumstance among men, a similarity which, where it exists, tends to bring about identity in all judgments and feelings. It is unmeaning to say that what is beautiful to one man *ought* to be beautiful to another. If their senses are the same, their associations and dispositions similar, then the same thing will certainly be beautiful to both. If their natures are different, the form which to one will be entrancing will be to another even invisible, because his classifications and discriminations in perception will be different, and he may see a hideous detached fragment or a shapeless aggregate of things, in what to another is a perfect whole—so entirely are the unities of objects unities of function and use. It is absurd to say that what is invisible to a given being *ought* to seem beautiful to him. Evidently this obligation of recognizing the same qualities is conditioned by the possession of the same faculties. But no two men have exactly the same faculties, nor can things have for any two exactly the same values.

What is loosely expressed by saying that anyone ought to see this or that beauty is that he would see it if his disposition, training, or attention were what our ideal demands for him; and our ideal of what anyone should be has complex but discoverable sources. We take, for instance, a certain pleasure in having our own judgments supported by those of others; we are intolerant, if not of the existence of a nature different from our own, at least of its expression in words and judgments. We are confirmed or made happy in our doubtful opinions by seeing them accepted universally. We are unable to find the basis of our taste in our own experience and therefore refuse to look for it there. If we were sure of our ground, we should be willing to acquiesce in the naturally different feelings and ways of others, as a man who is conscious of speaking his language with the accent of the capital confesses its arbitrariness with gaiety, and is pleased and interested in the variations of it he observes in provincials; but the provincial is always zealous to show that he has reason and ancient authority to justify his oddities. So people who have no sensations, and do not know why they judge, are always trying to show that they judge by universal reason.

Thus the frailty and superficiality of our own judgments cannot brook contradiction. We abhor another man's doubt when we cannot tell him why we ourselves believe. Our ideal of other men tends therefore to include the agreement of their judgments with our own; and although we might acknowledge the fatuity of this demand in regard to natures very different from the human, we may be unreasonable enough to require that all races should admire the same style of architecture, and all ages the same poets.

The great actual unity of human taste within the range of conventional history helps the pretension. But in principle it is untenable. Nothing has less to do with the real merit of a work of imagination than the capacity of all men to appreciate it; the true test is the degree and kind of satisfaction it can give to him who appreciates it most. The symphony would lose nothing if half mankind had always been deaf, as nine-tenths of them actually are, to the intricacies of its harmonies; but it would have lost much if no Beethoven had existed. And more: incapacity to appreciate certain types of beauty may be the condition *sine qua non* for the appreciation of another kind; the greatest capacity both for enjoyment and creation is highly specialized and exclusive, and hence the greatest ages of art have often been strangely intolerant.

The invectives of one school against another, perverse as as they are philosophically, are artistically often signs of health, because they indicate a vital appreciation of certain kinds of beauty, a love of them that has grown into a jealous passion. The architects that have pieced out the imperfections of ancient buildings with their own thoughts, like Charles V when he raised his massive palace beside the Alhambra, may be condemned from a certain point of view. They marred much by their interference; but they showed a splendid confidence in their own intuitions, a proud assertion of their own taste, which is the greatest evidence of aesthetic sincerity. On the contrary, our own gropings, eclecticism, and archaeology are the symptoms of impotence. If we were less learned and less just, we might be more efficient. If our appreciation were less general, it might be more real, and if we trained our imagination into exclusiveness, it might attain to character.

...[Could we] so transform our taste as to find beauty everywhere, because, perhaps, the ultimate nature of things is as truly exemplified in one thing as in another, we should, in fact, have abolished taste altogether. For the ascending series of aesthetic satisfactions we should have substituted a monotonous judgment of identity. If things were beautiful not by virtue of their differences but by virtue of an identical something which they equally contained, then there could be no discrimination in beauty. Like substance, beauty would be everywhere one and the same, and any tendency to prefer one thing to another would be a proof of finitude and illusion. When we try to make our judgments absolute, what we do is to surrender our natural standards and categories, and slip into another genus, until we lose ourselves in the satisfying vagueness of mere being.

Relativity to our partial nature is therefore essential to all our definite thoughts, judgments, and feelings. And when once the human bias is admitted as a legitimate, because for us a necessary, basis of preference, the whole wealth of nature is at once organized by that standard into a hierarchy of values. Everything is beautiful because everything is capable in some degree of interesting and charming our attention; but things differ immensely in this capacity to please us in the contemplation of them, and therefore they differ immensely in beauty. Could our nature be fixed and determined once for all in every particular, the scale of aesthetic values would become certain. We should not dispute about tastes, no longer because a common principle of preference could not be discovered, but rather because any disagreement would then be impossible.

As a matter of fact, however, human nature is a vague abstraction; that which is common to all men is the least part of their natural endowment. Aesthetic capacity is accordingly very unevenly distributed; and the world of beauty is much vaster and more complex to one man than to another. So long, indeed, as the distinction is merely one of development, so that we recognize in the greatest connoisseur only the refinement of the judgments of the rudest peasant, our aesthetic principle has not changed; we might say that, thus far, we had a common standard more or less widely applied. We might say so, because that standard would be an implication of a common nature more or less fully developed.

But men do not differ only in the degree of their susceptibility, they differ also in its direction. Human nature branches into opposed and incompatible characters. And taste follows this bifurcation. We cannot, except whimsically, say that a taste for music is higher or lower than a taste for sculpture. A man might be a musician and a sculptor by turns; that would only involve a perfectly conceivable enlargement in human genius. But the union thus effected would be an accumulation of gifts in the observer, not a combination of beauties in the object. The excellence of sculpture and that of music would remain entirely independent and heterogeneous. Such divergences are like those of the outer senses to which these arts appeal. Sound and colour have analogies only in their lowest depth, as vibrations and excitement; as they grow specific and objective, they diverge; and although the same consciousness perceives them, it perceives them as unrelated and uncombinable objects.

The ideal enlargement of human capacity, therefore, has no tendency to constitute a single standard of beauty. These standards remain the expression of diverse habits of sense and imagination. The man who combines the greatest range with the greatest endowment in each particular, will, of course, be the critic most generally respected. He will express the feelings of the greater number of men. The advantage of scope in criticism lies not in the improvement of our sense in each particular field; here the artist will detect the amateur's shortcomings. But no man is a specialist with his whole soul. Some latent capacity he has for other perceptions; and it is for the awakening of these, and their marshalling before him, that the student of each kind of beauty turns to the lover of them all.

The temptation, therefore, to say that all things are really equally beautiful arises from an imperfect analysis, by which the operations of the aesthetic consciousness are only partially disintegrated. The dependence of the *degrees* of beauty upon our nature is perceived, while the dependence of its *essence* upon our nature is still ignored. All things are not equally beautiful because the subjective bias that discriminates between them is the cause of their being beautiful at all. The principle of personal preference is the same as that of human taste; real and objective beauty, in contrast to a vagary of individuals, means only an affinity to a more prevalent and lasting susceptibility, a response to a more general and fundamental demand. And the keener discrimination, by which the distance between beautiful and ugly things is increased, far from being a loss of aesthetic insight, is a development of that faculty by the exercise of which beauty comes into the world.

It is the free exercise of the activity of apperception that gives so peculiar an interest to indeterminate objects, to the vague, the incoherent, the suggestive, the variously interpretable. The more this effect is appealed to, the greater wealth of thought is presumed in the observer, and the less mastery is displayed by the artist. A poor and literal mind cannot enjoy the opportunity for reverie and construction given by the stimulus of indeterminate objects; it lacks the requisite resources. It is nonplussed and annoyed, and turns away to simpler and more transparent things with a feeling of helplessness often turning into contempt. And, on the other hand, the artist who is not artist enough, who has too many irrepressible talents and too little technical skill, is sure to float in the region of the indeterminate. He sketches and never paints; he hints and never expresses; he stimulates and never informs. This is the method of individuals and of nations that have more genius than art.

The consciousness that accompanies this characteristic is the sense of profundity, of mighty significance. And this feeling is not necessarily an illusion. The nature of our materials —be they words, colours, or plastic matter—imposes a limit and bias upon our expression. The reality of experience can never be quite rendered through these media. The greatest mastery of technique will therefore come short of perfect adequacy and exhaustiveness; there must always remain a penumbra and fringe of suggestion if the most explicit representation is to communicate a truth. When there is real profundity—when the living core of things is most firmly grasped—there will accordingly be a felt inadequacy of expression, and an appeal to the observer to piece out our imperfections with his thoughts. But this should come only after the resources of a patient and well-learned art have been exhausted; else what is felt as depth is really confusion and incompetence. The simplest thing becomes unutterable, if we have forgotten how to speak. And a habitual indulgence in the inarticulate is a sure sign of the philosopher who has not learned to think, the poet who has not learned to write, the painter who has not learned to paint, and the impression that has not learned to express itself—all of which are compatible with an immensity of genius in the inexpressible soul.

Our age is given to this sort of self-indulgence, and on both the grounds mentioned. Our public, without being really trained—for we appeal to too large a public to require training in it—, is well informed and eagerly responsive to everything; it is ready to work pretty hard, and do its share towards its own profit and entertainment. It becomes a point of pride with it to understand and appreciate everything. And our art, in its turn, does not overlook this opportunity. It becomes disorganized, sporadic, whimsical, and experimental. The crudity we are too distracted to refine, we accept as originality, and the vagueness we are too pretentious to make accurate, we pass off as sublimity. This is the secret of making great works on novel principles, and of writing hard books easily...

While we gain this mastery of the formless, however, we should not lose the more necessary capacity of seeing form in those things which happen to have it. In respect to most of those things which are determinate as well as natural, we are usually in that state of aesthetic unconsciousness which the peasant is in in respect to the landscape. We treat human life and its environment with the same utilitarian eye with which he regards the field and mountain. That is beautiful which is expressive of convenience and wealth; the rest is indifferent. If we mean by love of nature aesthetic delight in the world in which we casually live (and what can be more *natural* than man and all his arts?), we may say that the absolute love of *nature* hardly exists among us. What we love is the stimulation of our own personal emotions and dreams; and landscape appeals to us, as music does to those who have no sense for musical form.

There would seem to be no truth in the saying that the ancients loved nature less than we. They loved landscape less —less, at least, in proportion to their love of the definite things it contained. The vague and changing effects of the atmosphere, the masses of mountains, the infinite and living complexity of forests, did not fascinate them. They had not that preponderant taste for the indeterminate that makes the landscape a favourite subject of contemplation. But love of nature, and comprehension of her, they had in a most eminent degree; in fact, they actually made explicit that objectification of our own soul in her, which for the romantic poet remains a mere vague and shifting suggestion. What are the celestial gods, the nymphs, the fauns, the dryads, but the definite apperceptions of that haunting spirit which we think we see in the sky, the mountains, and the woods? We may think that our vague intuition grasps the truth of what their childish imagination turned into a fable. But our belief, if it is one, is just as fabulous, just as much a projection of human nature into material things; and if we renounce all positive conception of quasi-mental principles in nature, and reduce our moralizing of her to a poetic expression of our own sensations, then can we say that our verbal and illusive images are comparable as representations of the life of nature to the precision, variety, humour, and beauty of the Greek mythology?

THE RELATION OF UTILITY TO BEAUTY

[The] natural harmony between utility and beauty, when its origin is not understood, is of course the subject of much perplexed and perplexing theory. Sometimes we are told that utility is itself the essence of beauty, that is, that our consciousness of the practical advantages of certain forms is the ground of our aesthetic admiration of them. The horse's legs are said to be beautiful because they are fit to run, the eye because it is made to see, the house because it is convenient to live in. An amusing application—which might pass for a *reductio ad absurdum*—of this dense theory is put by Xenophon into the mouth of Socrates. Comparing himself with a youth present at the same banquet, who was about to receive the prize of beauty, Socrates declares himself more beautiful and more worthy of the crown. For utility makes beauty, and eyes bulging from the head, like his, are the most advantageous for seeing; nostrils wide and open to the air, like his, most appropriate for smelling; and a mouth large and voluminous, like his, best fitted for both eating and kissing.*

Now since these things are, in fact, hideous, the theory that shows they *ought to be* beautiful is vain and ridiculous. But that theory contains this truth: that had the utility of Socratic features been so great that men of all other types must have perished, Socrates would have been beautiful. He would have represented the human type. The eye would have been then accustomed to that form, the imagination would have taken it as the basis of its refinements, and accentuated its naturally effective points. The beautiful does not depend on the useful; it is constituted by the imagination in ignorance and contempt of practical advantage; but it is not independent of the necessary, for the necessary must also be the habitual and consequently the basis of the type, and of all its imaginative variations.

* *Symposium of Xenophon*, v.

There are, moreover, at a late and derivative stage in our aesthetic judgment, certain cases in which the knowledge of fitness and utility enters into our sense of beauty. But it does so very indirectly, by convincing us that we should tolerate what practical conditions have imposed on an artist, by arousing admiration for his ingenuity, or by suggesting the interesting things themselves with which the object is known to be connected. Thus a cottage-chimney, stout and tall, with the smoke floating from it, pleases because we fancy it to mean a hearth, a rustic meal, and a comfortable family. But that is all extraneous association. The most ordinary way in which utility affects us is negatively; if we know a thing to be useless and fictitious, the uncomfortable haunting sense of waste and trickery prevents all enjoyment, and therefore banishes beauty. But this is also an adventitious complication. The intrinsic value of a form is in no way affected by it.

Opposed to this utilitarian theory stands the metaphysical one that would make the beauty or intrinsic rightness of things the source of their efficiency and of their power to survive. Taken literally, as it is generally meant, this idea must, from our point of view, appear preposterous. Beauty and rightness are relative to our judgment and emotion; they in no sense exist in nature or preside over her. She everywhere appears to move by mechanical law. The types of things exist by what, in relation to our approbation, is mere chance, and it is our faculties that must adapt themselves to our environment and not our environment to our faculties. Such is the naturalistic point of view which we have adopted.

To say, however, that beauty is in some sense the ground of practical fitness, need not seem to us wholly unmeaning. The fault of the Platonists who say things of this sort is seldom that of emptiness. They have an intuition; they have sometimes a strong sense of the facts of consciousness. But they turn their discoveries into so many revelations, and the veil of the infinite and absolute soon covers their little light of specific truth. Sometimes, after patient digging, the student comes upon the treasure of some simple fact, some common experience, beneath all their mystery and unction. And so it may be in this case. If we make allowances for the tendency to express experience in allegory and myth, we shall see that the idea of beauty and rationality presiding over nature and guiding her, as it were, for their own greater glory, is a projection and a writing large of a psychological principle.

The mind that perceives nature is the same that understands and enjoys her; indeed, these three functions are really elements of one process. There is therefore in the mere perceptibility of a thing a certain prophecy of its beauty; if it were not on the road to beauty, if it had no approach to fitness to our faculties of perception, the object would remain eternally unperceived. The sense, therefore, that the whole world is made to be food for the soul; that beauty is not only its own, but all things' excuse for being; that universal aspiration towards perfection is the key and secret of the world, —*that* sense is the poetical reverberation of a psychological fact, of the fact that our mind is an organism tending to unity, to unconsciousness of what is refractory to its action, and to assimilation and sympathetic transformation of what is kept within its sphere. The idea that nature could be governed by an aspiration towards beauty is, therefore, to be rejected as a confusion, but at the same time we must confess that this confusion is founded on a consciousness of the subjective relation between the perceptibility, rationality, and beauty of things.

This subjective relation is, however, exceedingly loose. Most things that are perceivable are not perceived so distinctly as to be intelligible, nor so delightfully as to be beautiful. If our eye had infinite penetration, or our imagination infinite elasticity, this would not be the case; to see would then be to understand and to enjoy. As it is, the degree of determination needed for perception is much less than that needed for comprehension or ideality. Hence there is room for hypothesis and for art. As hypothesis organizes experience imaginatively in ways in which observation has not been able to do, so art organizes objects in ways to which nature, perhaps, has never condescended.

The chief thing which the imitative arts add to nature is permanence, the lack of which is the saddest defect of many natural beauties. The forces which determine natural forms, therefore, determine also the forms of the imitative arts. But the non-imitative arts supply organisms different in kind from those which nature affords. If we seek the principle by which these objects are organized, we shall generally find that it is likewise utility. Architecture, for instance, has all its forms suggested by practical demands. Use requires our buildings to assume certain determinate forms; the mechanical properties of our materials, the exigency of shelter, light, accessibility, economy, and conveniences, dictate the arrangements of our buildings.

Houses and temples have an evolution like that of animals and plants. Various forms arise by mechanical necessity, like the cave, or the shelter of overhanging boughs. These are perpetuated by a selection in which the needs and pleasures of man are the environment to which the structure must be adapted. Determinate forms thus establish themselves, and the eye becomes accustomed to them. The line of use, by habit of apperception, becomes the line of beauty. A striking example may be found in the pediment of the Greek temple and the gable of the northern house. The exigencies of climate determine these forms differently, but the eye in each case accepts what utility imposes. We admire height in one and breadth in the other, and we soon find the steep pediment heavy and the low gable awkward and mean.

It would be an error, however, to conclude that habit alone establishes the right proportion in these various types of building. We have the same intrinsic elements to consider as in natural forms. That is, besides the unity of type and correspondence of parts which custom establishes, there are certain appeals to more fundamental susceptibilities of the human eye and imagination. There is, for instance, the value of abstract form, determined by the pleasantness and harmony of implicated retinal or muscular tensions. Different structures contain or suggest more or less of this kind of beauty, and in that proportion may be called intrinsically better or worse. Thus artificial forms may be arranged in a hierarchy like natural ones, by reference to the absolute values of their contours and masses. Herein lies the superiority of a Greek to a Chinese vase, or of Gothic to Saracenic construction. Thus although every useful form is capable of proportion and beauty, once its type is established, we cannot say that this beauty is always potentially equal; and an iron bridge, for instance, although it certainly possesses and daily acquires aesthetic interest, will probably never, on the average, equal a bridge of stone.

Beauty of form is the last to be found or admired in artificial as in natural objects. Time is needed to establish it, and training and nicety of perception to enjoy it. Motion or colour is what first interests a child in toys, as in animals; and the barbarian artist decorates long before he designs. The cave and wigwam are daubed with paint, or hung with trophies, before any pleasure is taken in their shape; and the appeal to the detached senses, and to associations of wealth and luxury, precedes by far the appeal to the perceptive harmonies of form. In music we observe the same graduation; first, we appreciate its sensuous and sentimental value; only with education can we enjoy its form. The plastic arts begin, therefore, with adventitious ornament and with symbolism. The aesthetic pleasure is in the richness of the material, the profusion of the ornament, the significance of the shape—in everything, rather than in the shape itself.

We have, accordingly, in works of art two independent sources of effect. The first is the useful form, which generates the type, and ultimately the beauty of form, when the type has been idealized by emphasizing its intrinsically pleasing traits. The second is the beauty of ornament, which comes from the excitement of the senses, or of the imagination, by colour, or by profusion or delicacy of detail. Historically, the latter is first developed, and applied to a form as yet merely useful. But the very presence of ornament attracts contemplation; the attention lavished on the object helps to fix its form in the mind, and to make us discriminate the less from the more graceful. The two kinds of beauty are then felt, and, yielding to that tendency to unity which the mind always betrays, we begin to subordinate and organize these two excellences. The ornament is distributed so as to emphasize the aesthetic essence of the form; to idealize it even more, by adding adventitious interests harmoniously to the intrinsic interest of the lines of structure.

There is here a great field, of course, for variety of combination and compromise. Some artists are fascinated by the decoration, and think of the structure merely as the background on which it can be most advantageously displayed. Others, of more austere taste, allow ornament only to emphasize the main lines of the design, or to conceal such inharmonious elements as nature or utility may prevent them from eliminating. We may thus oscillate between decorative and structural motives, and only in one point, for each style, can we find the ideal equilibrium, in which the greatest strength and lucidity is combined with the greatest splendour.

A less subtle, but still very effective, combination is that hit upon by many Oriental and Gothic architects, and found, also, by accident perhaps, in many buildings of the Plateresque style; the ornament and structure are both presented with extreme emphasis, but locally divided; a vast rough wall, for instance, represents the one, and a profusion of mad ornament huddled around a central door or window represents the other.

Gothic architecture offers us in the pinnacle and flying buttress a striking example of the adoption of a mechanical feature, and its transformation into an element of beauty. Nothing could at first sight be more hopeless than the external half-arch propping the side of a pier, or the chimney-like weight of stones pressing it down from above; but a courageous acceptance of these necessities, and a submissive study of their form, revealed a new and strange effect: the bewildering and stimulating intricacy of masses suspended in mid-air; the profusion of line, variety of surface, and picturesqueness of light and shade. It needed but a little applied ornament judiciously distributed; a moulding in the arches; a florid canopy and statue amid the buttresses; a few grinning monsters leaning out of unexpected nooks; a leafy budding of the topmost pinnacles; a piercing here and there of some little gallery, parapet, or turret into lacework against the sky—and the building became a poem, an inexhaustible emotion. Add some passing cloud casting its moving shadow over the pile, add the circling of birds about the towers, and you have an unforgettable type of beauty; not perhaps the noblest, sanest, or most enduring, but one for the existence of which the imagination is richer, and the world more interesting.

In this manner we accept the forms imposed upon us by utility, and train ourselves to apperceive their potential beauty. Familiarity breeds contempt only when it breeds inattention. When the mind is absorbed and dominated by its perceptions, it incorporates into them more and more of its own functional values, and makes them ultimately beautiful and expressive. Thus no language can be ugly to those who speak it well, no religion unmeaning to those who have learned to pour their life into its moulds.

Of course these forms vary in intrinsic excellence; they are by their specific character more or less fit and facile for the average mind. But the man and the age are rare who can choose their own path; we have generally only a choice between going ahead in the direction already chosen, or halting and blocking the path for others. The only kind of reform usually possible is reform from within; a more intimate study and more intelligent use of the traditional forms. Disaster follows rebellion against tradition or against utility, which are the basis and root of our taste and progress. But, within the given school, and as exponents of its spirit, we can adapt and perfect our works, if haply we are better inspired than our predecessors. For the better we know a given thing, and the more we perceive its strong and weak points, the more capable we are of idealizing it.

FORM IN WORDS

The main effect of language consists in its meaning, in the ideas which it expresses. But no expression is possible without a presentation, and this presentation must have a form. This form of the instrument of expression is itself an element of effect, although in practical life we may overlook it in our haste to attend to the meaning it conveys. It is, moreover, a condition of the kind of expression possible, and often determines the manner in which the object suggested shall be apperceived. No word has the exact value of any other in the same or in another language.* But the intrinsic effect of language does not stop there. The single word is but a stage in the series of formations which constitute language, and which preserve for men the fruit of their experience, distilled and concentrated into a symbol.

This formation begins with the elementary sounds themselves, which have to be discriminated and combined to make recognizable symbols. The evolution of these symbols goes on spontaneously, suggested by our tendency to utter all manner of sounds, and preserved by the ease with which the ear discriminates these sounds when made. Speech would be an absolute and unrelated art, like music, were it not controlled by utility. The sounds have indeed no resemblance to the objects they symbolize; but before the system of sounds can represent the system of objects, there has to be a correspondence in the groupings of both. The structure of language, unlike that of music, thus becomes a mirror of the structure of the world as presented to the intelligence.

Grammar, philosophically studied, is akin to the deepest metaphysics, because in revealing the constitution of speech

* Not only are words untranslatable when the exact object has no name in another language, as 'home' or 'mon ami', but even when the object is the same, the attitude toward it, incorporated in one word, cannot be rendered by another. Thus, to my sense, 'bread' is as inadequate a translation of the human intensity of the Spanish 'pan' as 'Dios' is of the awful mystery of the English 'God'. This latter word does not designate an object at all, but a sentiment, a psychosis, not to say a whole chapter of religious history. English is remarkable for the intensity and variety of the colour of its words. No language, I believe, has so many words specifically poetic.

it reveals the constitution of thought, and the hierarchy of those categories by which we conceive the world. It is by virtue of this parallel development that language has its function of expressing experience with exactness, and the poet—to whom language is an instrument of art—has to employ it also with a constant reference to meaning and veracity; that is, he must be a master of experience before he can become a true master of words. Nevertheless, language is primarily a sort of music, and the beautiful effects which it produces are due to its own structure, giving, as it crystallizes in a new fashion, an unforeseen form to experience.

Poets may be divided into two classes: the musicians and the psychologists. The first are masters of significant language as harmony; they know what notes to sound together and in succession; they can produce, by the marshalling of sounds and images, by the fugue of passion and the snap of wit, a thousand brilliant effects out of old materials. The Ciceronian orator, the epigrammatic, lyric, and elegiac poets, give examples of this art. The psychologists, on the other hand, gain their effect not by the intrinsic mastery of language, but by the closer adaptation of it to things. The dramatic poets naturally furnish an illustration.

But however transparent we may wish to make our language, however little we may call for its intrinsic effects, and direct our attention exclusively to its expressiveness, we cannot avoid the limitations of our particular medium. The character of the tongue a man speaks, and the degree of his skill in speaking it, must always count enormously in the aesthetic value of his compositions; no skill in observation, no depth of thought or feeling, but is spoiled by a bad style and enhanced by a good one. The diversities of tongues, and their irreducible aesthetic values, begin with the very sound of the letters, with the mode of utterance, and the characteristic inflections of the voice; notice, for instance, the effect of the French of these lines of Alfred de Musset:

> Jamais deux yeux plus doux n'ont du ciel le plus pur
> Sondé la profondeur et réfléchi l'azur;

and compare with its flute-like and treble quality the breadth, depth, and volume of the German in this inimitable stanza of Goethe's:

> Ueber allen Gipfeln
> Ist Ruh,
> In allen Wipfeln
> Spürest du
> Kaum einen Hauch;
> Die Vögelein schweigen im Walde.
> Warte nur, balde
> Ruhest du auch.

Even if the same tune could be played on both these vocal instruments, the difference in their *timbre* would make the value of the melody entirely distinct in each case.

The known impossibility of adequate translation appears here at the basis of language. The other diversities are superadded upon this diversity of sound. The syntax is the next source of effect. What could be better than Homer, or what worse than almost any translation of him? And this holds even of languages so closely allied as the Indo-European, which, after all, have certain correspondences of syntax and inflection. If there could be a language with other parts of speech than ours—a language without nouns, for instance—how would that grasp of experience, that picture of the world, which all our literature contains, be reproduced in it? Whatever beauties that language might be susceptible of, none of the effects produced on us, I will not say by poets, but even by nature itself, could be expressed in it.

Nor is such a language inconceivable. Instead of summarizing all our experiences of a thing by one word, its name, we should have to recall by appropriate adjectives the various sensations we had received from it; the objects we think of would be disintegrated, or, rather, would never have been unified. For 'sun', they would say 'high, yellow, dazzling, round, slowly moving', and the enumeration of these qualities (as we call them), without any suggestion of a unity at their source, might give a more vivid and profound, if more cumbrous, representation of the facts. But how could the machinery of such an imagination be capable of repeating the effects of ours, when the objects to us most obvious and real would be to those minds utterly indescribable?

The same diversity appears in the languages we ordinarily know, only in a lesser degree. The presence or absence of case-endings in nouns and adjectives, their difference of gender, the richness of inflections in the verbs, the frequency of particles and conjunctions—all these characteristics make one language differ from another entirely in genius and capacity of expression. Greek is probably the best of all languages in melody, richness, elasticity, and simplicity; so much so that, in spite of its complex inflections, when once a vocabulary is acquired, it is more easy and natural for a modern than his ancestral Latin itself. Latin is the stiffer tongue; it is by nature at once laconic and grandiloquent, and the exceptional condensation and transposition of which it is capable make its effects entirely foreign to a modern, scarcely inflected, tongue. Take, for instance, these lines of Horace:

me tabula sacer
votiva paries indicat uvida
suspendisse potenti
vestimenta maris deo,

or these of Lucretius:

Jamque caput quassans grandis suspirat arator
Crebrius incassum magnum cecidisse laborem.

What conglomerate plebeian speech of our time could utter the stately grandeur of these Lucretian words, every one of which is noble, and wears the toga?

As a substitute for the inimitable interpenetration of the words in the Horatian strophe, we might have the external links of rhyme; and it seems, in fact, to be a justification of rhyme that besides contributing something to melody and to the distribution of parts, it gives an artificial relationship to the phrases between which it obtains, which, but for it, would run away from one another in a rapid and irrevocable flux. In such a form as the sonnet, for instance, we have, by dint of assonance, a real unity forced upon the thought; for a sonnet in which the thought is not distributed appropriately to the structure of the verse has no excuse for being a sonnet. By virtue of this interrelation of parts, the sonnet, the *non plus ultra* of rhyme, is the most classic of modern poetical forms: much more classic in spirit than blank verse, which lacks almost entirely the power of synthesizing the phrase, and making the unexpected seem the inevitable.

This beauty given to the ancients by the syntax of their language, the moderns can only attain by the combination of their rhymes. It is a bad substitute perhaps, but better than the total absence of form, favoured by the atomic character of our words, and the flat juxtaposition of our clauses. The art which was capable of making a gem of every prose sentence—the art which, carried perhaps to a pitch at which it became too conscious, made the phrases of Tacitus a series of cameos—that art is inapplicable to our looser medium; we cannot give clay the finish and nicety of marble. Our poetry and speech in general, therefore, start out upon a lower level; the same effort will not, with this instrument, attain the same beauty. If equal beauty is ever attained, it comes from the wealth of suggestion, or the refinement of sentiment. The art of words remains hopelessly inferior. And what best proves this is that, when, as in our time, a reawakening of the love of beauty has prompted a refinement of our poetical language, we pass so soon into extravagance, obscurity, and affectation. Our modern languages are not susceptible of great formal beauty.

WHAT IS AESTHETICS?

An accomplished mathematician, who is certainly free from those prejudices which his science might be expected to foster, once said that all problems are divided into two classes, soluble questions, which are trivial, and important questions, which are insoluble. This epigram, if we chose for the moment to take it seriously, might help us to deal in a quick and trenchant fashion with the topic before us. Our problem would indeed be soluble and trivial, if we wished merely to fix the relation of an aesthetics arbitrarily defined to other sciences of our own delimitation. It would be all a question of dragooning reality into a fresh verbal uniform. We should have on our hands, if we were successful, a regiment of ideal and non-existent sciences, to which we should be applying titles more or less pre-empted by actual human studies; but in its flawless articulation and symmetry our classification would absolve itself from any subservience to usage, and would ignore the historic grouping and genealogy of existing pursuits.

Thus, for instance, in the recent *Estetica*, by Benedetto Croce, we learn that aesthetics is purely and simply the science of expression; expression being itself so defined as to be identical with every form of apperception, intuition, or imaginative synthesis. This imagined aesthetics includes the theory of speech and of all attentive perception, while it has nothing in particular to do with art or with beauty or with any kind of preference. Such system-making may be a most learned game, but it contributes nothing to knowledge. The inventor of Volapük might exhibit considerable acquaintance with current languages, and much acumen in comparing and criticizing their grammar, but his own grammar would not on that account describe any living speech. So the author of some new and ideal articulation of the sciences merely tells us how knowledge might have fallen together, if it had prophetically conformed to a scheme now suggesting itself to his verbal fancy; much as if a man fond by nature of architectural magnificence, but living by chance in a house built of mud and rubble, should plaster it on the outside, and, by the aid of a little paint, should divide it into huge blocks conjoined with masterly precision and apparently fit to outlast the ages. When this brilliant effect was achieved, and the speculative eye had gloated sufficiently on its masterpiece, the truly important question would still remain—namely, what the structure of that house really was and how long it could be expected to retain traces of the unmeaning checker-work with which its owner's caprice had overlaid it.

Perhaps we may pursue our subject to better advantage if we revert to our mathematical friend, and try to turn his satirical dictum into something like a sober truth. Some questions, let us say, are important and soluble, because the subject-matter can control the answer we give to them; others are insoluble and merely vexatious, because the terms they are stated in already traduce and dislocate the constitution of things. Now the word 'aesthetics' is nothing but a loose term lately applied in academic circles to everything that has to do with works of art or with the sense of beauty. The man who studies Venetian painting is aesthetically employed; so is he who experiments in a laboratory about the most pleasing division of a strip of white paper. The latter person is undoubtedly a psychologist; the former is nothing but a miserable amateur, or at best a historian of art. Aesthetic too would be any speculation about the dialectical relation of the beautiful to the rational or to the absolutely good; so that a theologian, excogitating the emanation of the Holy Ghost from the Son and from the Father, might be an aesthetician into the bargain, if only the Holy Ghost turned out to mean the fullness of life realized in beauty, when deep emotion suffuses luminous and complex ideas.

The truth is that the group of activities we can call aesthetic is a motley one, created by certain historic and literary accidents. Wherever consciousness becomes at all imaginative and finds a flattering unction in its *phantasmagoria*, or whenever a work, for whatever purpose constructed, happens to have notable intrinsic values for perception, we utter the word 'aesthetic'; but these occasions are miscellaneous, and there is no single agency in nature, no specific organ in sense, and no separable task in spirit, to which the aesthetic quality can be attributed. Aesthetic experience is so broad and so incidental, it is spread so thin over all life, that like life itself it opens out for reflection into divergent vistas. The most important natural division in the field of reflection is that between the vista of things found and the vista of things only conceived or desired. These are two opposite and centrifugal directions in which reasoned knowledge may expand; both diverge from the common root furnished by practical knowledge, memory, and history; one, proceeding by observation, yields natural science, and the other yields ideal science, which proceeds by dialectic. Yet even these two regions, the most disparate possible in speculation, covered respectively by pre-Socratic and by Socratic philosophy, are themselves far from separable, since before external facts can be studied they have to be arrested by attention and translated into terms having a fixed intent, so that relations and propositions may be asserted about them; while these terms in discourse, these goals of intent or attention, must in turn be borne along in the flux of existence, and must interpret its incidental formations.

Now, much that is aesthetic is factual—for instance, the phenomena of art and taste; and all this is an object for natural history and natural philosophy; but much also is ideal, like the effort and intent of poetic composition, or the interpretation of music, all of which is concerned only with fulfilling intent and establishing values. That psychology may occasionally deal with aesthetic questions is undeniable. No matter how clearly objects may originally stand out in their own proper and natural medium, in retrospect they may be made to retreat into the experience which discovered them. Now, to reduce everything to the experience which discloses it is doubtless the mission of psychology—a feat on which current idealism is founded; so that the subject-matter of aesthetics, however various in itself, may be swallowed up in the psychological vortex, together with everything else that exists. But mathematics or history or judgments of taste can fall within the psychological field only adventitiously and for a third person. An eventual subsumption of the whole universe under psychological categories would still leave every human pursuit standing and every field of experience or faith distinct in its native and persisting hypostasis. Intelligence is centrifugal. Every part of rational life, in spite of all afterthoughts and criticisms, remains in the presence of its own ideal, conscious of the objects it itself envisages rather than of the process imputed to it by another. Aesthetic experience will therefore continue to elude and overflow psychology in a hundred ways, although in its own way psychology might eventually survey and represent all aesthetic experience.

If psychology must sometimes consider aesthetic facts, so must moral philosophy sometimes consider aesthetic values. As mathematical dialectic, starting with simple intuitions, develops their import, so moral dialectic, starting with an animal will, develops its ideals. Now a part of man's ideal, an ingredient in his ultimate happiness, is to find satisfaction for his eyes, for his imagination, for his hand or voice aching to embody latent tendencies in explicit forms. Perfect success in this vital, aesthetic undertaking is possible, however, only when artistic impulse is quite healthy and representative—that is, when it is favourable to all other interests and is in turn supported by them all. If this harmony fails, the aesthetic activity collapses inwardly by inanition—since every other impulse is fighting against it—while for the same reason its external products are rendered trivial, meretricious, and mean. They will still remain symptomatic, as excrements are, but they will cease to be works of rational art, because they will have no further vital function, no human use. It will become impossible for a mind with the least scope to relish them, or to find them even initially beautiful. Aesthetic good is accordingly no separable value; it is not realizable by itself in a set of objects not otherwise interesting. Anything which is to entertain the imagination must first have exercised the senses; it must first have stimulated some animal reaction, engaged attention, and intertwined itself in the vital process; and later this aesthetic good, with animal and sensuous values imbedded in it and making its very substance, must be swallowed up in a rational life; for reason will immediately feel itself called upon to synthesize those imaginative activities with whatever else is valuable. As the underlying sensuous good must be necessarily merged in the imaginative (their product being what we call aesthetic charm), so in a cultivated mind ulterior rational interests, never being out of sight, will merge in the same total and immediate appreciation. It will be as impossible wholly to welcome what is cruel or silly, what is groundless, mindless, and purely aesthetical, as wholly to welcome what gives physical pain. Reason suffers us to approve with no part of our nature what is offensive to any other part; and even mathematical cogency, for instance, becomes trivial, in so far as mathematical being is irrelevant to human good. The whole of wisdom must colour a judgment which is to be truly imaginative and is to express adequately an enlightened and quick sensibility.

The question whether aesthetics is a part of psychology or a philosophic discipline apart is therefore an insoluble question, because aesthetics is neither. The terms of the problem do violence to the structure of things. The lines of cleavage in human history and art do not isolate any such block of experience as aesthetics is supposed to describe.

What exists in the ideal region in lieu of an aesthetic science is the art and function of criticism. This is a reasoned appreciation of human works by a mind not wholly ignorant of their subject or occasion, their school, and their process of manufacture. Good criticism leans on a great variety of considerations, more numerous in proportion to the critic's competence and maturity. Nothing relevant to the object's efficacy should be ignored, and an intelligent critic must look impartially to beauty, propriety, difficulty, originality, truth, and moral significance in the work he judges. In other words, as each thing, by its existence and influence, radiates effects over human life, it acquires various functions and values, sometimes cumulative, sometimes alternative. These values it is the moral philosopher's business to perceive and to combine as best he can in a harmonious ideal, to be the goal of human effort and a standard for the relative estimation of things. Under the authority of such a standard arts and their products fall of necessity, together with everything else that heaven or earth may contain. Towards the rational framing of this standard must go, together with every other interest and delight, the interest and delight which men find in the beautiful, either to watch it or to conceive and to produce it. Aesthetic sensibility and artistic impulse are two gifts distinguishable from each other and from other human gifts; the pleasures that accompany them may of course be separated artificially from the massive pleasures and fluid energies of life. But to pride oneself on holding a single interest free from all others, and on being lost in that specific sensation to the exclusion of all its affinities and effects, would be to pride oneself on being a voluntary fool. Isolated, local sensibility, helplessness before each successive stimulus, is precisely what foolishness consists in. To attempt, then, to abstract a so-called aesthetic interest from all other interests, and a so-called work of art from whatever work ministers, in one way or another, to all human good, is to make the aesthetic sphere contemptible. There has never been any art worthy of notice without a practical basis and occasion, or without some intellectual or religious function. To divorce in a schematic fashion one phase of rational activity from the rest is to render each part and the whole again irrational; such a course would lead in the arts, if it led to anything, to works with no subject or meaning or moral glow. It would lead in other fields to a mathematics without application in nature, to a morality without roots in life, and to other fantastic abstractions wholly irrelevant to one another and useless for judging the world.

Nor would such an insulation of the aesthetic ideal secure any permanent division of functions, nor even attain an ultimate technical analysis. For after the alleged aesthetic sphere had been abstracted, at the cost of making it a region of pure idiocy, it would turn out that an aesthetic element had remained imbedded in men's other thoughts and actions. Their steam-engines, their games, their prose, and their religion would prove incorrigibly, inherently, beautiful or ugly. So that side by side with pure aestheticism—something so dubious and inhuman—we should have to admit the undeniable beauties of the non-aesthetic, of everything that was fit, lucid, beneficent, or profound. For what is practically helpful soon acquires a gracious presence; the eye learns to trace its form, to piece out its characteristics with a latent consciousness of their function, and, if possible, to remodel the object itself so as to fit it better to the abstract requirements of vision, that so excellent a thing may become altogether congenial. Aesthetic satisfaction thus comes to perfect all other values; they would remain imperfect if beauty did not supervene upon them, but beauty would be absolutely impossible if they did not underlie it. For perception, while in itself a process, is not perception if it means nothing or has no ulterior function; and so the pleasures of perception are not beauties if they are attached to nothing substantial and rational, to nothing with a right of citizenship in the natural or in the moral world. But happily the merit of immediate pleasantness tends to diffuse itself over what otherwise is good, and to become, for refined minds, a symbol of total excellence. And simultaneously, knowledge of what things are, of what skill means, of what man has endured and desired, re-enters like a flood that no-man's-land of mere aestheticism; and what we were asked to call beautiful out of pure affectation and pedantry, now becomes beautiful indeed.

In moral philosophy, then, there is as little room for a special discipline called 'aesthetics' as there is among the natural sciences. Just as we may consider, among other natural facts, the pleasures incident to imagination and art, as we may describe their occasions and detail their varieties, so in moral philosophy we may train ourselves to articulate the judgments vaguely called aesthetic, to enlarge and clarify them, to estimate their weight, catch their varying message, and find their congruity or incongruity with other interests. This will be an exercise of moral judgment, of idealizing reason; and its very function of attributing worth reflectively and with comprehensive justice will forbid its arrest at the face value of dumb sensation, or of abstract skill, or of automatic self-expression; whatever distinguishable interests may be covered by these terms will be only ingredients in the total appreciation our criticism is to reach. The critic's function is precisely to feel and to confront all values, bringing them into relation, and if possible into harmony.

REASON IN ART

THE BASIS OF ART IN INSTINCT AND EXPERIENCE

...Utility, like significance, is an eventual harmony in the arts and by no means their ground. All useful things have been discovered as ancient China discovered roast pig; and the casual feat has furthermore to be supported by a situation favourable to maintaining the art. The most useful act will never be repeated unless its secret remains embodied in structure. Practice and endeavour will not help an artist to remain long at his best; and many a performance is applauded which cannot be imitated. To create the requisite structure two preformed structures are needed: one in the agent, to give him skill and perseverance, and another in the material, to give it the right plasticity. Human progress would long ago have reached its goal if every man who recognized a good could at once appropriate it, and possess wisdom for ever by virtue of one moment's insight. Insight, unfortunately, is in itself perfectly useless and inconsequential; it can neither have produced its own occasion nor now ensure its own recurrence. Nevertheless, being proof positive that whatever basis it needs is actual, insight is also an indication that the extant structure, if circumstances maintain it, may continue to operate with the same moral results, maintaining the vision which it has once supported.

When men find that by chance they have started a useful change in the world, they congratulate themselves upon it and call their persistence in that practice a free activity. And the activity is indeed rational, since it subserves an end. The happy organization which enables us to continue in that rational course is the very organization which enabled us to initiate it. If this new process was formed under external influences, the same influences, when they operate again, will reconstitute the process each time more easily; while if it was formed quite spontaneously, its own inertia will maintain it quietly in the brain and bring it to the surface whenever circumstances permit. This is what is called learning by experience. Such lessons are far from indelible and are not always at command. Yet what has once been done may be repeated; repetition reinforces itself and becomes habit; and a clear memory of the benefit once attained by fortunate action, representing as it does the trace left by that action in the system, and its harmony with the man's usual impulses (for the action is felt to be *beneficial*), constitutes a strong presumption that the act will be repeated automatically on occasion; i.e. that it has really been learned. Consciousness, which willingly attends to results only, will judge either the memory or the benefit, or both confusedly, to be the ground of this readiness to act; and only if some hitch occurs in the machinery, so that rational behaviour fails to take place, will a surprised appeal be made to material accidents, or to a guilty forgetfulness or indocility in the soul.

The idiot cannot learn from experience at all, because a new process, in his liquid brain, does not modify structure; while the fool uses what he has learned only inaptly and in frivolous fragments, because his stretches of linked experience are short and their connections insecure. But when the cerebral plasm is fresh and well disposed and when the paths are clear, attention is consecutive and learning easy; a multitude of details can be gathered into a single cycle of memory or of potential regard. Under such circumstances action is the unimpeded expression of healthy instinct in an environment squarely faced. Conduct from the first then issues in progress, and, by reinforcing its own organization at each rehearsal, makes progress continual. For there will subsist not only a readiness to act and a great precision in action, but if any significant circumstance has varied in the conditions or in the interests at stake, this change will make itself felt; it will check the process and prevent precipitate action. Deliberation or well-founded scruple has the same source as facility—a plastic and quick organization. To be sensitive to difficulties and dangers goes with being sensitive to opportunities.

Of all reason's embodiments art is therefore the most splendid and complete. Merely to attain categories by which inner experience may be articulated, or to feign analogies by which a universe may be conceived, would be but a visionary triumph if it remained ineffectual and went with no actual remodelling of the outer world, to render man's dwelling more appropriate and his mind better fed and more largely transmissible. Mind grows self-perpetuating only by its expression in matter. What makes progress possible is that rational action may leave traces in nature, such that nature in consequence furnishes a better basis for the Life of Reason; in other words, progress is art bettering the conditions of existence. Until art arises, all achievement is internal to the brain, dies with the individual, and even in him spends itself without recovery, like music heard in a dream. Art, in establishing instruments for human life beyond the human body, and moulding outer things into sympathy with inner values, establishes a ground whence values may continually spring up; the thatch that protects from today's rain will last and keep out tomorrow's rain also; the sign that once expresses an idea will serve to recall it in future.

Not only does the work of art thus perpetuate its own function and produce a better experience, but the process of art also perpetuates itself, because it is teachable. Every animal learns something by living; but if his offspring inherit only what he possessed at birth, they have to learn life's lessons over again from the beginning, with at best some vague help given by their parents' example. But when the fruits of experience exist in the common environment, when new instruments, unknown to nature, are offered to each individual for his better equipment, although he must still learn for himself how to live, he may learn in a humaner school, where artificial occasions are constantly open to him for expanding his powers. It is no longer merely hidden inner processes that he must reproduce to attain his predecessors' wisdom; he may acquire much of it more expeditiously by imitating their outward habit—an imitation which, furthermore, they have some means of exacting from him. Wherever there is art there is a possibility of training. A father who calls his idle sons from the jungle to help him hold the plough, not only inures them to labour but compels them to observe the earth upturned and refreshed, and to watch the germination there; their wandering thought, their incipient rebellions, will be met by the hope of harvest; and it will not be impossible for them, when their father is dead, to follow the plough of their own initiative and for their own children's sake. So great is the sustained advance in rationality made possible by art which, being embodied in matter, is teachable and transmissible by training; for in art the values secured are recognized the more easily for having been first enjoyed when other people furnished the means to them; while the maintenance of these values is facilitated by an external tradition imposing itself contagiously or by force on each new generation.

Art is action which transcending the body makes the world a more congenial stimulus to the soul. All art is therefore useful and practical, and the notable aesthetic value which some works of art possess, for reasons flowing for the most part out of their moral significance, is itself one of the satisfactions which art offers to human nature as a whole. Between sensation and abstract discourse lies a region of deployed sensibility or synthetic representation, a region where more is seen at arm's length than in any one moment could be felt at close quarters, and yet where the remote parts of experience, which discourse reaches only through symbols, are recovered and recomposed in something like their native colours and experienced relations. This region, called imagination, has pleasures more airy and luminous than those of sense, more massive and rapturous than those of intelligence. The values inherent in imagination, in instant intuition, in sense endowed with form, are called aesthetic values; they are found mainly in nature and living beings, but often also in man's artificial works, in images evoked by language, and in the realm of sound.

Productions in which an aesthetic value is or is supposed to be prominent take the name of fine art; but the work of fine art so defined is almost always an abstraction from the actual object, which has many non-aesthetic functions and values. To separate the aesthetic element, abstract and dependent as it often is, is an artifice which is more misleading than helpful; for neither in the history of art nor in a rational estimate of its value can the aesthetic function of things be divorced from the practical and moral. What had to be done was, by imaginative races, done imaginatively; what had to be spoken or made, was spoken or made fitly, lovingly, beautifully. Or, to take the matter up on its psychological side, the ceaseless experimentation and ferment of ideas, in breeding what it had a propensity to breed, came sometimes on figments that gave it delightful pause; these beauties were the first knowledges and these arrests the first hints of real and useful things. The rose's grace could more easily be plucked from its petals than the beauty of art from its subject, occasion, and use. An aesthetic fragrance, indeed, all things may have, if in soliciting man's senses or reason they can awaken his imagination as well; but this middle zone is so mixed and nebulous, and its limits are so vague, that it cannot well be treated in theory otherwise than as it exists in fact—as a phase of man's sympathy with the world he moves in. If art is that element in the Life of Reason which consists in modifying its environment the better to attain its end, art may be expected to subserve all parts of the human ideal, to increase man's comfort, knowledge, and delight. And as nature, in her measure, is wont to satisfy these interests together, so art, in seeking to increase that satisfaction, will work simultaneously in every ideal direction. Nor will any of these directions be on the whole good, or tempt a well-trained will, if it leads to estrangement from all other interests. The aesthetic good will be accordingly hatched in the same nest with the others, and incapable of flying far in a different air.

PLASTIC REPRESENTATION

...Imitation cannot, of course, result in a literal repetition of the object that suggests it. The copy is secondary; it does not iterate the model by creating a second object on the same plane of reality, but reproduces the form in a new medium and gives it a different function. In these latter circumstances lies the imitative essence of the second image: for one leaf does not imitate another nor is each twin the other's copy. Like sensibility, imitation remodels a given being so that it becomes, in certain formal respects, like another being in its environment. It is a response and an index, by which note is taken of a situation or of its possible developments. When a man involuntarily imitates other men, he does not become those other persons; he is simply modified by their presence in a manner that allows him to conceive their will and their independent existence, not without growing similar to them in some measure and framing a genuine representation of them in his soul. He enacts what he understands, and his understanding consists precisely in knowing that he is re-enacting something which has its collateral existence elsewhere in nature. An element in the percipient repeats the total movement and tendency of the person perceived. The imitation, though akin to what it imitates, and reproducing it, lies in a different medium, and accordingly has a specific individuality and specific effects. Imitation is far more than similarity, nor does its ideal function lie in bringing a flat and unmeaning similarity about. It has a representative and intellectual value because in reproducing the forms of things it reproduces them in a fresh substance to a new purpose.

If I imitate mankind by following their fashions, I add one to the million and improve nothing: but if I imitate them under proper inhibitions and in the service of my own ends, I really understand them, and, by representing what I do not bodily become, I preserve and enlarge my own being and make it relevant ideally to what it physically depends upon. Assimilation is a way of drifting through the flux or of letting it drift through oneself; representation, on the contrary, is a principle of progress. To grow by accumulating passions and fancies is at best to grow in bulk: it is to become what a colony or a hydra might be. But to make the accretions which time brings to your being representative of what you are not, and do not wish to be, is to grow in dignity. It is to be wise and prepared. It is to survey a universe without ceasing to be a mind.

A product of imitative sensibility is accordingly on a higher plane than the original existences it introduces to one another—the ignorant individual and the unknown world. Imitation in softening the body into physical adjustment stimulates the mind to ideal representation. This is the case even when the stimulus is a contagious influence or habit, though the response may then be slavish and the representation vague. Sheep jumping a wall after their leader doubtless feel that they are not alone; and though their action may have no purpose it probably has a felt sanction and reward. Men also think they invoke an authority when they appeal to the *quod semper et ubique et ab omnibus*, and a conscious unanimity is a human if not a rational joy. When, however, the stimulus to imitation is not so pervasive and touches chiefly a single sense, when what it arouses is a movement of the hand or eye retracing the object, then the response becomes very definitely cognitive. It constitutes an observation of fact, an acquaintance with a thing's structure amounting to technical knowledge; for such a survey leaves behind it a power to reconstitute the process it involved. It leaves an efficacious idea. In an idle moment, when the information thus acquired need not be put to instant use, the new-born faculty may work itself out spontaneously. The sound heard is repeated, the thing observed is sketched, the event conceived is acted out in pantomime. Then imitation rounds itself out; an uninhibited sensation has become an instinct to keep that sensation alive, and plastic representation has begun.

The secret of representative genius is simple enough. All hangs on intense, exhaustive, rehearsed sensation. To paint is a way of letting vision work; nor should the amateur imagine that while he lacks technical knowledge he can have in his possession all the ideal burden of an art. His reaction will be personal and adventitious, and he will miss the artist's real inspiration and ignore his genuine successes. You may instruct a poet about literature, but his allegiance is to emotion. You may offer the sculptor your comparative observations on style and taste; he may or may not care to listen, but what he knows and loves is the human body. Critics are in this way always one stage behind or beyond the artist; their operation is reflective and his is direct. In transferring to his special medium what he has before him his whole mind is lost in the object; as the marksman, to shoot straight, looks at the mark. How successful the result is, or how appealing to human nature, he judges afterwards, as an outsider might, and usually judges ill; since there is no life less apt to yield a broad understanding for human affairs or even for the residue of art itself, than the life of a man inspired, a man absorbed, as the genuine artist is, in his own travail. But into this travail, into this digestion and reproduction of the thing seen, a critic can hardly enter. Having himself the ulterior office of judge, he must not hope to rival nature's children in their sportiveness and intuition.

In an age of moral confusion, these circumstances may lead to a strange shifting of roles. The critic, feeling that something in the artist has escaped him, may labour to put himself in the artist's place. If he succeeded, the result would only be to make him a biographer; he would be describing in words the very intuitions which the artist had rendered in some other medium. To understand how the artist felt, however, is not criticism; criticism is an investigation of what the work is good for. Its function may be chiefly to awaken certain emotions in the beholder, to deepen in him certain habits of apperception; but even this most aesthetic element in the value of art does not borrow its value from the possible fact that the artist also shared those habits and emotions. If he did, and if they are desirable, so much the better for him; but his work would still have its value entirely in its power to propagate such good effects, whether they were already present in him or not. All criticism is therefore moral, since it deals with benefits and their relative weight. Psychological penetration and reconstructed biography may be excellent sport; if they do not reach historic truth they may at least exercise dramatic talent. Criticism, on the other hand, is a serious and public function; it shows the race assimilating the individual, dividing the immortal from the mortal part of a soul.

Representation naturally repeats those objects which are most interesting in themselves. Even the medium, when a choice is possible, is usually determined by the sort of objects to be reproduced. Instruments lose their virtue with their use and a medium of representation, together with its manipulation, is nothing but a vehicle. It is fit if it makes possible a good rendition. All accordingly hangs on what life has made interesting to the senses, on what presents itself persuasively to the artist for imitation; and living arts exist only while well-known, much-loved things imperatively demand to be copied, so that their reproduction has some honest non-aesthetic interest for mankind. Although subject-matter is often said to be indifferent to art, and an artist, when his art is secondary, may think of his technique only, nothing is really so poor and melancholy as art that is interested in itself and not in its subject. If any remnant of inspiration or value clings to such a performance, it comes from a surviving taste for something in the real world. Thus the literature that calls itself purely aesthetic is in truth prurient; without this half-avowed weakness to play upon, the coloured images evoked would have had nothing to marshal or to sustain them...

JUSTIFICATION OF ART

...Art actually segregates classes of men and masses of matter to serve its special interests. This involves expense; it impedes some possible activities and imposes others. On this ground, from the earliest time until our own, art has been occasionally attacked by moralists, who have felt that it fostered idolatry or luxury or irresponsible dreams. Of these attacks the most interesting is Plato's, because he was an artist by temperament, bred in the very focus of artistic life and discussion, and at the same time a consummate moral philosopher. His aesthetic sensibility was indeed so great that it led him, perhaps, into a relative error, in that he overestimated the influence which art can have on character and affairs. Homer's stories about the gods can hardly have demoralized the youths who recited them. No religion has ever given a picture of deity which men could have imitated without the grossest immorality. Yet these shocking representations have not had a bad effect on believers. The deity was opposed to their own vices; those it might itself be credited with offered no contagious example. In spite of the theologians, we know by instinct that in speaking of the gods we are dealing in myths and symbols. Some aspect of nature or some law of life, expressed in an attribute of deity, is what we really regard, and to regard such things, however sinister they may be, cannot but chasten and moralize us. The personal character that such a function would involve, if it were exercised willingly by a responsible being, is something that never enters our thoughts. No such painful image comes to perplex the plain sense of instinctive, poetic religion. To give moral importance to myths, as Plato tended to do, is to take them far too seriously and to belittle what they stand for. Left to themselves they float in an ineffectual stratum of the brain. They are understood and grow current precisely by not being pressed, like an idiom or a metaphor. The same aesthetic sterility appears at the other end of the scale, where fancy is anything but sacred. A Frenchman once saw in 'Punch and Judy' a shocking proof of British brutality, destined further to demoralize the nation; and yet the scandal may pass. That black tragedy reflects no very pretty manners, but puppets exercise no suasion over men.

To his supersensitive censure of myths Plato added strictures upon music and the drama: to excite passions idly was to enervate the soul. Only martial or religious strains should be heard in the ideal republic. Furthermore, art put before us a mere phantom of the good. True excellence was the function things had in use; the horseman knew the use and essence of a bridle better than the artisan did who put it together; but a painted bridle would lack even this relation to utility. It would rein in no horse, and was an impertinent sensuous reduplication of what, even when it had material being, was only an instrument and a means.

This reasoning has been little understood, because Platonists so soon lost sight of their master's Socratic habit and moral intent. They turned the good into an existence, making it thereby unmeaning. Plato's dialectic, if we do not thus abolish the force of its terms, is perfectly cogent: representative art has indeed no utility, and, if the good has been identified with efficiency in a military state, it can have no justification. Plato's Republic was avowedly a fallen state, a church militant, coming sadly short of perfection; and the joy which Plato as much as anyone could feel in sensuous art he postponed, as a man in mourning might, until life should be redeemed from baseness.

Never have art and beauty received a more glowing eulogy than is implied in Plato's censure. To him nothing was beautiful that was not beautiful to the core, and he would have thought to insult art—the remodelling of nature by reason—if he had given it a narrower field than all practice. As an architect who had fondly designed something impossible, or which might not please in execution, would at once erase it from the plan and abandon it for the love of perfect beauty and perfect art, so Plato wished to erase from pleasing appearance all that, when its operation was completed, would bring discord into the world. This was done in the ultimate interest of art and beauty, which in a cultivated mind are inseparable from the vitally good. It is mere barbarism to feel that a thing is aesthetically good but morally evil, or morally good but hateful to perception. Things partially evil or partially ugly may have to be chosen under stress of unfavourable circumstances, lest some worse thing come; but if a thing were ugly it would *thereby* not be wholly good, and if it were *altogether* good it would perforce be beautiful.

To criticize art on moral grounds is to pay it a high compliment by assuming that it aims to be adequate, and is addressed to a comprehensive mind. The only way in which art could disallow such criticism would be to protest its irresponsible infancy, and admit that it was a more or less amiable blatancy in individuals, and not *art* at all. Young animals often gambol in delightful fashion, and men also may, though hardly when they intend to do so. Sportive self-expression can be prized because human nature contains a certain elasticity and margin for experiment, in which waste activity is inevitable and may be precious: for this licence may lead, amid a thousand failures, to some real discovery and advance. Art, like life, should be free, since both are experimental. But it is one thing to make room for genius and to respect the sudden madness of poets through which, possibly, some god may speak, and it is quite another not to judge the result by rational standards. The earth's bowels are full of all sorts of rumblings; which of the oracles drawn thence is true can be judged only by the light of day. If an artist's inspiration has been happy, it has been so because his work can sweeten or ennoble the mind and because its total effect will be beneficent. Art being a part of life, the criticism of art is a part of morals.

Maladjustments in human society are still so scandalous, they touch matters so much more pressing than fine art, that maladjustments in the latter are passed over with a smile, as if art were at any rate an irresponsible miraculous parasite that the legislator had better not meddle with. The day may come, however, if the state is ever reduced to a tolerable order, when questions of art will be the most urgent questions of morals, when genius at last will feel responsible, and the twist given to imagination will seem the most crucial thing in life. Under a thin disguise, the momentous character of imaginative choices has already been fully recognized by mankind. Men have passionately loved their special religions, languages, and manners, and preferred death to a life flowering in any other fashion. In justifying this attachment forensically, with arguments on the low level of men's named and consecrated interests, people have indeed said, and perhaps come to believe, that their imaginative interests were material interests at bottom, thinking thus to give them more weight and legitimacy; whereas in truth material life itself would be nothing worth, were it not, in its essence and its issue, ideal.

It was stupidly asserted, however, that if a man omitted the prescribed ceremonies or had unauthorized dreams about the gods, he would lose his battles in this world and go to hell in the other. He who runs can see that these expectations are not founded on any evidence, on any observation of what actually occurs; they are obviously a *mirage* arising from a direct ideal passion, that tries to justify itself by indirection and by falsehoods, as it has no need to do. We all read facts in the way most congruous with our intellectual habit, and when this habit drives us to effulgent creations, absorbing and expressing the whole current of our being, it not merely biases our reading of this world but carries us into another world altogether, which we posit instead of the real one, or beside it.

Grotesque as the blunder may seem by which we thus introduce our poetic tropes into the sequence of external events or existences, the blunder is intellectual only; morally, zeal for our special rhetoric may not be irrational. The lovely Phoebus is no fact for astronomy, nor does he stand behind the material sun, in some higher heaven, physically superintending its movements; but Phoebus is a fact in his own region, a token of man's joyful piety in the presence of the forces that really condition his welfare. In the region of symbols, in the world of poetry, Phoebus has his inalienable rights. Forms of poetry are forms of human life. Languages express national character and enshrine particular ways of seeing and valuing events. To make substitutions and extensions in expression is to give the soul, in her inmost substance, a somewhat new constitution. A method of apperception is a spontaneous variation in mind, perhaps the origin of a new moral species...

There is consequently nothing fitted to colour human happiness more pervasively than art does, nor to express more deeply the mind's internal habit. In educating the imagination art crowns all moral endeavour, which from the beginning is a species of art, and which becomes a fine art more completely as it works in a freer medium...

THE CRITERION OF TASTE

Dogmatism in matters of taste has the same status as dogmatism in other spheres. It is initially justified by sincerity, being a systematic expression of a man's preferences; but it becomes absurd when its basis in a particular disposition is ignored and it pretends to have an absolute or metaphysical scope. Reason, with the order which in every region it imposes on life, is grounded on an animal nature and has no other function than to serve the same; and it fails to exercise its office quite as much when it oversteps its bounds, and forgets whom it is serving, as when it neglects some part of its legitimate province and serves its master imperfectly, without considering all his interests.

Dialectic, logic, and morals lose their authority and become inept if they trespass upon the realm of physics and try to disclose existences; while physics is a mere idea in the realm of poetic meditation. So the notorious diversities which human taste exhibits do not become conflicts, and raise no moral problem, until their basis or their function has been forgotten, and each has claimed a right to assert itself exclusively. This claim is altogether absurd, and we might fail to understand how so preposterous an attitude could be assumed by anybody did we not remember that every young animal thinks himself absolute, and that dogmatism in the thinker is only the speculative side of greed and courage in the brute. The brute cannot surrender his appetites nor abdicate his primary right to dominate his environment. What experience and reason may teach him is merely how to make his self-assertion well balanced and successful. In the same way taste is bound to maintain its preferences but free to rationalize them. After a man has compared his feelings with the no less legitimate feelings of other creatures, he can reassert his own with more complete authority, since now he is aware of their necessary ground in his nature, and of their affinities with whatever other interests his nature enables him to recognize in others and to co-ordinate with his own.

A criterion of taste is, therefore, nothing but taste itself in its more deliberate and circumspect form. Reflection refines particular sentiments by bringing them into sympathy with all rational life. There is consequently the greatest possible difference in authority between taste and taste, and while delight in drums and eagle feathers is perfectly genuine and has no cause to blush for itself, it cannot be compared in scope or representative value with delight in a symphony or an epic. The very instinct that is satisfied by beauty prefers one beauty to another; and we have only to question and purge our aesthetic feelings in order to obtain our criterion of taste. This criterion will be natural, personal, autonomous; a circumstance that will give it authority over our own judgment—which is all moral science is concerned about—and will extend its authority over other minds also, in so far as their constitution is similar to ours. In that measure what is a genuine instance of reason in us, others will recognize for a genuine expression of reason in themselves also.

Aesthetic feeling, in different people, may make up a different fraction of life and vary greatly in volume. The more nearly insensible a man is the more incompetent he becomes to proclaim the values which sensibility might have. To beauty men are habitually insensible, even while they are awake and rationally active. Tomes of aesthetic criticism hang on a few moments of real delight and intuition. It is in rare and scattered instants that beauty smiles even on her adorers, who are reduced for habitual comfort to remembering her past favours. An aesthetic glow may pervade experience, but that circumstance is seldom remarked; it figures only as an influence working subterraneously on thoughts and judgments which in themselves take a cognitive or practical direction. Only when the aesthetic ingredient becomes predominant do we exclaim, How beautiful! Ordinarily the pleasures which formal perception gives remain an undistinguished part of our comfort or curiosity.

Taste is formed in those moments when aesthetic emotion is massive and distinct; preferences then grown conscious, judgments then put into words, will reverberate through calmer hours; they will constitute prejudices, habits of apperception, secret standards for all other beauties. A period of life in which such intuitions have been frequent may amass tastes and ideals sufficient for the rest of our days. Youth in these matters governs maturity, and while men may develop their early impressions more systematically and find confirmations of them in various quarters, they will seldom look at the world afresh or use new categories in deciphering it. Half our standards come from our first masters, and the other half from our first loves. Never being so deeply stirred again, we remain persuaded that no objects save those we then discovered can have a true sublimity. These high-water marks of aesthetic life may easily be reached under tutelage. It may be some eloquent appreciations read in a book, or some preference expressed by a gifted friend, that may have revealed unsuspected beauties in art or nature; and then, since our own perception was vicarious and obviously inferior in volume to that which our mentor possessed, we shall take his judgments for our criterion, since they were the source and exemplar of all our own. Thus the volume and intensity of some appreciations, especially when nothing of the kind has preceded, makes them authoritative over our subsequent judgments. On those warm moments hang all our cold systematic opinions; and while the latter fill our days and shape our careers it is only the former that are crucial and alive.

A race which loves beauty holds the same place in history that a season of love or enthusiasm holds in an individual life. Such a race has a pre-eminent right to pronounce upon beauty and to bequeath its judgments to duller peoples...

Some persons, themselves inattentive, imagine, for instance, that Greek sculpture is abstract, that it has left out all the detail and character which they cannot find on the surface, as they might in a modern work. In truth it contains those features, as it were, in solution and in the resultant which, when reduced to harmony, they would produce. It embodies a finished humanity which only varied exercises could have attained, for as the body is the existent ground for all possible actions, in which as actions they exist only potentially, so a perfect body, such as a sculptor might conceive, which ought to be ready for all excellent activities, cannot present them all in act but only the readiness for them. The features that might express them severally must be absorbed and mastered, hidden like a sword in its scabbard, and reduced to a general dignity or grace. Though such immersed eloquence be at first overlooked and seldom explicitly acknowledged, homage is nevertheless rendered to it in the most unmistakable ways. When lazy artists, backed by no great technical or moral discipline, think they, too, can produce masterpieces by summary treatment, their failure shows how pregnant and supreme a thing simplicity is. Every man, in proportion to his experience and moral distinction, returns to the simple but inexhaustible work of finished minds, and finds more and more of his own soul responsive to it.

Human nature, for all its margin of variability, has a substantial core which is invariable, as the human body has a structure which it cannot lose without perishing altogether; for as creatures grow more complex a greater number of their organs become vital and indispensable. Advanced forms will rather die than surrender a tittle of their character; a fact which is the physical basis for loyalty and martyrdom. Any deep interpretation of oneself, or indeed of anything, has for that reason a largely representative truth. Other men, if they look closely, will make the same discovery for themselves. Hence distinction and profundity, in spite of their rarity, are wont to be largely recognized. The best men in all ages keep classic traditions alive. These men have on their side the weight of superior intelligence, and, though they are few, they might even claim the weight of numbers, since the few of all ages, added together, may be more than the many who in any one age follow a temporary fashion. Classic work is nevertheless always national, or at least characteristic of its period, as the classic poetry of each people is that in which its language appears most pure and free. To translate it is impossible; but it is easy to find that the human nature so inimitably expressed in each masterpiece is the same that, under different circumstance, dictates a different performance. The deviations between races and men are not yet so great as is the ignorance of self, the blindness to the native ideal, which prevails in most of them. Hence a great man of a remote epoch is more intelligible than a common man of our own time...

PENITENT ART

...Fortunately revivals now seem to be over. Ruins and museums are interesting to the antiquary; they stir the historical imagination, and dazzle us here and there with some ray of living beauty, like that of a jewel; but they cannot supply inspiration. In art, in poetry, unless you become as a little child you cannot enter the kingdom of heaven. Little children is what artists and poets are now striving hard to be; little children who instead of blowing a tin trumpet blow by chance through a whole orchestra, but with the same emotion as the child; or who, instead of daubing a geometrical skeleton with a piece of chalk, can daub a cross-eyed cross-section of the entire spectrum or a compound fracture of a nightmare. Such is Cubism: by no means an inexpert or meaningless thing. Before you can compose a chaos or paint the unnamable, you must train yourself to a severe abstention from all practical habits of perception; you must heroically suppress the understanding. The result, when the penance is genuinely performed, has a very deep and recondite charm; you revert to what the spinal column might feel if it had a separate consciousness, or to what the retina might see if it could be painlessly cut off from the brain; lights, patterns, dynamic suggestions, sights and memories fused together, hypnotic harmonies such as may visit a vegetative or even mineral sensibility; you become a thousand prisms and mirrors reflecting one another. This is one kind of aesthetic repentance. Vain, vain, it says to itself, was the attempt to depict or beautify external objects; let material things be what they will; what are they to the artist? Nature has the urgency of life, which art cannot rival; it has the lure, the cruelty, of actual existence, where all is sin and confusion and vanity, a hideous strife of forms devouring one another, in which all are mutilated and doomed. What is that to the spirit? Let it confess its own impotence in that field, and abandon all attempts to observe or preserve what are called *things*: let it devote itself instead to cleansing the inside of the cup, to purifying its sensibility, which is after all what Nature plays upon when she seems to us to be beautiful. Perhaps in that way spirit may abstract the gold of beauty and cast the dross away—all that alloy of preoccupation with material forms and external events and moral sentiments and vain animal adventures which has so long distracted the misguided artist, when he could paint the whole world and had lost his own soul. It is always the play of sensibility, and nothing else, that lends interest to external themes; and it was an evil obsession with alien things that dragged sensibility into a slavery to things which stifled and degraded it: *salvation lies in emancipating the medium.*

To renounce representation, or be representative only by accident, is accordingly one sort of penitent art; but there is another sort, more humble and humorous. This second sort makes no attempt to resist the impulse to observe and to express external things. It does not proudly imagine that the medium, which is the human contribution to representation, can be sufficient unto itself. On the contrary, in its sensuous orchestration, it is content to be rudimentary, to work in clay or in wood, and to dress in homespun. It is all feeling, all childlike tenderness, all sense of life. Persons and animals fascinate it. At the same time, warned by the fate of explicit poets and realistic painters, it does not attempt, in its portraiture, to give more than a pregnant hint, some large graphic sign, some profound caricature. Don't be rhetorical, it says; don't try to be exhaustive; all that is worth saying can be said in words of one syllable. Look long, and be brief. It is not in their material entirety and detail that things penetrate to the soul, but in their simple large identity, as a child knows his mother, nurse, or dog. Fresh inchoate forms, voices draped in mantles, people the mind, and return to it in dreams. Monsters and dwarfs were the first gods; the half, said a Greek proverb, is better than the whole. The implicit is alone important where life is concerned: nothing is more eloquent than an abstract posture, an immovable single gesture. Let art abandon reproduction and become indication. If it threatens thereby to become caricature, know that profound art can never be anything else. If men, when seen truly, take on the aspect of animals or puppets, it is because they are animals and puppets at bottom. But all caricature need not be unkind; it may be tender, or even sublime. The distortion, the single emphasis, the extreme simplification may reveal a soul which rhetoric and self-love had hidden in a false rationality. The absurd is the naked truth, the pathetic appeal of sheer fact, attempting to come into existence, like a featherless chick peeping out of its egg-shell. All this pompous drapery of convention was a disguise; strip it away. Do not make maps of your images; make companions of them, make idols. Be reticent, emphatic, moody, bold; *salvation lies in caricature.*

Accustomed as they are to revivals, some critics have called this form of aesthetic penance a revival of savage art; but the mood is reversed. Savages were never rudimentary on purpose; they were not experimenting in the distortion or simplification of forms; much less, of course, did they voluntarily eliminate all representation of objects in order to deepen sensibility for the medium. They simply painted as well as they could. We have got far beyond that. Penitent art, childish as it may seem at times, is a refinement, perhaps an over-refinement; it is not so much crude or incompetent, as ascetic or morbid. It is also sometimes a little vulgar; because one of the forms of caricature and self-revelation is to be brutal, to flaunt what is out of place, what spoils the picture. Tragedy used to be noble; there is a new refinement in seeing how often it is ignoble; there is a second tragedy in that. Perhaps what we regard at first sight as a terrible decline in art may be sometimes the awakening of this sort of self-scorn. See how ugly I am, it cries, how brutish, common, and deformed! There are remains of sculpture and paintings of the late Roman Empire in some respects like our latest experiments. The decorative splendour (which was very marked) is lost; we miss the coloured marbles, the gold, the embroideries, the barbaric armour and jewels; but the stunted pathetic human figures remain in crowds. It seems that the spirit had no joy in man any more; it hid him in hieratic garments or pityingly recorded his gregarious misery. He was a corpse laid out in pontifical vestments. We too are dying; but in nature the death of one thing is commonly the birth of another. Instead of decorating a Byzantine sanctuary, our artists do penance in a psychological desert, studying their own sensations, the mysteries of sheer light and sound; and as music was long ago divorced from poetry and instrumental music from singing, so a luxurious but strident art is detaching itself from everything but its own medium. This on the decorative side; in representation the same retrenchment stops at another level. Representation too has a psychological medium; fancy must create the images which the observer or reproducer of things conceives to be their forms. These images are not the forms of things at all; not only is their perspective created by the observer, but their character, when it is truly considered, is amazingly summary, variable, and fantastic—a mere wraith, a mere hint, a mere symbol. What we suppose we see, what we *say* things look like, is rather an inventory, collected in memory and language, of many successive observations; it is discursive study, registered perhaps in discursive painting. But as the total composition never was nor ever could be a living image, so its parts are not images any longer; in being arrested they have acquired new boundaries and lost half their primitive essence. We may paint the things we see, we cannot arrest the images by which we see them; all we can do—if the images and not the things are what interest us—is to paint something that, by some occult trick of optics, may revive the image in some particular; and then, although the picture when studied discursively may not resemble the thing at all, it may bring back to us, as it were by scent, the feeling which the thing originally gave us; and we may say that it has caught the *spirit* of the thing. It is the medium that in such a case animates the object, and seems to obscure it; and this medium which we call sense in so far as things affect us through it, we call spirit in so far as it modifies our view of the things. The more we transform things in seeing them, the more we seem to spiritualize them and turn them into forms of our own sensibility, regarding the living image in us as the dramatic essence of the object. It is the business of science to correct this illusion; but the penitent artist—who has taken refuge in the spirit and is not striving to stretch his apprehension into literal truth, since the effort to depict things discursively has proved a vain and arid ambition—the penitent artist is content with the rhythms, echoes, or rays which things awaken within him; and in proportion as these reverberations are actually renewed, the poem remains a cry, the story a dream, the building a glimpse, the portrait a caricature.

Selected Portraits

MY FATHER

. . . My father was educated at Valladolid, I don't know first under what schoolmaster, but eventually at the university there, where he studied law; and he at least learned Latin well enough to take pleasure in translating the tragedies of Seneca into Castilian blank verse; a pure work of love, since he could expect no advancement, perhaps rather the opposite, from such an exhibition of capricious industry. Nor was that his only taste; he also studied painting, and quite professionally, although he made no great progress in it. His feeling for the arts and sciences was extraordinarily different from that which prevailed in the 1880s in English-speaking circles. As to painting, all in England was a matter of culture, of the pathos of distance, of sentimental religiosity, Pre-Raphaelitism, and supercilious pose. Even the learned and gifted that I saw in Oxford were saturated with affectations. My friend Lionel Johnson was typical: although thirty years later, during the war, I had other distinguished friends in Oxford, Robert Bridges and Father Waggett, who were not in the least affected. But my father could not understand the English mind, greatly as he admired and respected the practical lordliness of Britain. Speaking once of Newman, he said he wondered why Newman broke with the Anglican establishment. Was it so as to wear a trailing red silk gown? I had some difficulty in making him admit that Newman could have been sincere; perhaps it was possible, if, as I said, Newman had never doubted the supernatural authority of the Church. But of inner unrest or faith suddenly born out of despair my father had absolutely no notion. Could he ever have read the Confessions of his patron saint, Saint Augustine? Was that not a natural sequel to the tragedies of Seneca?

As to painting, my father's ideas were absolutely those of the craftsman, the artisan, following his trade conscientiously with no thought or respect for the profane crowd of rich people who might be babbling about art in their ignorance.

This jealous professionalism did not exclude speculation and criticism; but they were the speculation and criticism of the specialist, scientific and materialistic. He viewed the arts in the manner of Leonardo, whom probably he had never read. In talking about the pictures in the Prado, which I had seen for the first time, he approved of an observation I made about 'El Pasmo de Sicilia', that all the figures were brick-coloured except that of Christ, which was whitish—a contrast that seemed artificial. He said I had been looking at the picture to some purpose. But he was disappointed when he questioned me about the Goyas, because I said nothing about the manner of painting, and only thought of the subjects, the ladies' fashions, and the sensuality of the eighteenth-century notion of happiness, coarser in Goya than in Watteau.

His methods were not less workmanlike than his thoughts. His easel, his colours, ground by himself with a glass pestle and carefully mixed with the oil, his palette and his brushes were objects of wonder to my childish heart. I was too young to catch the contagion and try to imitate him; but afterwards, when drawing became a pastime for me (as it still is), I wondered sometimes if my father's example and lessons would have helped me to make the progress in draughtsmanship which I have never made. And I doubt that they would have helped me. Because composition and ideal charm, which are everything to me in all the arts, seemed to be nothing to my father. I might have acquired a little more manual skill, and corrected a few bad mannerisms; but I should soon have broken away and turned to courses that he could not approve. Yet I think that he himself suffered in his painting, as in his life, from the absence of any ideal inspiration. He was arrested by the sheer mechanics of the art, as I was arrested by ignorance of them; and he remained an amateur all his life in his professionalism, because after measuring his drawing, and catching the likeness (since his paintings were all portraits) and laying on his first strata of colour, he would become uncertain and discouraged, without a clear vision of what might render his picture living, distinctive, harmonious, and in a word *beautiful.*

When I once asked him, apropos of his liberal politics, the hollowness of which I already began to feel, what ideal of society he would approve, he said he had no *ideal.* 'I don't know what I want, but I know what I don't want.' We laughed, and the matter ended there, since discussion with him was rendered difficult by his extreme deafness; and few things seem worth saying when one has to reduce them first to a few words, and to make and impose an express effort in order to communicate them. But in my reflections afterwards it has often occurred to me that this position, knowing what you don't like but not knowing what you like, may be sincere enough emotionally, but not intellectually. Rejection is a form of self-assertion. You have only to look back upon yourself as a person who hates this or that to discover what it is that you secretly love. Hatred and love are imposed on the spirit by the psyche; and though the spirit may have no image of the end pursued, but only of jolts and obstacles on the way, there could be no jolts or obstacles if the life of the psyche had not a specific direction, a specific good demanded, which when discovered to the spirit will become an ideal. Not to know what one wants is simple absence of self-knowledge. It is abdication—my father was inclined to abdicate—and the insistence on *not* wanting this, or *not* wanting that, becomes an unamiable exhibition of the seamy side of your nature, the fair face of which you have turned downwards. Now my father hated shams, among which he placed religion, and hated complicated purposes or ambitions, with all the havoc they make; from which expressed dislikes it would be easy to infer that he loved the garden of Epicurus, with simple natural pleasures, quietness, and a bitter-sweet understanding of everything. This garden of Epicurus, though my father would have denied it, was really a vegetable garden, a convent garden; and it seemed strange to me that a man who had been so much at sea, and seen many remote countries, should take such a narrow and stifled view of human nature. He was tolerant and kindly towards the minor vices and the physical ills of mankind; he was tightly and ferociously closed against all higher follies. But is it not an initial folly to exclude all happy possibilities and condemn oneself to limp through life on one leg? If it be legitimate to live physically, why isn't it legitimate to live morally? I am afraid that my father, unlike my mother, was not brave.

In some directions, however, my father was docile and conservative. He had a great respect for authority in science or letters, and would quote Quintilian in support of his own preference for limited views: *Ad cognoscendum genus humanum sufficit una domus*:* 'For exploring human nature one household is large enough.' Yet when authority made for boldness of thought or for ambitious aims, he mocked it. In the region of Avila, which is some 4000 feet above the sea level, the heath is strewn with many boulders, large and small, often fantastically piled one over another; and one day when we noticed a particularly capricious heap of them, I said what a pity it was that we hadn't a geologist at hand to tell us about the origin of this odd formation. 'What would be the use of that?' said my father. 'He would tell us his theory, but he wasn't there to see the fact.' Hobbes had said the same thing: 'No discourse whatsoever can end in absolute knowledge of fact'; and I have made the *authority of things*, as against the presumption of words or ideas, a principle of my philosophy. Yet we materialists cannot consistently reject the evidence of analogy between one thing and another, since materialism itself is an interpretation of appearance by certain analogies running through things, and helping us to trace their derivation. There are glaciers in movement today in other mountainous regions the effects of which on the rocks they carry with them may be observed, as also the effect of running streams and beating waves in rounding and smoothing pebbles: so that those boulders on the skirts of the Castilian mountains may be plausibly explained by analogy. But my father feared to be cheated: and whenever he suggested any-

* Probably a confused memory, mine or my father's, of Juvenal, *Satire XIII*, 159–60:

> Humani generis mores tibi nosse volenti
> Sufficit una domus.

thing a bit paradoxical, he would hasten to disown any personal responsibility for it. 'I haven't invented that myself,' he would say; 'I have read it in a printed book, *en letras de molde*.' There seemed to be a curious mixture in his mind of the primitive man's awe for any scripture, with the sceptic's distrust of every theory and every report. And yet this very distrust tempted him to odd hypotheses at times to explain the motives behind what people said or imagined. If a visiting lady told us something interesting, which in my relative innocence I supposed might be true, it would startle me to hear my father say, as soon as she had turned her back: 'I wonder *why* she said that.'

Respect for authorities is fatal when the doctors disagree and the pupil is not self-confident enough to give direction to this freedom. My father's style in painting, for instance, inclined to clear shadows, pure outlines, and fidelity to the model, with little thought of picturesque backgrounds or decorative patterns. Had he had greater decision and dared to follow the ideal that he denied he possessed; had he simplified his surfaces boldly and emphasized characteristic features and attitudes without exaggerating them, he would have painted like Manet. But perhaps when he was at work on a canvas that promised well, he would visit the Prado, and some lurid figures by Ribera would catch his eye, or the magic lights in darkness of Rembrandt, and he would come home and spoil his picture by incongruously deepening the shadows. Stronger imaginations than his have been distracted and defeated by rival contagions; he at least was conscious of his defeat, and finished very few of his portraits; and he deputed even these to be finished when in reality they were scarcely begun...

My father was as strong a liberal as my mother; but he had studied Roman law and looked upon government as an indispensable instrument for securing peace and prosperity. Arcadia and the state of nature were among the ideals that he refused to have. He had lived among the Malays in the Philippines, the most blameless of primitive peoples, and he spoke kindly of them; but the only Malays he respected were those that had become Mohammedan and warlike—pirates if you like—and had kept their independence. He was modest enough not to hate superiors, as my mother did; he admired them.

When I ask myself what it was that he admired, say in the English or in the Romans, and what he respected them for, I think it was not that he had any inner sympathy with their spirit. The English I know he didn't understand: their whole poetic, sporting, frank, gentle side was unknown to him. He thought them only stiff, determined, competent and formidable. They were all captains of frigates pacing the quarter deck. And they were all rich, oppressively rich; because in his respect and admiration for the English there was an undercurrent of contempt—as towards people who are too well dressed. If you wish to be thought a gentleman among the English, he would say, you must shave and change your linen every morning, and never eat with your knife. The only time I remember him to have been annoyed with me was during my first visit to him in 1883, when we had made an excursion to the Escorial, going third class at night from Avila, because in the morning, before we had breakfast, I wanted to wash my face and hands, and asked the waitress for some soap. '*¡Cuantos requisitos!*' he exclaimed. How many requirements!

As to the Romans, I am uncertain of his feelings. He often quoted them as great authorities, especially the line of Lucretius about *Tantum religio potuit suadere malorum*. But it was the thought, the political wisdom in them, that he cared for. He took their Greek refinements, as the true Romans took them, for mere accessories and matters of fashion. When I once wrote out for him (he had few books) the well-known little ode to Pyrrha in the first book of Horace, he was arrested at the word *uvida*, and remarked on the interweaving of the concordance between adjectives and nouns. Of the poetry, of the Epicurean blasé sentiment, he said nothing. If I had written out the first ode of the fourth book, through which so much pierces that is disquieting, what would he have said? He might have shrugged his shoulders at pagan corruption: societies are like human bodies, they all rot in the end, unless you burn them up in time. But he was no soldier, not merely no soldier temperamentally in that personally he shrank from conflicts, but no soldier morally or religiously in that he saw nothing worth fighting for. Of course, you fought for your life, if attacked: that was a mechanical reaction of the organism. But he could have felt no sympathy with the martial regimen and martial patriotism of an ancient city. There was something sporting about it, a club of big boys, only hereditary, sanctified, made eloquent and mysterious by religion. The Spaniard is an individualist; he can be devout mystically, because that is his own devotion to his own deity; but socially, externally, he distrusts everything and everybody, even his priests and his kings; and he would have distrusted the *Numina* of Romulus and Remus...

All this formed a meagre, old-fashioned, almost indifferent stage-setting to my father's life: the real drama was his health. He was a wiry and (for a Spaniard) a tall man, and lived to the age of seventy-nine; and long walks and long sea-voyages in comfortless old sailing vessels were nothing to him. Yet he was a hypochondriac, always watching his symptoms, and fearing that death was at hand. Whether this was congenital or the effect of insidious ailments proper to tropical climates, I do not know: but the sense of impediment, of insecurity, was constant in him. It defeated any clear pleasure in any project, and mixed a certain bitterness with such real pleasures as he enjoyed. They were snatched, as it were, from the fire with a curious uneasiness, as if they were forbidden and likely to be punished. And this when theoretically he was absolutely rationalistic, materialistic, and free from moral or physical superstition. Perhaps, if a man's bowels are treacherous, he cannot trust anything else. Dysentery removes all the confidence that the will has in itself: the alien, the irresistibly dissolving, force is too much within you. Moreover, my father had other obvious discouragements to face: poverty, deafness, semi-blindness: yet these, if his digestion had been good and strong, I don't think would have cowed him. He had plenty of Castilian indifference to circumstances and to externals, plenty of independence and capacity to live content with little and quite alone. But the firmness of the inner man must not be undermined by a sour stomach: that, at least, seems to have been my father's experience. Intelligence and brave philosophy were mixed strangely with this discouragement. On one of the many occasions when he thought, or dreaded, that he might be on his deathbed, he felt a sudden desire for some boiled chicken, without in the least giving up his asseveration that he was dying; and as his deafness prevented him from properly modulating his voice, he cried out with a shout that resounded through the whole house: *¡La Unción y la gallina!*, 'Extreme Unction and a chicken!' Extreme Unction only, be it observed. That is the last Sacrament, to be received passively, without saying a word. It would put him to no inconvenience. To have asked for confession and communion would have implied much talking; he was too far gone for that. Extreme Unction would do perfectly to avoid all unpleasantness regarding his funeral and burial in holy ground. Nobody would need to be distressed about his soul. And meantime, since these were his last moments, and the consequences of any imprudence would make no difference, why not boldly indulge himself one last time, and have some boiled chicken? That, I am confident, was his thought. And he had the chicken. The last Sacrament, this time, was not required.

MY MOTHER[1]

. . . The date of my mother's birth, according to her official papers, was 1828, but there is reason to believe that in reality it was 1826. When she was brought to Spain in 1835 the shocking fact appeared that she had never been christened. Was there no Catholic priest in Glasgow in those days, and none in Winchester, Virginia? Had no travelling ecclesiastic been met with in all those wanderings? No doubt her father's enlightened principles made him regard all religious practices, morally and philosophically, as indifferent, while socially it was advisable that everyone should be affiliated to the religious customs prevalent in his country. But what was to be my mother's country? If it were to be Scotland or Virginia, she ought to be christened and brought up a Protestant: if it were to be Spain, it was imperative that she should be a Catholic. The matter therefore had to be suspended until the question of final residence was settled: although it may seem singular that my grandmother should have wholly acquiesced in this view and allowed her daughter to grow up, as they say in Spain, a Moor. Now, however, the matter had to be patched up as expeditiously and quietly as possible. Friends and relations, even clerical advisers, are very accommodating in Spain and very ingenious. The age of seven, the canonical age of reason, when one begins to sin of one's own accord, was the right age for confirmation; young Josefina was small for her age; let her official age be reduced to seven years, let a private christening, to supply the place of the missing documents, be smuggled in before the confirmation, and then the child would be launched quite legally and becomingly in her religious career, with confession and communion to follow immediately. This wealth of sacraments, raining down on her unprepared and extraordinarily self-reliant little soul, seems not to have left much hunger for further means of grace. My mother always spoke of such things as of troublesome and

[1] Much extraneous material that Santayana included has had to be omitted.

empty social requirements; and even ordinary social requirements, like visiting, rather annoyed her, as if they interfered with her liberty and interrupted her peace.

On the whole, however, her ten years or more of girlhood in Barcelona seem to have been gay and happy—the only frankly happy period of her life. Without being robust, her health was perfect, her needlework exquisite, her temper equable and calm; she loved and was loved by her girl-friends; she read romantic verses and select novels; above all, she danced. That was the greatest pleasure in life for her: not for the sake of her partners—those were surely only round dances, and the partners didn't count; what counted was the joy of motion, the sense of treading lightly, in perfect time, a sylph in spotless muslin, enriched with a ribbon or a flower, playing discreetly with her fan, and sailing through the air with feet that seemed scarcely to touch the ground. Even in her old age my mother never walked, she stepped. And she would say in her quaint, perhaps Virginian English: 'Will you step in?' She was not beautiful, and prematurely regarded herself as an old woman, and put on a white lace cap; but she had good points and made a favourable ideal impression, even if she did not positively attract. I can imagine her in her young days, agile of foot and hand, silent and enigmatic behind her large sunken blue eyes, thin lips, and brown corkscrew curls, three on a side, setting off her white complexion. If men did not often make love to her, especially not the men who care specifically for women, she amply took her revenge. Her real attachments, apart from her devotion to her father, were to her women friends, not to crowds of them, but to two or three and for life. To men as men, even to her two husbands, she seems to have been cold, critical and sad, as if conscious of yielding to some inevitable but disappointing fatality...

In the decline of his life, he [her father] was suddenly transferred to a tropical climate[1] entirely new to him, without advice or such resources, medical or other, as even a tropical

[1] He was appointed governor to the Batan islands in 1846. His daughter accompanied him there.

colony would have afforded in its capital city; and he succumbed. His wife also had meantime died in Barcelona; and my mother was left an orphan, without property or friends, alone at the age of twenty in a remote island peopled only by Indians. It was at this crisis that she first gave proof of her remarkable courage and strength of character. With what ready money she could scrape together, and with her jewels for security, she bought or hired a small sailing vessel, engaged a native skipper and supercargo, and began to send hemp for sale in Manila. If she was without friends in a social sense, the people round her were friendly. Two of her servants, her man cook and her maid, offered to remain with her without wages; and her skipper and agent proved faithful; so much so that in a short time a small fund was gathered, and she began to feel secure and independent in her singular position...

That solitude, at once tragic and protective, was one day disturbed by a fresh arrival. Batan had remained without a governor; but at last a new governor, a young man, was sent out from Manila. Now two white persons, a young man and a young lady without a chaperon, alone together on a tropical island formed an idyllic but dangerous picture; and it became necessary for that young lady in order to avoid scandal to return to a corrupt civilization. Thus the life of pure virtue, as I might show if I were Hegel, by its inner ironical dialectic transformed itself into conventional life; and fate laughed at the antithesis that prudence and decorum opposed to its decrees: because, though my mother proudly turned her back on that young intruder, and went to live with friends [the Iparraguirres] in Manila, he nevertheless was destined, many years later, to become her second husband and my father...

My mother always spoke contemptuously of love-making and match-making: yet she herself was twice married, and not by any simple concatenation of circumstances but in spite of serious obstacles. Passion may inspire determination in a Romeo and a Juliet; in my mother I think determination rather took passion's place. She decided what was best, and then defied all difficulties in doing it. Now it was certainly not best, or even possible to remain forever a guest of the Iparraguirres. Victorina any day might be married and what would the orphaned Josefina do then? Go to Montevideo to keep house for her uncle, the parish priest? Wouldn't it be wiser and more natural herself to marry? Certainly not any one of those Creole youths or Spanish officials who in the first place did not particularly court her, and in the second place were not virtuous. However, there was one wholly exceptional young man in Manila, tall, blond, aquiline, blue-eyed, an American, a Protestant, and unmistakably virtuous.[1] And that young man, probably as little passionate as herself, and as little trustful of the Spanish young women as she was of the Spanish young men, could not but be visited by kindred thoughts. Was not this grave, silent, proud orphan wholly unlike the other young girls? Was she not blue-eyed like himself? Did she not speak English? Had she not lived in Virginia, which if not as reassuring as Boston, still was in the United States? And as he found on inquiry, if she was not a Protestant, at least she was no bigoted Catholic, but a stern, philosophical, virtuous soul. Was she not courage personified, and had she not suddenly found herself alone and penniless and, like Benjamin Franklin, made her own way in the world? Was she not a worthy, a safe, a suitable, even an exceptionally noble and heroic person to marry? And was it not safer, more suitable and more virtuous for a merchant in the Far East to be married to a foreigner than not to be married at all? Such convergent reflections found ways of expressing themselves, and the logical conclusion was easily drawn. A virtuous marriage meant safety and peace for him in his old bonds, and it meant safety and peace for her, who had no dread of novelty, in new bonds rationally chosen...

The loss of her first-born did not affect my mother as it would any mother, especially a Spanish mother. There were no violent fits of lamentation, no floods of tears, no exag-

[1] George Sturgis, whom she married in 1849.

gerated cult of the grave or relics of the departed. Especially in a woman who has or is expecting other children, as was the case here, such wild sorrow has its period: the present and the future soon begin to gain healthily upon the past. But with my mother this event was crucial. It made a radical revolution in her heart. It established there a reign of silent despair, permanent, devastating, ruffled perhaps by fresh events on the surface, but always dark and heavy beneath, like the depths of the sea. Her husband, with his sanguine disposition and American optimism, couldn't understand it. He wrote worried letters home, expressing his fears for her life or her reason. He didn't see the strength of this coldness. Her health was not affected. She continued to bear children at frequent intervals —five in seven years. She did not neglect her appearance, her embroidery, her friends, or her flowers. She spoke little, but she never had been loquacious: and when, in a brief interval between babies, he proposed a voyage to Boston, to present her and the children to his family, she readily agreed. This marriage for him had been extremely happy. He described his domestic bliss in glowing terms in his letters. Was it not a happy marriage for her also? Of course it was. Why then this deadly calm, this strange indifference? Why these silent steps, grave bows, and few words, such as people exchange at a funeral?

Many Spanish women live in this way the life of a Mater Dolorosa, and are devout for that reason to Our Lady of the Seven Sorrows, with seven swords fixed in her heart. They give a religious or pictorial turn to their despair; but at bottom they have the same experience that my mother congealed into a stoical philosophy. She knew that her father's positivism and humanism and thirst for progress had a black lining; and she had the courage to wear his mantle with the black side out. Let the world see the truth of its own madness. She at least would not pretend not to see it.

However, let me not exaggerate. This second life, this mystic unmasking of the commonplace and the obvious, was not explicit in my mother. She didn't know what her real philosophy was: her verbal philosophy remained the most trite and superficial positivism. Her depth was entirely psychic, passionately dispassionate, intensely determined and cold; but her intelligence had no depth. It was borrowed, and borrowed not from the best sources, but from the intellectual fashions of her father's time. Therefore, in her outward life and actions, she showed a persistent attachment to persons and to principles that really meant very little to her... That which she saw and prized in Boston was only what the Sturgises represented: wealth, kindness, honesty, and a general air of being competent and at home in the world. They belonged to the aristocracy of commerce, the only one my mother respected and identified with the aristocracy of virtue. The titular nobility of Spain and other European countries, which she knew only by hearsay, was only the aristocracy of undeserved privilege and luxurious vice. It was detestable; it was also out of reach; and she felt doubly virtuous, being cut off from it physically as well as morally. In Boston her friends were at the top, where they deserved to be; and although her friendship with them was little more than nominal, she was content to be counted among them; and this feeling made her heroic resolution to break away from all her associations and go to live in America very much easier than it might have seemed. Climatically, socially, intellectually she was moving into a strange world, but m rally she felt she was moving into her true sphere. It was the sphere of her principles and her imagination. She soon found that in practice she could play no part in it; but that did not change her theoretical conviction that it was the *right* place to live in. There the mighty had fallen from their seat, and the righteous had been filled with good things.

A superstitious person might have been alarmed at the omens and accompaniments of this first visit to Boston; for Old Nathaniel, her father-in-law, whom they presumably went to see, died soon after their arrival, and George Sturgis, her husband, died soon after their return to Manila not only prematurely and unexpectedly, for he was scarcely forty, but in the midst of a disastrous commercial venture, which left the widow with inadequate means. My mother, however, had not a vestige of superstition; and her courage and coolness, her quick and intrepid action, on this occasion contrasted oddly with the utter apathy and despair that had overcome her on the death of Pepín. The pathetic but not uncommon loss of an infant had paralysed her; the loss of a young husband, the prospect of a complicated journey half round the world, alone with four little children, and the prospect of life in a strange society and a strange climate in reduced circumstances, seemed to revive her energies and to make her more alert and self-possessed than ever.

Yet such a crisis had occurred once before, on the death of her father, when she had no experience and no resources, which this time was not the case: for now she was not penniless: her brother-in-law Robert gave her a present of ten thousand dollars to help her over the crisis and she had recently made the acquaintance of the whole Sturgis family in Boston, where a share, one-eleventh, of her father-in-law's estate remained for her support. She would have to give up her easy colonial life with numerous servants and old friends, and with nothing exacted of her except the usual charities. Yet she was not in the least perturbed. I almost think that she was relieved, liberated, happy to abandon burdensome superfluities and reduce her life to the essentials; and as to the demands that her new environment would make on her, perhaps she did not foresee them, and in any case she had ample strength to resist them. The admiration she aroused at this time was well deserved but not very intelligent. People supposed her to be bearing up under a terrible sorrow and cutting herself off from the dearest ties, in order to do her duty by her children; but the fact was that the most tragic events now could not move her deeply, and the most radical outward changes could disturb her inner life and daily habits very little. She had undergone a veritable conversion, a sweeping surrender of all earthly demands or attachments; she retained her judgments and her standards, but without hope. I am confident of this, because at about the same age I underwent a similar transformation, less obviously, because in my case there were no outer events to occasion it, except the sheer passage of time, the end of youth and friendship, the sense of being harnessed for life like a beast of burden. It did not upset me, as the revolution in her circumstances did not upset my mother; but it separated the inner self from the outer, and rendered external things comparatively indifferent. I recorded this conversion in my Platonizing sonnets; my mother expressed it silently in the subsequent fifty years of her life...

CHARLES ELIOT NORTON

Of the older Harvard worthies, I was on good terms with two: Charles Eliot Norton and William James. They were perhaps the most distinguished, but not the most trusted; they too had had to be swallowed. They too, although in my time their position was established, had seemed at first questionable and irregular. Norton, with ten generations of local magnates behind him, had his inspirations and sympathies far away. He worshipped Greek art, he worshipped Christian art, he loved refined English life. He spoke rarefied English. He loved Turner and Ruskin. His personal friends were Burne-Jones, Carlyle and Matthew Arnold. To me he showed the most exquisite paternal kindness. He encouraged and praised me whenever he could do so conscientiously: when he wished to warn or admonish me, he did it through his nephew, Frank Bullard, who was one of my best friends. He feared that I lived too much among dreams. When my extravagant drama, *Lucifer*, was published,[1] I of course sent him a copy; and in thanking me he said that the value of it, in its substance, could not be known for the present, but that the versification was that of a master. This was flattery, but not absurd flattery, from an old man with Victorian standards in literature. 'Versification' was the right word in this case, for mine is not what English-speaking people now call poetry: it is not a dissolution and fresh concretion of language. Verbally it is ordinary speech made rhythmical and harmonious. Where I break through convention, whether in verse or prose, is in my themes or sentiments, as here in *Lucifer*. Norton very modestly and prudently refused to judge on this point. He was not at home in metaphysics or religion; the dissolution of common sense and a fresh concretion of myths seemed to him, I suspect, a waste of time. Here he had the prejudices of a positivist; yet he was cultivated and courteous enough to conceal them when speaking to a young man, like me, who

[1] In 1899.

possessed imagination without trusting it to reveal truth. My scepticism reconciled him to my mythology, and made him more benevolent than he might have been to a fanatic; and he was always benevolent, even when grieved.

At the funeral of C. C .Everett, an old professor at the Harvard Divinity School, a Unitarian and a Fichtean, I happened to join Norton as we came out. 'All this', he said with his usual sweetness, 'must make a sad impression on you.' I admitted that of course death was sad, but my acquaintance with Everett had been very slight, and it was not, at his age, a loss to our philosophical forces. 'I don't mean the death of Dr Everett. He was a good man, but he had no intellect-u-al power' (Norton pronounced with this extreme accuracy, but easily; and the habit sometimes gave a satirical force to his words). 'What I meant,' he continued, 'was this survival of superstition among us. Mr Cruthers has compared Dr Everett to an eagle.' Cruthers was the Unitarian minister in Cambridge and couldn't help being saturated with complacency and with unctuous flattery of everything mediocre; but he was hardly superstitious. To compare that old theological or anti-theological professor to St John was absurd or, if you like, blasphemous: but the primary evil was the insensibility to St John, not the obituary fulsomeness about Everett. Fulsomeness and complete lack of perspective had become habitual in American appreciation of Americans. There was a conspiracy of flattery; free lances were sometimes broken against it, but the phalanx might be expected to sweep the field, and to form public opinion. This, I think, was what made Norton sad.

Norton was president of the Tavern Club, which occasionally gave dinners in compliment to some person not a member. I recollect two such occasions on which Norton presided, and made the inevitable complimentary speech. Here he ran serious danger of falling into the 'superstition' that saddened him in others. But he had a means of safety; he was not without wit, a mild irony that saved him from platitudes. One dinner was in honour of John Fiske, a local disciple of Herbert Spencer, who had passed from popular science to history, and published first a book on *Cosmic Evolution* and later a *History of the United States*. Norton, in his speech, after paddling about as usual in the backwaters of anecdote, said that Fiske had been an industrious author. 'I wish his style had been a little chastened,* but the substance has been solid. He began by giving us a history of the universe; he proceeded to give us a history of the United States; and we may hope that in this upward progress he may end by giving us a history of Cambridge, Massachusetts.' The distrust of speculative pretensions, the positivism, the love of home and country (which was profound in Norton, and the cause of his melancholy) were all expressed in these words, with which he ended his speech.

The other dinner was in honour of Rudyard Kipling. Hard luck for Norton, I thought at first; why hadn't he pretended to be ill and let someone else praise what must be odious to him? But not at all. Norton was quite happy, not in his remarks, but in his mood. He had known and liked Kipling's mother, and he was prepared *a priori* to accept the bard of imperialism as a distinguished lover of humanity. Kipling sympathized with the Hindus; he was democratic; a glib prophet with warm feelings and popular rhythms; and Norton was so saturated with morality that when anything seemed to him morally right, he couldn't notice whether it was vulgar. That which seemed paramount in Norton, his fastidious retrospective nostalgia, was in reality secondary. Fundamental still was his fidelity to the conscience of his ancestors.

* Norton said 'chassened', doubtless to indicate that the word means castigated and not made chaste.

WILLIAM JAMES

William James enjoyed in his youth what are called advantages: he lived among cultivated people, travelled, had teachers of various nationalities. His father was one of those somewhat obscure sages whom early America produced; mystics of independent mind, hermits in the desert of business, and heretics in the churches. They were intense individualists, full of veneration for the free souls of their children, and convinced that everyone should paddle his own canoe, especially on the high seas. William James accordingly enjoyed a stimulating if slightly irregular education: he never acquired that reposeful mastery of particular authors and those safe ways of feeling and judging which are fostered in great schools and universities. In consequence he showed an almost physical horror of club sentiment and of the stifling atmosphere of all officialdom. He had a knack for drawing, and rather the temperament of the artist; but the unlovely secrets of nature and the troubles of man preoccupied him, and he chose medicine for his profession. Instead of practising, however, he turned to teaching physiology, and from that passed gradually to psychology and philosophy.

In his earlier years he retained some traces of polyglot student days at Paris, Bonn, Vienna, or Geneva; he slipped sometimes into foreign phrases, uttered in their full vernacular; and there was an occasional afterglow of Bohemia about him, in the bright stripe of a shirt or the exuberance of a tie. On points of art or medicine he retained a professional touch and an unconscious ease which he hardly acquired in metaphysics. I suspect he had heartily admired some of his masters in those other subjects, but had never seen a philosopher whom he would have cared to resemble. Of course there was nothing of the artist in William James, as the artist is sometimes conceived in England, nothing of the aesthete, nothing affected or limp. In person he was short rather than tall, erect, brisk, bearded, intensely masculine. While he shone in expression and would have wished his style to be noble if it could also be strong, he preferred in the end to be spontaneous, and to leave it at that; he tolerated slang in himself rather than primness. The rough, homely, picturesque phrase, whatever was graphic and racy, recommended itself to him; and his conversation outdid his writing in this respect. He believed in improvisation, even in thought; his lectures were not minutely prepared. Know your subject thoroughly, he used to say, and trust to luck for the rest. There was a deep sense of insecurity in him, a mixture of humility with romanticism: we were likely to be more or less wrong anyhow, but we might be wholly sincere. One moment should respect the insight of another, without trying to establish too regimental a uniformity. If you corrected yourself tartly, how could you know that the correction was not the worse mistake? All our opinions were born free and equal, all children of the Lord, and if they were not consistent that was the Lord's business, not theirs. In reality, James was consistent enough, as even Emerson (more extreme in this sort of irresponsibility) was too. Inspiration has its limits, sometimes very narrow ones. But James was not consecutive, not insistent; he turned to a subject afresh, without egotism or pedantry; he dropped his old points, sometimes very good ones; and he modestly looked for light from others, who had less light than himself.

His excursions into philosophy were accordingly in the nature of raids, and it is easy for those who are attracted by one part of his work to ignore other parts, in themselves perhaps more valuable. I think that in fact his popularity does not rest on his best achievements. His popularity rests on three somewhat incidental books, *The Will to Believe*, *Pragmatism*, and *The Varieties of Religious Experience*, whereas, as it seems to me, his best achievement is his *Principles of Psychology*. In this book he surveys, in a way which for him is very systematic, a subject made to his hand. In its ostensible outlook it is a treatise like any other, but what distinguishes it is the author's gift for evoking vividly the very life of the mind. This is a work of imagination; and the subject as he conceived it, which is the flux of immediate experience in men in general, requires imagination to read it at all. It is a literary subject, like autobiography or psychological fiction, and can be treated only poetically; and in this sense Shakespeare is a better psychologist than Locke or Kant. Yet this gift of imagination is not merely literary; it is not useless in divining the truths of science, and it is invaluable in throwing off prejudice and scientific shams. The fresh imagination and vitality of William James led him to break through many a false convention. He saw that experience, as we endure it, is not a mosaic of distinct sensations, nor the expression of separate hostile faculties, such as reason and the passions, or sense and the categories; it is rather a flow of mental discourse, like a dream, in which all divisions and units are vague and shifting, and the whole is continually merging together and drifting apart. It fades gradually in the rear, like the wake of a ship, and bites into the future, like the bow cutting the water. For the candid psychologist, carried boldly on this voyage of discovery, the past is but a questionable report, and the future wholly indeterminate; everything is simply what it is experienced as being...

In *The Varieties of Religious Experience*...normal religious experience is hardly described...Religious experience, for the great mass of mankind, consists in simple faith in the truth and benefit of their religious traditions. But to James something so conventional and rationalistic seemed hardly experience and hardly religious; he was thinking only of irruptive visions and feelings as interpreted by the mystics who had them. These interpretations he ostensibly presents, with more or less wistful sympathy, for what they were worth; but emotionally he wished to champion them. The religions that had sprung up in America spontaneously—communistic, hysterical, spiritistic, or medicinal—were despised by select and superior people. You might enquire into them, as you might go slumming, but they remained suspect and distasteful. This picking up of genteel skirts on the part of his acquaintances prompted William James to roll up his sleeves—not for a knock-out blow, but for a thorough clinical demonstration. He would tenderly vivisect the experiences in question, to show how living they were, though of course he could not guarantee, more than other surgeons do, that the patient would survive the operation. An operation that eventually kills may be technically successful, and the man may die cured; and so a description of religion that showed it to be madness might first show how real and how warm it was, so that if it perished, at least it would perish understood.

I never observed in William James any personal anxiety or enthusiasm for any of these dubious tenets. His conception even of such a thing as free will, which he always ardently defended, remained vague; he avoided defining even what he conceived to be desirable in such matters. But he wished to protect the weak against the strong, and what he hated beyond everything was the *non possumus* of any constituted authority. Philosophy for him had a Polish constitution; so long as a single vote was cast against the majority, nothing could pass. The suspense of judgment which he had imposed on himself as a duty, became almost a necessity. I think it would have depressed him if he had had to confess that any important question was finally settled. He would still have hoped that something might turn up on the other side, and that just as the scientific hangman was about to despatch the poor convicted prisoner, an unexpected witness would ride up in hot haste, and prove him innocent. Experience seems to most of us to lead to conclusions, but empiricism has sworn never to draw them...Besides, a philosopher who is a teacher of youth is more concerned to give people a right start than a right conclusion. James fell in with the hortatory tradition of college sages; he turned his psychology, whenever he could do so honestly, to purposes of edification; and his little sermons on habit, on will, on faith, and...on the latent capacities of men, were fine and stirring, and just the sermons to preach to the young Christian soldier. He was much less sceptical in morals than in science. He seems to have felt sure that certain thoughts and hopes—those familiar to a liberal Protestantism—were every man's true friends in life. This assumption would have been hard to defend if he or those he habitually addressed had ever questioned it; yet his whole argument for voluntarily cultivating those beliefs rests on this assumption, that they are beneficent. Since, whether we will or no, we cannot escape the risk of error, and must succumb to some human or pathological bias, at least we might do so gracefully and in the form that would profit us most, by clinging to those prejudices which help us to lead what we all feel is a good life. But what is a good life? Had William James, had the people about him, had modern philosophers anywhere, any notion of that? I cannot think so. They had much experience of personal goodness, and love of it; they had standards of character and right conduct; but as to what might render human existence good, excellent, beautiful, happy, and worth having as a whole, their notions were utterly thin and barbarous. They had forgotten the Greeks, or never known them...

William James shared the passions of liberalism. He belonged to the left, which, as they say in Spain, is the side of the heart, as the right is that of the liver; at any rate there was much blood and no gall in his philosophy. He was one of those elder Americans still disquieted by the ghost of tyranny, social and ecclesiastical. Even the beauties of the past troubled him; he had a puritan feeling that they were tainted. They had been cruel and frivolous, and must have suppressed far better things. But what, we may ask, might these better things be? It may do for a revolutionary politician to say: 'I may not know what I want—except office—but I know what I don't want'; it will never do for a philosopher. Aversions and fears imply principles of preference, goods acknowledged; and it is the philosopher's business to make these goods explicit. Liberty is not an art, liberty must be used to bring some natural art to fruition. Shall it be simply eating and drinking and wondering what will happen next? If there is some deep and settled need in the heart of man, to give direction to his efforts, what else should a philosopher do but discover and announce what that need is?

There is a sense in which James was not a philosopher at all. He once said to me: 'What a curse philosophy would be if we couldn't forget all about it!' In other words, philosophy was not to him what it has been to so many, a consolation and sanctuary in a life which would have been unsatisfying without it. It would be incongruous, therefore, to expect of him that he should build a philosophy like an edifice to go and live in for good. Philosophy to him was rather like a maze in which he happened to find himself wandering, and what he was looking for was the way out. In the presence of theories of any sort he was attentive, puzzled, suspicious, with a certain inner prompting to disregard them. He lived all his life among them, as a child lives among grown-up people; what a relief to turn from those stolid giants, with their prohibitions and exactions and tiresome talk, to another real child or a nice animal! Of course grown-up people are useful, and so James considered that theories might be; but in themselves, to live with, they were rather in the way, and at bottom our natural enemies. It was well to challenge one or another of them when you got a chance; perhaps that challenge might break some spell, transform the strange landscape, and simplify life. A theory while you were creating or using it was like a story you were telling yourself or a game you were playing; it was a warm, self-justifying thing then; but when the glow of creation or expectation was over, a theory was a phantom, like a ghost, or like the minds of other people. To all other people, even to ghosts, William James was the soul of courtesy; and he was civil to most theories as well, as to more or less interesting strangers that invaded him. Nobody ever recognized more heartily the chance that others had of being right, and the right they had to be different. Yet when it came to understanding what they meant, whether they were theories or persons, his intuition outran his patience; he made some brilliant impressionistic sketch in his fancy and called it by their name. This sketch was as often flattered as distorted, and he was at times the dupe of his desire to be appreciative and give the devil his due; he was too impulsive for exact sympathy; too subjective, too romantic, to be just. Love is very penetrating, but it penetrates to possibilities rather than to facts. The logic of opinions, as well as the exact opinions themselves, were not things James saw easily, or traced with pleasure. He liked to take things one by one, rather than to put two and two together. He was a mystic, a mystic in love with life. He was comparable to Rousseau and to Walt Whitman; he expressed a generous and tender sensibility, rebelling against sophistication, and preferring daily sights and sounds, and a vague but indomitable faith in fortune, to any settled intellectual tradition calling itself science or philosophy.

A prophet is not without honour save in his own country; and until the return wave of James's reputation reached America from Europe, his pupils and friends were hardly aware that he was such a distinguished man. Everybody liked him, and delighted in him for his generous, gullible nature and brilliant sallies. He was a sort of Irishman among the Brahmins, and seemed hardly imposing enough for a great man. They laughed at his erratic views and his undisguised limitations. Of course a conscientious professor ought to know everything he professes to know, but then, they thought, a dignified professor ought to seem to know everything. The precise theologians and panoplied idealists, who exist even in America, shook their heads. What sound philosophy, said they to themselves, could be expected from an irresponsible doctor, who was not even a college graduate, a crude empiricist, and vivisector of frogs? On the other hand, the solid men of business were not entirely reassured concerning a teacher of youth who seemed to have no system in particular—the ignorant rather demand that the learned should have a system in store, to be applied at a pinch; and they could not quite swallow a private gentleman who dabbled in hypnotism, frequented mediums, didn't talk like a book, and didn't write like a book, except like one of his own. Even his pupils, attached as they invariably were to his person, felt some doubts about the profundity of one who was so very natural, and who after some interruption during a lecture—and he said life was a series of interruptions—would slap his forehead and ask the man in the front row 'What *was* I talking about?' Perhaps in the first years of his teaching he felt a little in the professor's chair as a military man might feel when obliged to read the prayers at a funeral. He probably conceived what he said more deeply than a more scholastic mind might have conceived it; yet he would have been more comfortable if someone else had said it for him. He liked to open the window, and look out for a moment. I think he was glad when the bell rang, and he could be himself again until the next day. But in the midst of this routine of the class-room the spirit would sometimes come upon him, and, leaning his head on his hand, he would let fall golden words, picturesque, fresh from the heart, full of the knowledge of good and evil. Incidentally there would crop up some humorous characterization, some candid confession of doubt or of instinctive preference, some pungent scrap of learning; radicalisms plunging sometimes into the subsoil of all human philosophies; and, on occasion, thoughts of simple wisdom and wistful piety, the most unfeigned and manly that anybody ever had.

HOWARD STURGIS

...I had been expressly summoned[1] in order that I might make the acquaintance of Howard Sturgis, 'Cousin Lucy's' youngest brother, who might well have been her son, being then thirty-three years of age. Howard, too, comes properly under the head of friendship, since I began the next year to make him almost yearly visits, sometimes reduplicated, at his house in Windsor: but since I first saw him in America, and it was my Sturgis connection that established a kind of family intimacy between us, I will say something about him here.

He had come to America for a complete change of scene, hoping it might help to heal the wound that, in his excessively tender heart, had been left by the death of his mother. She had not been, from all I have gathered, at all a remarkable woman, but luxurious and affectionate, surrounded in London by a few rich American friends, especially the daughters of Motley, the historian, who were married to Englishmen, and surrounded beyond them, more by hearsay than acquaintance, by the whole British aristocracy. Howard had been her last and permanent baby. The dear child was sensitive and affectionate, with abundant golden hair, large blue eyes, and well-turned chubby arms and legs. Her boudoir became his nursery and his playroom. As if by miracle, for he was wonderfully imitative, he became, save for the accident of sex, which was not yet a serious encumbrance, a perfect young lady of the Victorian type. He acquired a good accent in French, German and Italian, and instinctively embraced the proper liberal humanitarian principles in politics and history. There was an absolutely right and an absolutely wrong side in every war and every election; only the wicked, selfish, and heartless still prevented the deserving from growing rich, and maintained an absurd and cruel ascendency of birth, superstition, and

[1] To Cotuit on Cape Cod, in 1889, where Mrs Lucy Codman, a Sturgis connection, had a country house.

military power. These were the sentiments of the Great Merchants, economists and reformers of the early nineteenth century, and Howard would have embraced them in any case because they appealed to his heart, and his feminine nature would never have allowed his intellect, no matter how keen, to do anything but defend his emotions. When women's opinions waver, it means that their hearts are not at rest. Let them once settle their affections and see their interests, and theoretical doubt becomes impossible for them. Howard's affections and interests were inextricably bound up with the liberal epoch; and no evidence would ever have convinced him that this was the only ground for his liberal dogmatism.

This was not all that he imbibed from his mother's circle. He was not only imitative, but he also had a theory that there was nothing women did that a man couldn't do better. Pride therefore seconded inclination in making him vie with the ladies and surpass them. He learned to sew, to embroider, to knit, and to do crochet; these occupations were not only guiltless of any country's blood, but helped to pass away the empty hours. He became wedded to them, and all his life, whether he sat by the fire or in his garden, his work-basket stood by his low chair. His needlework was exquisite, and he not only executed gorgeous embroideries, but designed them, for he was clever also with the pencil. Imitation, or a sort of involuntary caricature, sometimes went further with him. He would emit little frightened cries, if the cab he was in turned too fast round a corner, and in crossing a muddy road he would pick up the edge of his short covert-coat, as the ladies in those days picked up their trailing skirts.

Some of these automatisms were so extreme and so ridiculous that I can't help suspecting that there was something hypnotic or somnambulistic about them. He was too intelligent and too satirical to have done such things if he could have helped it. There may have been some early fixation at work, probably to his mother, of the kind that induces dreams, and develops into grotesque exaggerations and symbolic fancies. He mimicked people, sometimes on purpose, but often involuntarily: and his imagination penetrated their motives and thoughts, as his novels show, not necessarily with truth, but plausibly and with an endless capacity for extensions. He may have been at times the victim of this dramatic fertility in his own person, and found himself playing a part that the real circumstances did not call for.

He had not yet written his best novels, only an ultra-pathetic story about a little boy 'Tim'; but one morning we found him sitting in the porch outside the living-room, on one of the wicker chairs with red-cotton cushions that adorned it, and that he copied later in the addition made to Queen's Acre; and we found him armed, not with his usual work-basket, but with a red leather writing-case. He had an absorbed and far-away air. He was writing poetry: verses about the loss of his mother. We asked him to read them: he would not have brought them downstairs if he wished them to bloom and die unseen. He read them very nicely, without self-consciousness or affectation: the sentiment was intimate, but the form restrained and tactful.

Courage and distinction will save a man in almost any predicament; and Howard had been at Eton, where he acquired distinction and showed remarkable courage. Sending him there must have been a last desperate measure insisted on by his brothers, to cure him of his girlishness. A cruel remedy, it might seem, as if he had been sent to sea before the mast. Why hadn't his father and mother corrected him sooner? His father's mind had been growing feeble, and his mother probably thought the lad sweeter as he was. After all, too, they were Bostonians; and would it have been *right* to correct dear little sweet Howard for girlishness, when girlishness wasn't *morally wrong*? Let him go to Eton, properly safeguarded, if his brothers thought it absolutely necessary. And this heroic remedy didn't prove in the least cruel, or in the least efficacious. Young Howard calmly defied all those schoolboys with his feminine habits and arts, which he never dreamt of disguising. He was protected by his wit and intellectual assurance; while his tutor, Mr Ainger, author of the *Carmen*

Etonense, and the two Misses Ainger, adopted him and screened him from the rude mob. Besides, Howard attracted affection, and however astonished one might be at first, or even scornful, one was always won over in the end.

After Eton, Trinity College, Cambridge was plain sailing, and confirmed his humanitarian principles and aristocratic habits. His studies don't seem to have been serious; but he remembered what he had read of *belles-lettres*, just as ladies do. He had even dipped into Berkeley's philosophy and had laid it aside, not unwisely, as an academic curiosity. To see interesting people, or at least fashionable people, and to hear about them, made his chief entertainment later. Of course he had travelled abroad and seen everything that everybody should see; he remained old-fashioned, without Pre-Raphaelite affectations, in matters of art. His novels were exquisitely felt and observed, full of delicately satirical phrases, and not without an obvious moral aimed against domestic prejudice and social tyranny: but his writing had hardly force enough, either in style or in thought, to leave a lasting impression...

JOHN FRANCIS STANLEY RUSSELL[1]

Because the windows of my room in Hollis Hall looked out directly on the brick path that led from the Harvard Yard to Jervis field, then the college playground; or because, for an undergraduate, I was thought comparatively articulate; or because I was a foreigner and known to write verses; or because the guide to whom the young Earl Russell was entrusted was a good friend of mine, that exceptional nobleman, grandson and heir of Lord John Russell, was brought to see me, when on being 'sent down' from Oxford in 1886 he visited America in charge of a tutor. He was the first Englishman I had ever spoken to or that had ever spoken to me. That of itself would have made him notable in my eyes; but this Englishman was remarkable on his own account.

He was a tall young man of twenty, still lithe though large of bone, with abundant tawny hair, clear little steel-blue eyes, and a florid complexion. He moved deliberately, gracefully, stealthily, like a tiger well fed and with a broad margin of leisure for choosing his prey. There was precision in his indolence; and mild as he seemed, he suggested a latent capacity to leap, a latent astonishing celerity and strength, that could crush at one blow. Yet his speech was simple and suave, perfectly decided and strangely frank. He had some thoughts, he said, of becoming a clergyman. He seemed observant, meditative, as if comparing whatever he saw with something in his mind's eye. As he looked out of the window at the muddy paths and shabby grass, the elms standing scattered at equal intervals, the ugly factory-like buildings, and the loud-voiced youths passing by, dressed like shop assistants, I could well conceive his thoughts, and I said apologetically that after Oxford all this must seem to him rather mean; and he replied curtly: 'Yes, it does.' I explained our manner of life, our

[1] Second Earl Russell, elder brother of Bertrand Russell.

social distinctions, our choice of studies, our sports, our food, our town amusements. He listened politely, obviously rather entertained and not displeased to find that, according to my description, all I described might be dismissed forever without further thought. Then he sat good-naturedly on the floor and began to look at my books—a rather meagre collection in some open shelves. He spied Swinburne's *Poems*, and took out the volume. Did I like Swinburne? Yes, perhaps he was rather verbose; but did I know the choruses in *Atalanta in Calydon*? No? Then he would read me one. And he read them all, rather liturgically, with a perfect precision and clearness, intoning them almost, in a sort of rhythmic chant, and letting the strong meaning shine through the steady processional march of the words. It seemed the more inspired and oracular for not being brought out by any human change of tone or of emphasis. I had not heard poetry read in this way before. I had not known that the English language could become, like stained glass, an object and a delight in itself.

He stayed a long time, until, the daylight having decidedly failed, he remembered that he was to dine at the Jameses'. My own dinner was long since cold. He was off the next day, he said; but I must look him up whenever I came to London. I saw no more of him at that time; but I received through the post a thin little book bound in white vellum, *The Bookbills of Narcissus*, by Richard Le Gallienne, inscribed 'from R.' And William James not long afterwards took occasion to interrupt himself, as his manner was, as if a sudden thought had struck him, and to say to me: 'I hear you have seen this young grandson of Lord John Russell's. He talked about you; you seem to have made an impression.' The impression I had made was that I was capable of receiving impressions. With young Russell, who completely ignored society and convention, this was the royal road to friendship.

When late in March of the following year, 1887, after the winter semester at Berlin, I reached England for the holidays, Russell was not in town, but wrote that he was bringing a boat down from the engineers at Newbury to the boatbuilders in London. They were merely patched up for the journey; it would be a three days' trip, one on a canal and two on the Thames. He feared he couldn't offer me much accommodation and I should have to sleep ashore, but it would be a good chance of seeing the river. It was finally arranged that I should join him on the second day at Reading. Muddy and sordid streets led from the dismal railway station to the Kennet Canal Office where Russell's small yacht, the *Royal*, was to lie for the night. After various inquiries I found my way over a shaky plank (very little to my taste) to a narrow strip of deck surrounding the cabin skylight. There I found my host in conversation with a workman. My arrival was noticed, and I was asked if I had duly deposited my bag at the inn. All being well, I was left to stand about, while the conversation with the workman continued. I stood by for a while and listened; but seeing that the business gave no signs of coming to an end, and was not very intelligible or interesting, I sat on the edge of the cockpit and took to sketching the hulks, masts and chimneys visible from the river. In those days I always carried a note-book and pencil in my pocket for setting down sudden inspirations. I had full time for exhausting the dreary beauties of the scene and my small skill in expressing them. At length the worthy workman departed (I suppose his working hours were up) and Russell called me, quite affectionately, slipped his arm into mine, and took me to look at the cabin and the engine-room and the galley, which was also the place where one washed. My ignorant questions were answered briefly, clearly, with instant discernment of what I knew and didn't know about ships. Then we went ashore for tea.

Russell said he should not have been a peer but an engineer. At the time I thought this a little joke, remembering him reading the choruses in *Atalanta* and wishing to be a parson; but now I see that there was a genuine feeling in it. When he died [in 1931], one of the notices in the newspapers referred to his 'scientific training' and its value in his political career.[1]

[1] He became Parliamentary Under-Secretary of State to the India Office in 1929, a post he held until the fall of the Labour government.

What was this scientific training? Surely nothing that he acquired at Winchester or Oxford, but what he learned while refitting his steam-yacht and talking to workmen, as he had that afternoon. He took up each mechanical novelty as it arose, experimented, became more or less expert. He carved, drove and steered admirably; he would have made an excellent naval officer and gunner. When he lived at Broom Hall and had a private electric plant for charging his launch and supplying his light, I remember asking him what electricity was. And he said, 'I will show you', and after making me leave my watch at a distance, he brought me close to the large magnet that formed part of the machinery, until I felt a strong pull; and then he said triumphantly, 'That is what it is.' In one sense, a scholastic and verbal answer; yet there was the scientific humility and peace in it that is satisfied with dark facts. And there was another side to his pleasure in engineering: the sense of mastery. Matter can be wooed, coaxed, and mastered like a woman, and this without being in the least understood sympathetically. On the contrary the keen edge of the pleasure comes from defiance. If matter can crush us when ignored, it can be played with and dragged about when once caught in its own meshes: and this skilful exercise of compulsion was dear to Russell. When he acted as Leader of the Opposition in the House of Lords he was not half so happy or in his element. The peers could not so easily be engineered.

At the inn he began to lavish endearments on the cat, who returned his advances disdainfully, and after purring a little when stroked found the thing a bore and scooted into parts unknown. The barmaid then had her turn for a moment, and would doubtless have proved more responsive; but the other servants had to be spoken to about the tea—the tea was very important—and the smiling barmaid and the ungrateful cat were alike forgotten. Tea was a wonderful sedative; and the post and the newspapers were brought in at the same time. Russell opened his letters with the tips of his strong fingers, without haste, without one needless movement or the least unnecessary force. A brief glance usually sufficed, and the letter was dropped, as if into eternal oblivion, upon the floor. But now and then something called for a comment, and then my presence seemed providential. I was invited to observe the stupidity of the correspondent or the folly of the government, or the outrage it was to have such prolonged bad weather. What did I think of the absurd language of the Scottish housekeeper who asked: 'Will I light the fire?' And could I conceive anything more annoying than the position of a young man who hadn't yet come into his money and whose grandmother (Lady Russell, and not Lady Stanley) was a fool? In all this fault-finding there was nothing really troubled or querulous. It was all serene observation of the perversity of things, the just perceptions and judgments of a young god to whom wrongness was hateful on principle, but who was not in the least disturbed about it in his own person. Was it not his own choice to move in this ridiculous world, where there were imperfect inns and yachts to be refitted and untrustworthy tradesmen and faithless cats and silly, disappointed barmaids? What difference could such incidents of travel make to a transcendental spirit, fixed and inviolate in its own centre?...

My position as a familiar friend who was not a nuisance was not established without some preliminary slips. One was a slip in the literal sense of the word. Russell had at Hampton, where he then lived, an electric launch for scurrying at a surprising speed along the river. Electric launches were novelties in those days, and with his good steering and perfect serenity, he attracted the admiring attention of the good people in the boats or on the banks. But nature had endowed him with a more surprising ability of another kind. He could walk along the edges and ledges of roofs, and up inclined poles, like a cat. I suppose all boys, except me, have had a desire to do such things, and have tried their hand at them at a certain age, and then abandoned feline ambitions for things more human. But in Russell, for some reason, feline instincts survived, and developed into habits. He performed his acrobatic feats as a matter of course, without training and without comment. He never boasted of them; he only thought it a singular deficiency in others not to be able to do them. One Sunday afternoon we had landed at Richmond for tea, and on our return found the launch removed from the landing—there was naturally a crowd of trippers on that day—and it lay at a little distance from the sloping bank, which didn't allow it to come nearer. For Russell this created no problem. One long boat-hook was turned into a bridge from the launch to the shore, and seizing the other as a *picador* does his lance, and sticking the prong through the clear water into the sand, he walked calmly and quickly aboard. But how was I to get in? In the same way of course. In vain did I protest, like Rosencrantz and Guildenstern, that I hadn't the skill. Hamlet said it was as easy as lying. If I had insisted on making them turn about, and wait for their chance to come up to the landing so that I might step aboard easily, I should have been making myself a nuisance. Seeing my hesitation. Russell said encouragingly: 'Come on. Try it. I'll lend you a hand.' I knew I should fall in; but I might as well try it, since the only alternative was to wade across, and I must get wet in any case. The pole was rather steep, I had on ordinary boots, not tennis shoes like Russell, and no experience in walking the tight rope. So I took the boat-hook and gave Russell my other hand. The result was tragic, but not what either of us expected. I fell in, inevitably, but I pulled him in after me; and while I only got my legs wet, he fell in backwards head over heels, with a tremendous splash, which caused great laughter among the sundry trippers lined up on the shore. There was no danger, even in a complete immersion; two feet of water at most, and a warm summer afternoon. We both climbed in easily; but Russell flew into an indescribable rage. His language showed that the society of working men had not been wasted upon him; or rather that he must have overheard a good deal that no working man would knowingly have said in his presence. Where? Or could nature have endowed him with Billingsgate as it had endowed him with somnambulism when awake? For that inexhaustible flow of foul words and blasphemous curses was somnambulistic: he didn't know what he was saying or why. It was an automatism let loose, as was his acrobatic instinct.

I thought at the time that what maddened him was having been baulked and made a fool of in public; but now that I know him better I believe that he had no idea that he was in the least to blame. He felt innocent and injured. It was all my fault for being such an incredible muff. I had ducked him in the Thames and was keeping him wet to the skin in the cool breeze all the way home. His memory for injuries, however—and he thought everybody injured him—was remarkably short. As soon as he got into dry clothes his wrath subsided. Still, he had been so outrageously abusive, and so persistent, that I was cut to the quick. Not that I minded his words, which I had hardly distinguished and couldn't remember; they had no real application to me and couldn't stick. What I feared was that the sting of his own folly had made him hate me, and that all might be over between us. But not in the least. He didn't understand why that evening I could hardly swallow my food, or why I was leaving the next morning.

There was some difficulty about getting my things to the station. It wasn't far, and I had only a bag, but it was rather heavy. 'I'll carry it for you', he said; and he actually did so, most of the way. And he continued to send me little notes, inviting me to this or that so long as I remained in England; and before long, instead of signing them 'yours sincerely', he began to sign them 'yours ever'. This was not meant for a mute apology, kindness vanquishing resentment. He behaved exactly in the same way with his worst enemies, such as Lady Scott: forgot terrible injuries, and reverted spontaneously to a deeper impulse, which events had obscured for a moment. I accepted all his invitations. My ego was no less absolute than his, and calmer. If he allowed me my inabilities, I could allow him his explosions. That the wild animal and the furious will should exist beneath his outwardly exact and critical intelligence was so much added, a double *virtù*. I liked it and I didn't fear it.

The astonishing thing about this incident was that Russell completely forgot it. Years after, when I once referred to having pulled him into the water at Richmond, he denied it, and didn't know what I was talking about. This again was not a case of legal oblivion, such as lawyers command a man to scatter over his past when he is about to give evidence: it was a genuine blank. A blank, that is, in his conscious memory; for in his inner man the thing must have left its trace, because he never afterwards urged me to do anything to which I was not inclined or taxed me with any defect. He respected my freedom unconditionally and gladly, as I respected his. This was one of the reasons why our friendship lasted so many years, weathering all changes in our circumstances, in spite of the few points of contact between our characters and the utter diversity in our lives. Neither of us was ever a nuisance to the other...[1]

[1] It is worth recalling that in London in 1896, and at considerable risk to his career, Santayana testified as 'a friend' in a scandalous libel action connected with Russell's first marriage and divorce. Santayana's evidence helped Russell win his case.

LIONEL JOHNSON

[Lionel Johnson] was then in his first year at New College.[1] He had rooms at the top of the new buildings overlooking Holywell. Over the roofs of the low houses opposite, the trees in the Parks were visible in places, as well as the country beyond: and pointing to the distant horizon Lionel Johnson said sadly: 'Everything above that line is right, everything below it is wrong.' These were almost the first words he spoke to me, and they formed an admirable preface to a religious conversion.

He was rather a little fellow, pale, with small sunken blinking eyes, a sensitive mouth, and lank pale brown hair. His child-like figure was crowned by a smooth head, like a large egg standing on its small end. His age was said to be sixteen, and I readily believed the report. His genius was the kind that may be precocious, being an inward protest against external evidence; and his aspect, though thoughtful, was very youthful: yet his real age seems to have been twenty, only a year and a half younger than Russell and three years younger than I. He said he lived on eggs in the morning and nothing but tea and cigarettes during the rest of the day. He seldom went out, but when he did, it was for a walk of twenty miles in the country: and on those days he dined. There was also conspicuous on a centre table a jug of Glengarry whisky between two open books: *Les Fleurs du Mal* and *Leaves of Grass*. Two large portraits hung on the wall: Cardinal Newman and Cardinal Wiseman. When he was of age he intended to become a Catholic and a monk: at present his people, who were Welsh, objected. This intention he carried out in part; but instead of becoming a monk he became a Fenian; for at the same time that he was converted from a legal Protestant to a legal Catholic, he was mystically transformed from a Welshman into an Irishman. It was the same thing, he said, being Celtic. Perhaps, too, being Irish was closer to his inner man,

[1] Oxford, April 1887.

and certainly more congruous with Catholicism and with whisky.

Our acquaintance was never close, but it seemed to gain in interest, for both of us, as it receded. Some years later he honoured me with a poem *To a Spanish Friend*, beginning with the words 'Exiled in America', and ending with an exhortation to return to Saint Theresa and her 'holy Avila'. I returned often, and should gladly have grown old in that atmosphere, yet not in order to indulge the impulse to dream awake: rather in order to remove the pressure of reality (of which I was only too well aware) and to leave my reflection free to survey that reality fairly, at arm's length. Lionel Johnson lived only in his upper storey, in a loggia open to the sky; and he forgot that he had climbed there up a long flight of flinty steps, and that his *campanile* rested on the vulgar earth. The absence of all foundations, of all concreteness, of all distinction between fiction and truth, makes his poetry indigestible. I see that it is genuine poetry—an irresponsible flux of impassioned words: and his religion too was genuine religion, if we admit that religion must be essentially histrionic. Let everything that comes, it says, be to thee an Angel of the Lord; embroider upon it in that sense, and let the vulgar world recede into a distant background for an endless flapping of angelic wings and chanting of angelic voices. The age had given Lionel Johnson enough verbal culture and knowledge of literature to raise his effusions in that angelic choir to a certain level of refinement and fancy; but he was not a traditional Catholic, accepting good-naturedly a supernatural economy that happened to prevail in the universe, as political and domestic economy prevail in one's earthly fortunes. Nor was he a philosopher, enduring the truth. He was a spiritual rebel, a spiritual waif who couldn't endure the truth, but demanded a lovelier fiction to revel in, invented or accepted it, and called it revelation. In part like Shelley, in part like Rimbaud, he despised the world and adored the unreal.

Had the first saying of his to me, that everything above the horizon was right and everything below it wrong, represented his primary and constant mind, he might have become a monk as he had intended; because that is the foundation of Christianity. There is a divine world *surrounding us*; but there is sin and damnation *in us*. Lionel Johnson never seemed to me to feel this as, for instance, St Paul and St Augustine felt it. What he felt was rather the opposite, that everything within him was right, and everything outside wrong; and if he made an exception of the blank sky, this was only because he could fill it at will with his poetry. In other words, he was a transcendentalist and a humanist; for that reason he seemed a prophet to Russell;[1] and at bottom nothing could be more contrary to Christian humility and to Catholic discipline. I know that an effort has been made to represent him as a saint, hushing the sad reality: it is part of the general practice of bluff, and the *claque* in journalistic criticism...

After two years of Oxford, Johnson had developed an element of banter, and favoured me with the following letter:

Hunter's Inn,
August 2nd (1888) *Hedder's Mouth, Barnstaple.*

My dear Santayana,

Forgive my not writing earlier: I have been for weeks a wanderer, with letters chasing me about the world in vain.

I wish I could be in Oxford in August; but only, be sure, for the sake of meeting you. Unhappily it is impossible. I am bound, hand and foot, to a 'reading party' in an obscure corner of Devonshire; and see no prospect of escape. Can you not find your way to our pastoral retreat? or be in Oxford in October? You will not go back to our dear America just yet, mon ami?

Berenson charmed Oxford for a term, and vanished: leaving behind a memory of exotic epigrams and, so to speak, cynical music. It was a strangely curious time. He is something too misanthropic: but always adorable.

I missed Russell[1] lately by four hours: you know we have not met for many a year, almost. I incline to think it time for his drama of life to become critical in some way: at least, beyond disregarding all unities of time and space he does not appear to progress. This morning is very hot; the sea sparkles; Plato is beautiful; the world

[1] John Francis Russell.

very charming; but why go to America? Come to Oxford in October and learn of me how to live on nothing with nothing to do. I intend to teach Berenson: and neither of you shall set foot again in Boston, that Holy and self-satisfied city.

Do you read Shelley still, and have you renounced that stage devil, Byron, and all his works, except Don Juan? Kegan Paul, whom you met, asked me the question concerning you the other day. Ach! there is always Keats.

When next you hear from me you will probably hear that I am a Jesuit novice or a budding Carthusian or some such an one. Anyway, the Church will probably have claimed her own in me. But just now I am lazy and fond of life this side of death.

Will you let me know your movements? And pray think out ways and means to see us all before you go to the Land of the Lost, and leave us desolate!

Yours very sincerely,

Lionel Johnson

This was written at the moment when the vogue of aestheticism, pessimism, Pre-Raphaelitism, and amateur Catholicism was at its height. The superior young mind was bound to share these affectations, but might save itself by a mental reservation and a pervasively weary, all-knowing and all-mocking tone. Was Lionel Johnson laughing at Jesuits and Carthusians, at Plato, Shelley and Keats, no less than at Berenson and me? Or had something or somebody, Shelley perhaps or the Jesuits, really taken him in? I have no doubt that sincerity existed somewhere beneath all these poses, but the exact place of it is hard to discover. Russell at that moment, in the drama of his life, was making rapid progress in the direction of Byron's *Don Juan*: he had fallen into the clutches of a mature adventuress who was marrying him off to her daughter. In what direction was Lionel Johnson's sincere drama progressing?

I am not writing Johnson's life or Russell's or even my own, but only picking out such points as interest me now in my personal retrospect. I saw Lionel Johnson in later years only at long intervals and found him each time less accessible. My last glimpse of him was in the summer of 1897, in Russell's rooms in Temple Gardens. It was a tragic spectacle. He still looked very young, though he was thirty, but pale, haggard, and trembling. He stood by the fireplace, with a tall glass of whisky and soda at his elbow, and talked wildly of persecution. The police, he said, were after him everywhere. Detectives who pretended to be friends of his friend Murphy or of his friend MacLaughlin had to be defied. Without a signed letter of introduction he could trust nobody. He had perpetually to sport his oak. As he spoke, he quivered with excitement, hatred, and imagined terrors. He seemed to be living in a dream; and when at last he found his glass empty, it was with uncertainty that his hat sat on his head as with sudden determination he made for the door, and left us without saying good night.

I never saw him again, but he still lived for five years, and there may have been important changes in him before the end. Nor do I profess to have fathomed his Celtic inspiration or his Celtic Catholicism. He says in his lines on *Wales*:

> No alien hearts may know that magic, which acquaints
> Thy heart with splendid passion, a great fire of dreams;

and I am willing to believe him. But to my prosaic apprehension he remains a child of premature genius and perpetual immaturity; and I cannot forget what Oscar Wilde is reported to have said of him, that any morning at eleven o'clock you might see him come out very drunk from the Café Royal, and hail the first passing perambulator. Yet I should be the last to deride the haze in which he lived, on the ground that Bacchus had something to do with it. Bacchus too was a god; and the material occasion of inspiration makes no difference if the spirit is thereby really liberated. Lionel Johnson lived in the spirit; but to my sense his spirituality was that of a transcendental poet, not that of a saint. His mind was subjective in its presuppositions or in the absence of all presuppositions; so that after reading him through you are aware of a great wind of passionate language, but not of what was said or of what it all was about. And this vagueness was hardly due to absorption in something higher, because it did not liberate him from everything lower. So at least he tells us in *The Dark Angel*.

Because of thee, no thought, no thing
Abides for me undesecrate...
Of two defeats, of two despairs;
Less dread, a change to drifting dust,
Than thine eternity of cares.

And if we ask what the alternative to these two despairs may be, and what will issue from the triumph that he still hopes for, we find nothing positive, nothing specific, but only transcendental spirit, still open to every thought and to every torment:

Lonely, unto the Lone I go;
Divine, to the Divinity.

These words are the words of Plotinus and of Christian mystics; but here we do not feel them to be backed by either the Platonic or the Christian scheme of the universe: they are floating words. Even the firmness and constructive power of the Catholic faith could not *naturalize* Lionel Johnson in the Catholic world. The same emotional absolutism, the same hatred of everything not plastic to the fancy, which drove him from Victorian England into Celtic poetry and Catholic supernaturalism, kept him from accepting definition and limitation even there; he could not deny himself other dreams...

The passionate need of sinking into these dreams, and defying the false world that pretended to be more real, seems to me to have been the secret of Lionel Johnson in all his phases. It was what made him a pagan or a Buddhist at Winchester, a Baudelairean Catholic at Oxford, and a Fenian conspirator in London. In his verse he could modulate those dreams lyrically, but not logically, morally, and historically as the Church had modulated her original inspirations; and he dared to take them, as the Church did hers, for revelations of the truth. But his dreams had no such application to the facts and sorrows of life as had the Christian faith. Their passion remained dreamy, weak and verbal, and he perished, not a martyr to his inspiration, but a victim of it.

LOWES DICKINSON

My other friend at King's[1] [was] Lowes Dickinson. His classicism was not of the rough, coarse, realistic Roman kind, but Greek, as attenuated and Platonized as possible, and seen through Quaker spectacles. I liked his *Greek View of Life*, but it wasn't Greek life as depicted by Aristophanes or by Plutarch; it was what a romantic Puritan of our time would wish Greek life to have been. War, lust, cruelty and confusion were washed out of it. Dickinson was super-sensitive, hard-working, unhappy, and misguided. His gift was for form; his privately printed poems seemed to me admirable; but his subject-matter was perverse, even in those poems, and much more, I think, in his philosophy and politics. He prayed, watched, and laboured to redeem human life, and began by refusing to understand what human life is. Too weak to face the truth, he set himself a task too great for Titans: to shatter this world to bits, and put it together again on a moralistic plan. If at least that plan had been beautiful, he might have consoled himself for his practical impotence by being an avowed poet; but his plan was incoherent, negative, sentimental. It was that no one should suffer, and that all should love one another: in other words, that no one should be alive or should distinguish what he loved from what he hated.

Poor Dickinson came once or twice to America, the first time to give some Lowell Lectures in Boston. It was winter, and he suffered from the cold, as well as from the largeness and noise of the town. I remember his horror when the electric car we were in got into the subway, and the noise became deafening; also his misery when one evening we walked across the Harvard bridge, and he murmured, shivering: 'I have never been so cold in my life.' The cocktail, he said, was the only good thing in America. He hated the real, bumptious, cordial democracy that he found there; he would have liked a

[1] Santayana spent the academic year of 1896 at King's College, Cambridge, *in statu pupillari*. Lowes Dickinson was a tutor there.

silent, Franciscan, tender democracy, poor, clean, and inspired. If he could have visited New England sixty years earlier he might have found sympathetic souls at Concord or at Brook Farm. He wouldn't have liked them, reformers don't like one another; but at least he might have imagined that the world was moving towards something better. As it was, he found that it was sliding hellwards with a whoop of triumph.

BERTRAND RUSSELL[1]

Of all my friends, of all persons belonging at all to my world, Bertrand Russell was the most distinguished. He had birth, genius, learning, indefatigable zeal and energy, brilliant intelligence, and absolute honesty and courage. His love of justice was as keen as his sense of humour. He was at home in mathematics, in natural science, and in history. He knew well all the more important languages and was well informed about everything going on in the world of politics and literature. He ought to have been a leader, a man of universal reputation and influence. He was indeed recognized to be a distinguished man, having made his mark in mathematics and logic, and largely inspired the new philosophical sect of 'logical realists'. Yet on the whole, relative to his capacities, he was a failure. He petered out. He squandered his time and energy, and even his money, on unworthy objects. He left no monument—unless it be the early *Principia Mathematica* written in collaboration with Whitehead—that does justice to his powers and gives him a place in history.

In his physique he was a complete contrast to his brother, a Russell while his brother was a Stanley. Bertie was small, dark, brisk, with a lively air and a hyena laugh. According to some people he was the ugliest man they had ever seen. But I didn't find him ugly, because his mask, though grotesque, was expressive and engaging. You saw that he was a kind monster, that if he spit fire, it was a *feu-de-joie*. For so violent, so merciless a satirist, he made a charming companion. I, at least, was never afraid of him; and he was benevolence itself to the most humble and hopeless intellectual waifs. Though his laughter was savage, it was fed by the subtlest intellectual lights; that was the chief charm of his conversation, added to

[1] Santayana first met Bertrand Russell in 1893, and became most closely acquainted with him in Cambridge during the years immediately prior to the First World War, when Russell was a resident Fellow of Trinity College. They seem not to have met again after Santayana left England in 1919.

the sense of security that his faultless memory and universal knowledge gave in regard to any information that he might give. This information, though accurate, was necessarily partial, and brought forward in a partisan argument; he couldn't know, he refused to consider, everything; so that his judgments, nominally based on that partial information, were really inspired by passionate prejudice and were always unfair and sometimes mad. He would say, for instance, that the bishops supported the war because they had money invested in munition works; or that the United States government had called out troops, not to fight the Germans, but to support capitalism against the strikers. It was for this libel that he was sent to prison; and this wasn't the worst consequence of such rash assertions. They alienated opinion in high quarters and ruined his official career. 'I would go to the stake for that', he would cry sometimes in summing up a philosophical argument. But going only to Holloway, in the first division, hadn't the posthumous value of martyrdom; and the general feeling that his judgment was unsound and his allegiance misplaced defeated all his attempts to guide public opinion.

He had been beautifully educated by private tutors at Pembroke Lodge. After the dreadful experience she had had with her elder grandson,[1] who would throw her letters unread into the fire, Lady Russell dreaded the fatal influence of schools: Bertie at least must be preserved, pure, religious, and affectionate; he must be fitted to take his grandfather's place as Prime Minister and continue the sacred work of Reform. Bertie showed me his schoolroom at Pembroke Lodge, and his old notebooks on the various subjects that he had studied. It was perfect princely education, but a little like cultivating tropical flowers under electric light in a steaming greenhouse. The instruction was well selected, competently given, and absorbed with intense thirst; but it was too good for the outdoor climate. Moreover, there were obstacles that far from being surmounted were built upon as cornerstones of righteousness and sources of superior light. One was the

[1] John Francis Russell.

hereditary liberalism and Low Church piety of the family. Another was Bertie's microscopic intensity that narrowed each of his insights, no matter how varied these insights might be, lost the substance in the visible image, the sense in the logic of the words, and made him, though he might be many-sided, a many-sided fanatic.

Bertie, Stickney and Westenholz, the three best-educated persons I have known, never went to school. Bertie, however, did go to the University, and here he made those fruitful contacts that produced his best work and opened to him an academic career. Had he been an obscure and penniless person, such a career might have fulfilled his ambition and determined his path; but for him, destined by his grandmother to be Prime Minister and by himself to be an international Messiah, academic life was but a preparation or an interlude. His vocation was to reform radically the whole intellectual and social world.

I can imagine two ways in which Bertie might have proceeded to prove how great a man it was in him to be. One would have been to carry out his grandmother's plans, get early a safe seat in the House of Commons, moderate his zeal so far as not to denounce bishops, generals, admirals or even Tory ministers, unless he had proofs of their obliquity, and generally to identify himself (as he could well do emotionally) with the official interests of his country. He would not at once or always have been in office. These intervals of leisure would have sufficed for the intensive study and the literary work that were appropriate to a leader of reform; and when his party won an election, he would have been able to exert the power of government for the heroic purpose of diminishing that power. He might have prevented the collapse of the Liberal party, by transforming it into a labour party true to democratic, anti-military, anti-imperialistic, anti-clerical principles. He might have shown the world whether at least in England it were not possible for a modern civilization to exist with a maximum of liberty and a minimum of government.

The other way in which Bertie might conceivably have become a great man would have been by emulating people like Bacon, Hobbes, Spinoza or Auguste Comte. I don't mean in their doctrines but in their ambition. He might have undertaken an *instauratio magna* of scientific philosophy. He could have done it better than Bacon, inasmuch as the science at his command was so much more advanced; and the *Principia Mathematica*, a title challenging comparison with Newton's, seemed to foreshadow such a possibility. Why, then, didn't Bertie proceed in this course? Or why didn't he choose the other, the political path?

I can judge only superficially, and from a distance. I didn't know him as I knew his brother. But judging by the work that he has actually accomplished, I think that, penetrating as his analysis might be in particular cases, in fundamentals he could never shake himself free from his environment and from the miscellaneous currents of opinion in his day. Except in mathematics, he seemed to practise criticism only sporadically, caught and irresistibly excited by current discussions. His radical solutions were rendered vain by the conventionality of his problems. His outlook was universal, but his presuppositions were insular...

INDEX

References to a complete essay or extract are in bold type.
Italic type indicates other major references.

Index

Index